THE ∞ INFINITY GAUNTLET WARZONES!

STORY **GERRY DUGGAN** & **DUSTIN WEAVER**

ARTIST **DUSTIN WEAVER**

SCRIPT **GERRY DUGGAN**

LETTERER **COMICRAFT'S ALBERT DESCHESNE**

COVER ARTIST **DUSTIN WEAVER**

ASSISTANT EDITOR **DEVIN LEWIS**

EDITOR **NICK LOWE**

COLLECTION EDITOR: MARK D. BEAZLEY
ASSISTANT EDITOR: SARAH BRUNSTAD
ASSOCIATE MANAGING EDITOR: ALEX STARBUCK
EDITOR, SPECIAL PROJECTS: JENNIFER GRÜNWALD

SENIOR EDITOR, SPECIAL PROJECTS: JEFF YOUNGQUIST
SVP PRINT, SALES & MARKETING: DAVID GABRIEL
BOOK DESIGNER: ADAM DEL RE

EDITOR IN CHIEF: AXEL ALONSO
CHIEF CREATIVE OFFICER: JOE QUESADA
PUBLISHER: DAN BUCKLEY
EXECUTIVE PRODUCER: ALAN FINE

INFINITY GAUNTLET: WARZONES! Contains material originally published in magazine form as INFINITY GAUNTLET #1-5. First printing 2015. ISBN# 978-0-7851-9874-1. Published by MARVEL WORLDWIDE, INC., a subsidiary of MARVEL ENTERTAINMENT, LLC. OFFICE OF PUBLICATION: 135 West 50th Street, New York, NY 10020. Copyright © 2015 MARVEL. No similarity between any of the names, characters, persons, and/or institutions in this magazine with those of any living or dead person or institution is intended, and any such similarity which may exist is purely coincidental. Printed in Canada. ALAN FINE, President, Marvel Entertainment; DAN BUCKLEY, President, TV, Publishing and Brand Management; JOE QUESADA, Chief Creative Officer; TOM BREVOORT, SVP of Publishing; DAVID BOGART, SVP of Operations & Procurement, Publishing; C.B. CEBULSKI, VP of International Development & Brand Management; DAVID GABRIEL, SVP Print, Sales & Marketing; JIM O'KEEFE, VP of Operations & Logistics; DAN CARR, Executive Director of Publishing Technology; SUSAN CRESPI, Editorial Operations Manager; ALEX MORALES, Publishing Operations Manager; STAN LEE, Chairman Emeritus. For information regarding advertising in Marvel Comics or on Marvel.com, please contact Jonathan Rheingold, VP of Custom Solutions & Ad Sales, at jrheingold@marvel.com. For Marvel subscription inquiries, please call 800-217-9158. Manufactured between 10/9/2015 and 11/16/2015 by SOLISCO PRINTERS, SCOTT, QC, CANADA.

10 9 8 7 6 5 4 3 2 1

SECRET WARS

THE ∞ INFINITY GAUNTLET

CAST ACROSS THE FARTHEST REACHES OF THE COSMOS,
THE INFINITY STONES ARE A POWER BEYOND COMPARE.
WHEN BROUGHT TOGETHER, THEY GRANT THEIR USER COMPLETE
CONTROL OVER ALL OF REALITY. THE SINGULAR DEVICE THAT
CAN HOLD ALL THE STONES IS CALLED

THE MULTIVERSE WAS DESTROYED!

THE HEROES OF EARTH-616 AND EARTH-1610
WERE POWERLESS TO SAVE IT!

NOW, ALL THAT REMAINS....IS BATTLEWORLD!

A MASSIVE, PATCHWORK PLANET COMPOSED
OF THE FRAGMENTS OF WORLDS THAT
NO LONGER EXIST, MAINTAINED BY THE
IRON WILL OF ITS GOD AND MASTER,
VICTOR VON DOOM!

EACH REGION IS A DOMAIN UNTO ITSELF!

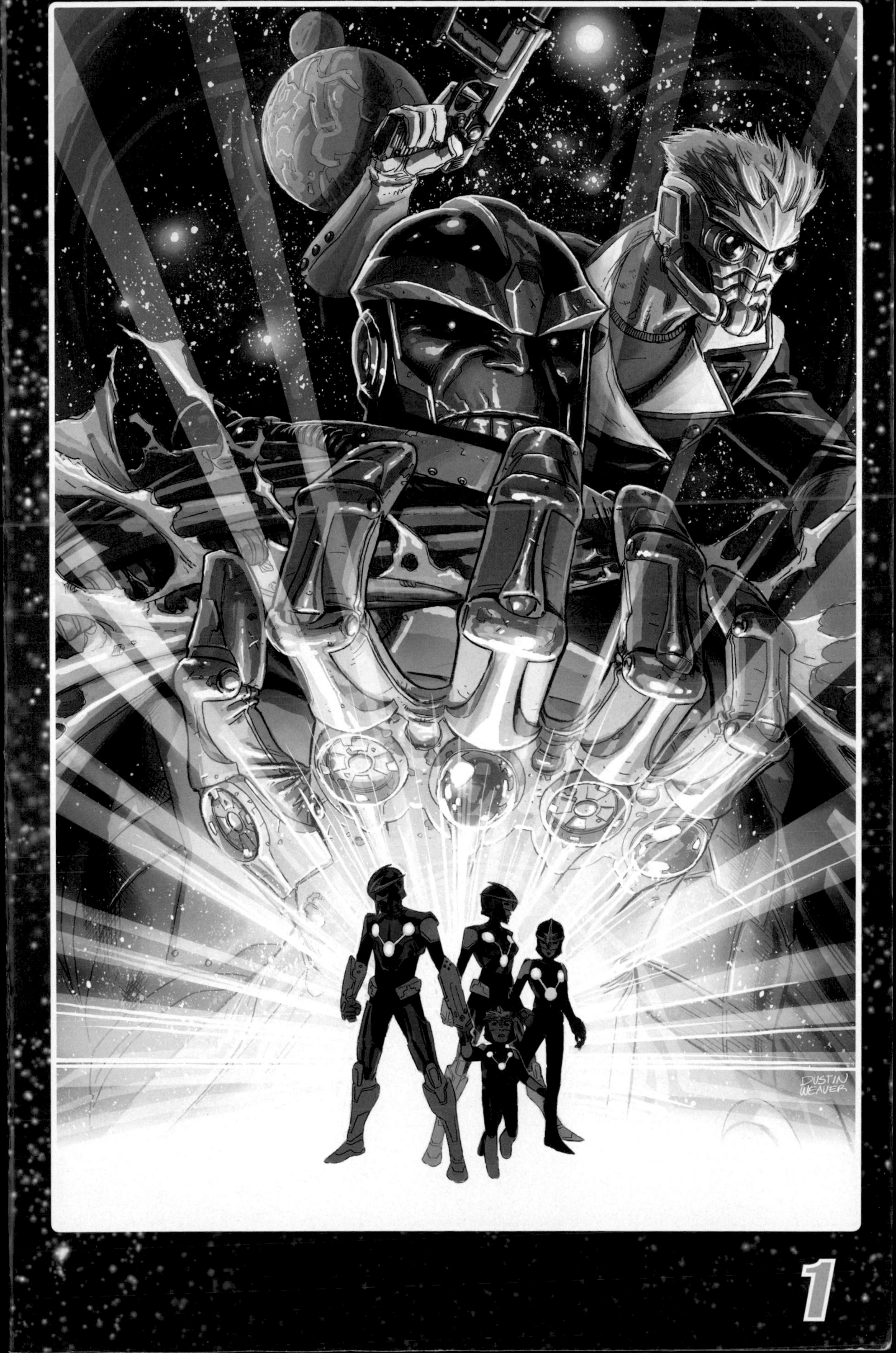
DUSTIN WEAVER

1

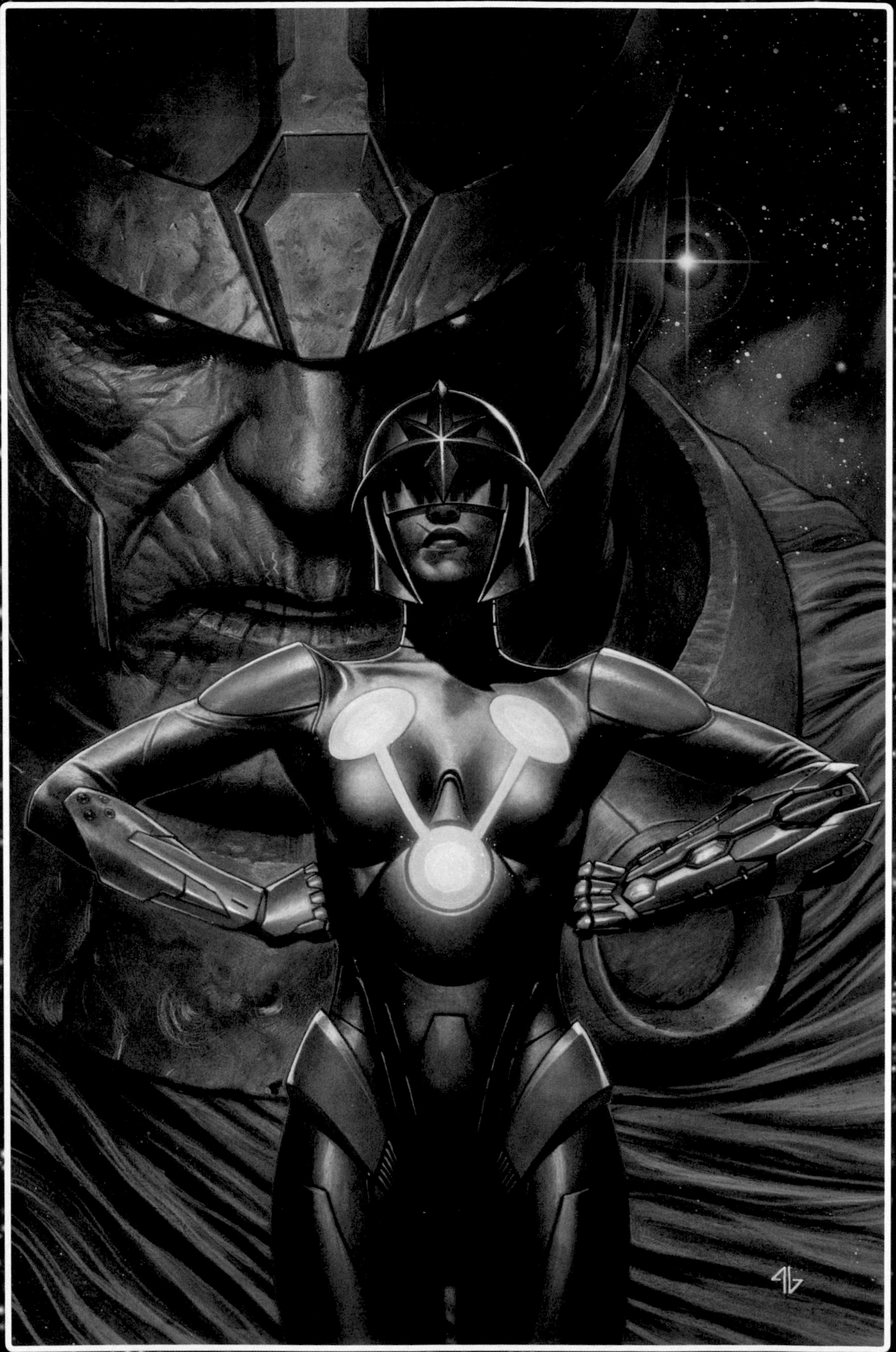

INFINITY GAUNTLET 1
VARIANT COVER BY ADI GRANOV

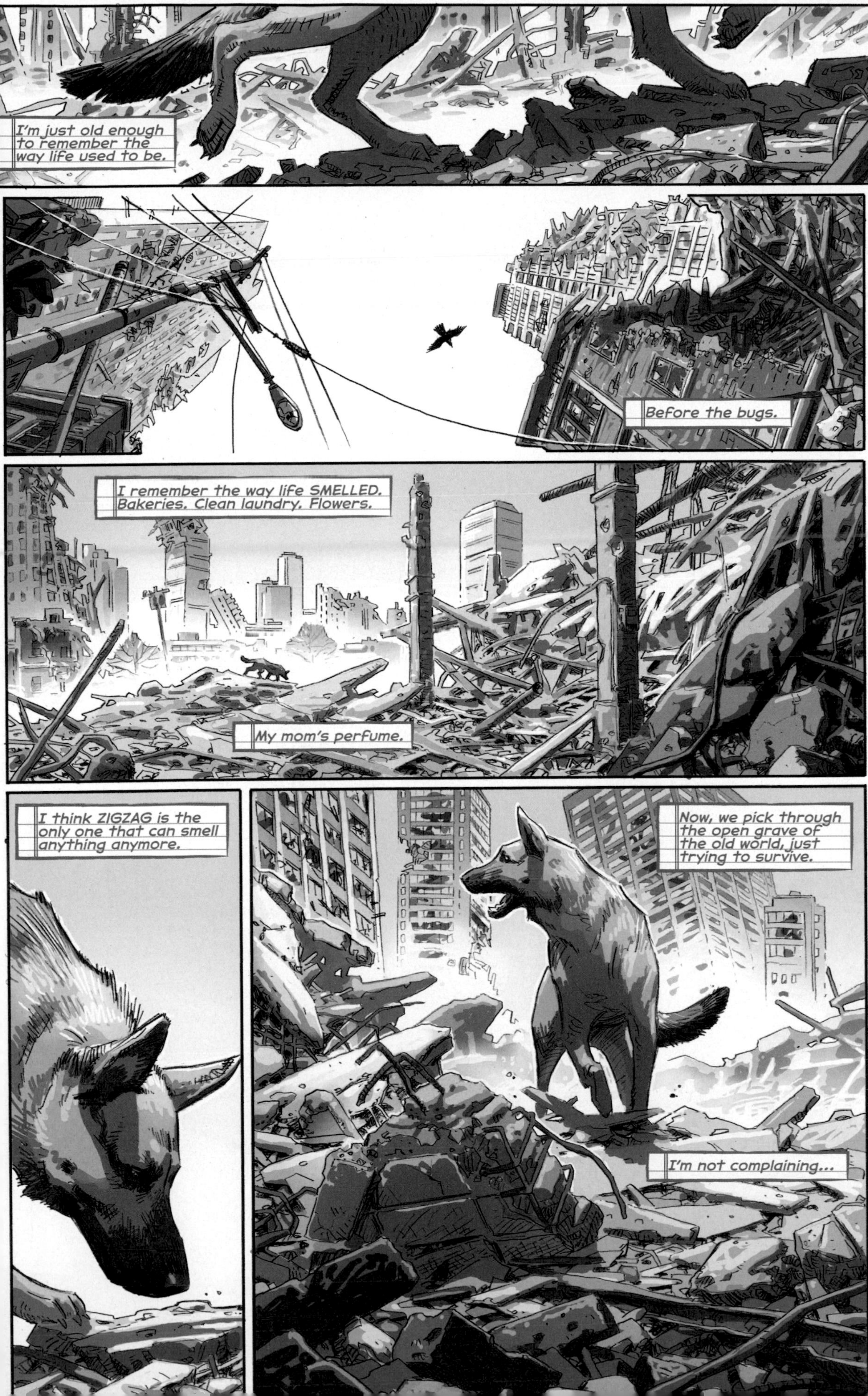
I'm just old enough to remember the way life used to be.
Before the bugs.
I remember the way life SMELLED. Bakeries. Clean laundry. Flowers.
My mom's perfume.
I think ZIGZAG is the only one that can smell anything anymore.
Now, we pick through the open grave of the old world, just trying to survive.
I'm not complaining...

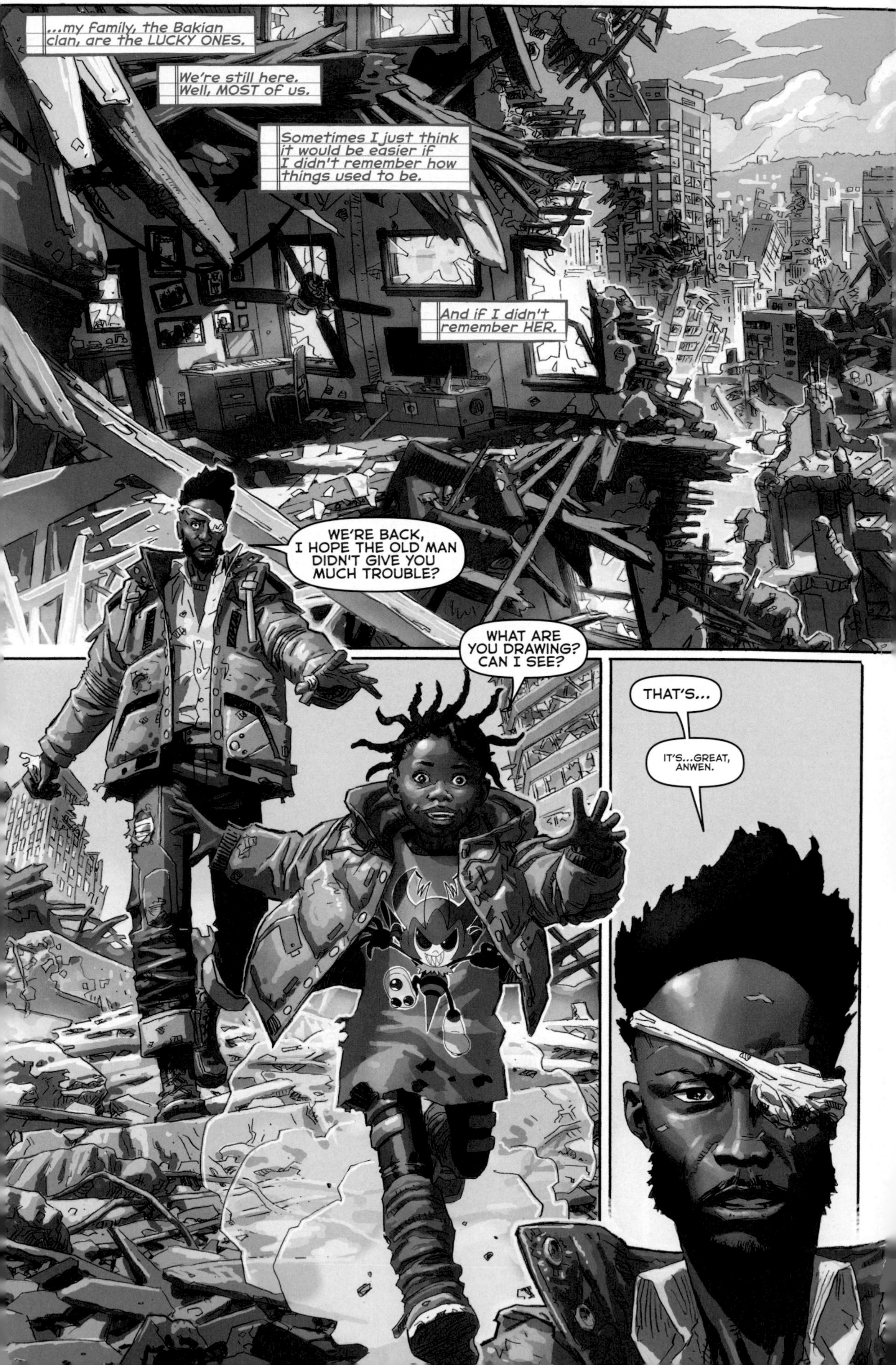
...my family, the Bakian clan, are the LUCKY ONES.
We're still here. Well, MOST of us.
Sometimes I just think it would be easier if I didn't remember how things used to be.
And if I didn't remember HER.
WE'RE BACK, I HOPE THE OLD MAN DIDN'T GIVE YOU MUCH TROUBLE?
WHAT ARE YOU DRAWING? CAN I SEE?
THAT'S...
IT'S...GREAT, ANWEN.

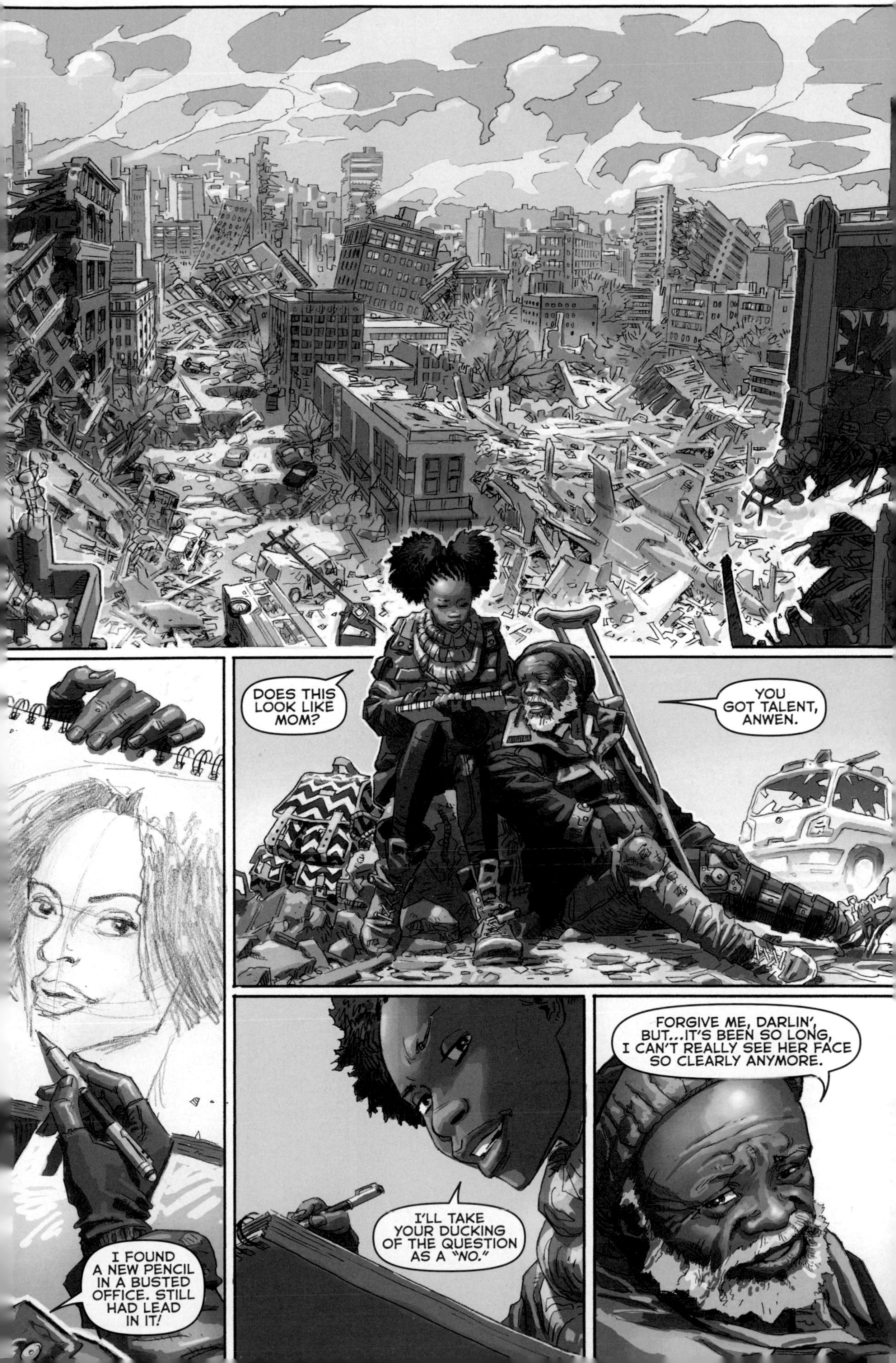
DOES THIS LOOK LIKE MOM?
YOU GOT TALENT, ANWEN.
I FOUND A NEW PENCIL IN A BUSTED OFFICE. STILL HAD LEAD IN IT!
I'LL TAKE YOUR DUCKING OF THE QUESTION AS A "NO."
FORGIVE ME, DARLIN', BUT...IT'S BEEN SO LONG, I CAN'T REALLY SEE HER FACE SO CLEARLY ANYMORE.

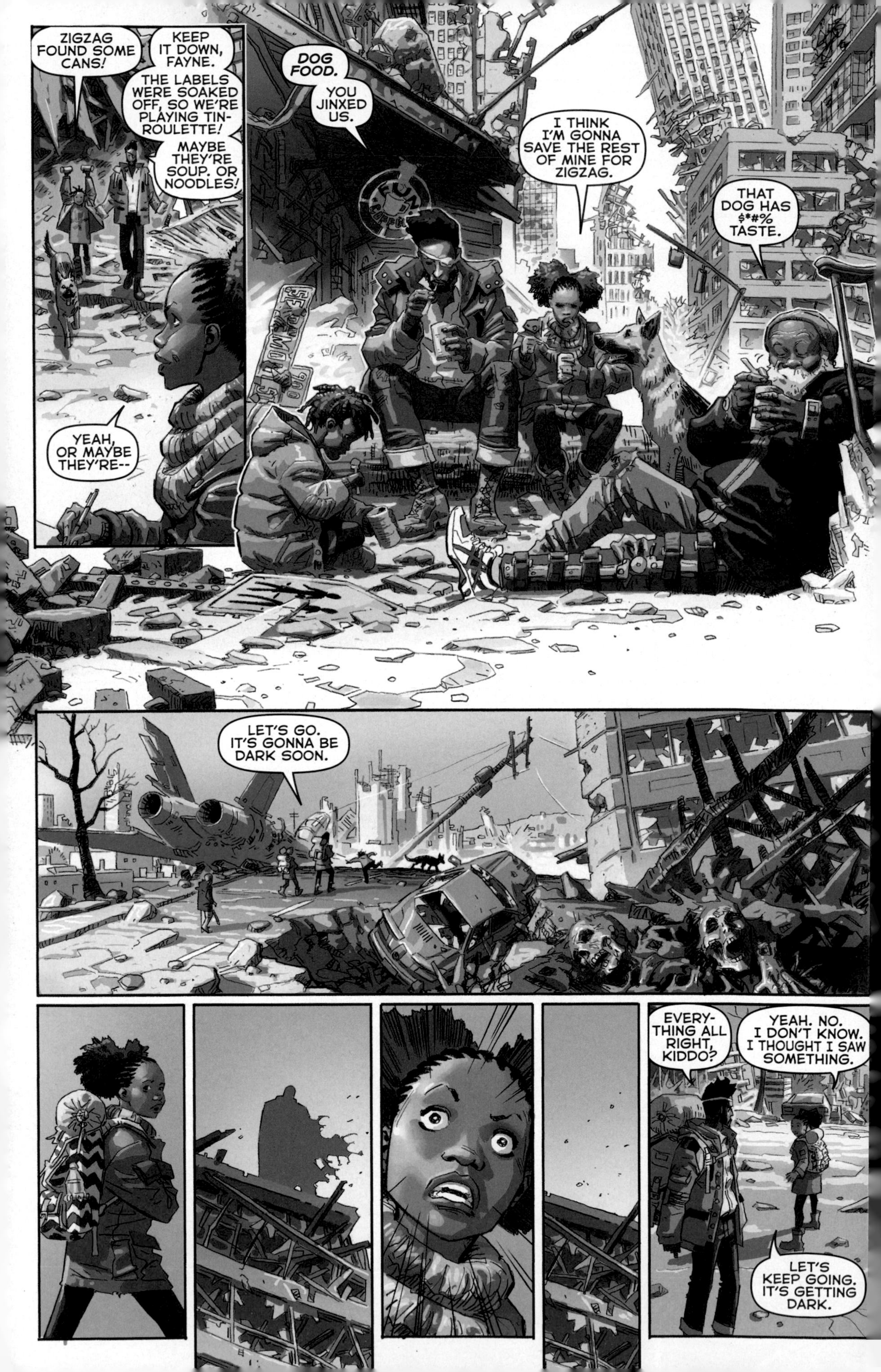
ZIGZAG FOUND SOME CANS!
KEEP IT DOWN, FAYNE.
THE LABELS WERE SOAKED OFF, SO WE'RE PLAYING TIN-ROULETTE!
MAYBE THEY'RE SOUP. OR NOODLES!
YEAH, OR MAYBE THEY'RE--
DOG FOOD.
YOU JINXED US.
I THINK I'M GONNA SAVE THE REST OF MINE FOR ZIGZAG.
THAT DOG HAS $*#% TASTE.
LET'S GO. IT'S GONNA BE DARK SOON.
EVERY-THING ALL RIGHT, KIDDO?
YEAH. NO. I DON'T KNOW. I THOUGHT I SAW SOMETHING.
LET'S KEEP GOING. IT'S GETTING DARK.

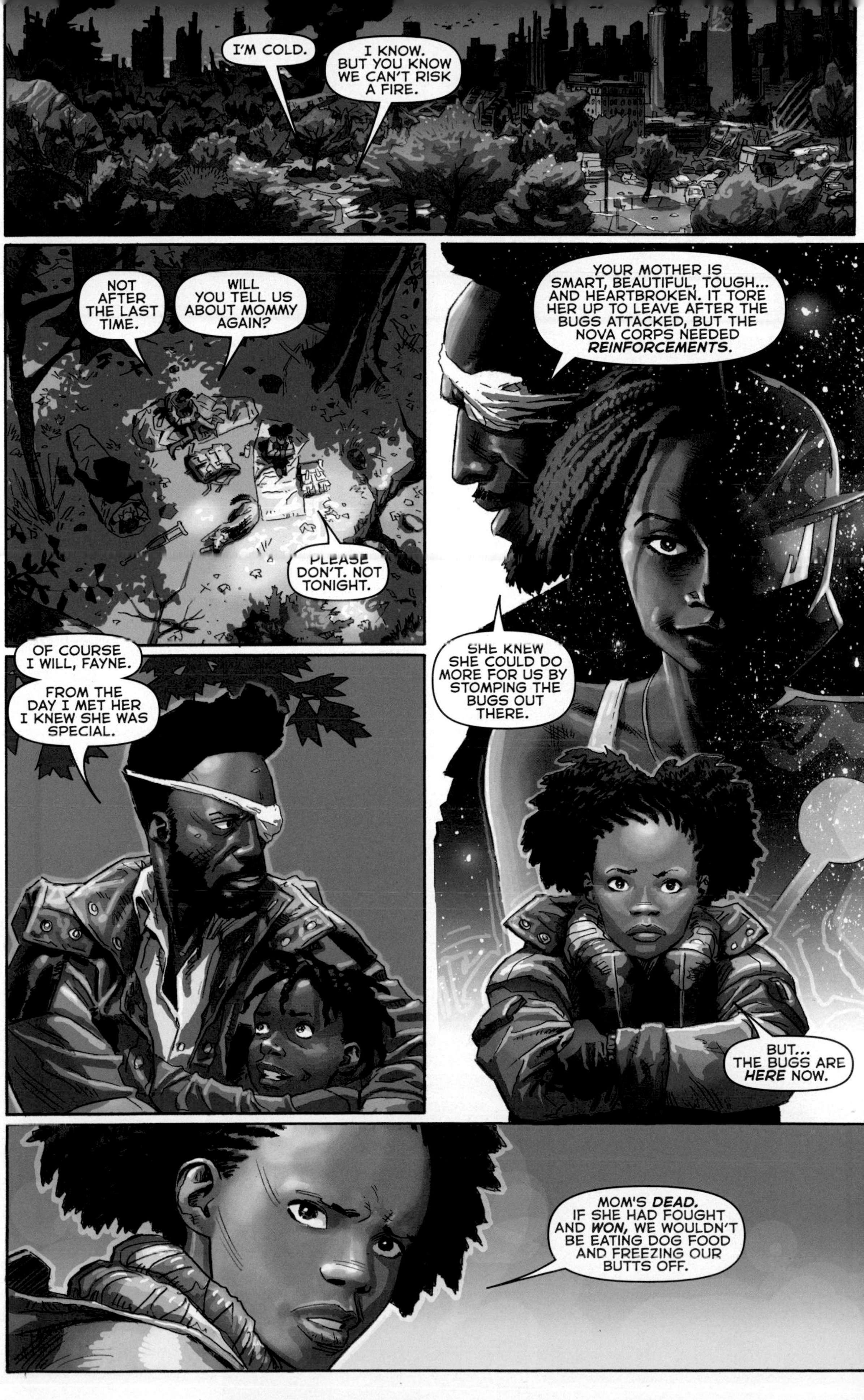
I'M COLD.
I KNOW. BUT YOU KNOW WE CAN'T RISK A FIRE.
NOT AFTER THE LAST TIME.
WILL YOU TELL US ABOUT MOMMY AGAIN?
PLEASE DON'T. NOT TONIGHT.
OF COURSE I WILL, FAYNE.
FROM THE DAY I MET HER I KNEW SHE WAS SPECIAL.
YOUR MOTHER IS SMART, BEAUTIFUL, TOUGH... AND HEARTBROKEN. IT TORE HER UP TO LEAVE AFTER THE BUGS ATTACKED, BUT THE NOVA CORPS NEEDED *REINFORCEMENTS*.
SHE KNEW SHE COULD DO MORE FOR US BY STOMPING THE BUGS OUT THERE.
BUT... THE BUGS ARE *HERE* NOW.
MOM'S *DEAD.* IF SHE HAD FOUGHT AND *WON,* WE WOULDN'T BE EATING DOG FOOD AND FREEZING OUR BUTTS OFF.

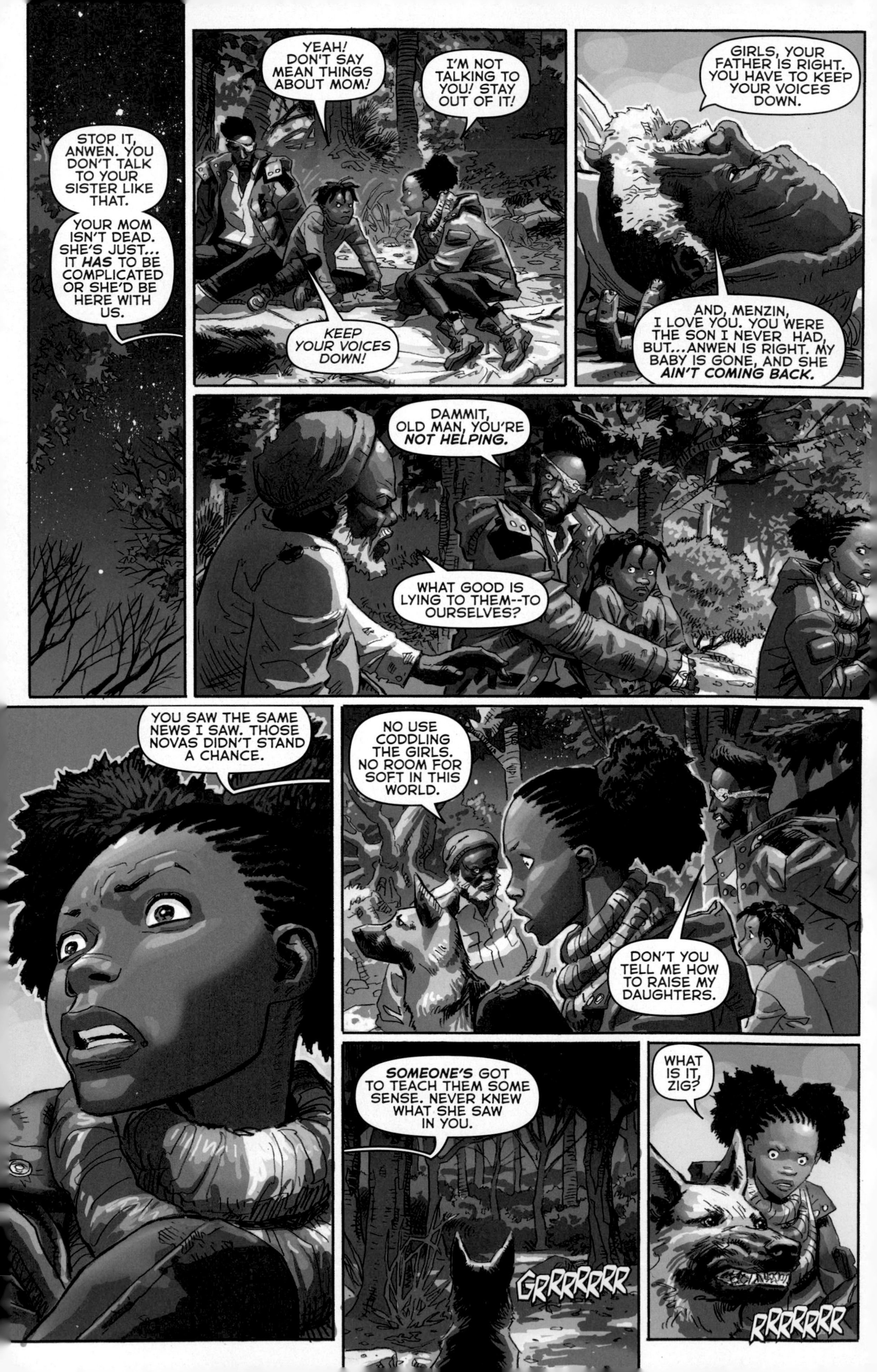

STOP IT, ANWEN. YOU DON'T TALK TO YOUR SISTER LIKE THAT.
YOUR MOM ISN'T DEAD. SHE'S JUST... IT HAS TO BE COMPLICATED OR SHE'D BE HERE WITH US.
YEAH! DON'T SAY MEAN THINGS ABOUT MOM!
I'M NOT TALKING TO YOU! STAY OUT OF IT!
KEEP YOUR VOICES DOWN!
GIRLS, YOUR FATHER IS RIGHT. YOU HAVE TO KEEP YOUR VOICES DOWN.
AND, MENZIN, I LOVE YOU. YOU WERE THE SON I NEVER HAD, BUT...ANWEN IS RIGHT. MY BABY IS GONE, AND SHE AIN'T COMING BACK.
DAMMIT, OLD MAN, YOU'RE NOT HELPING.
WHAT GOOD IS LYING TO THEM--TO OURSELVES?
YOU SAW THE SAME NEWS I SAW. THOSE NOVAS DIDN'T STAND A CHANCE.
NO USE CODDLING THE GIRLS. NO ROOM FOR SOFT IN THIS WORLD.
DON'T YOU TELL ME HOW TO RAISE MY DAUGHTERS.
SOMEONE'S GOT TO TEACH THEM SOME SENSE. NEVER KNEW WHAT SHE SAW IN YOU.
GRRRRRRR
WHAT IS IT, ZIG?
RRRRRRR

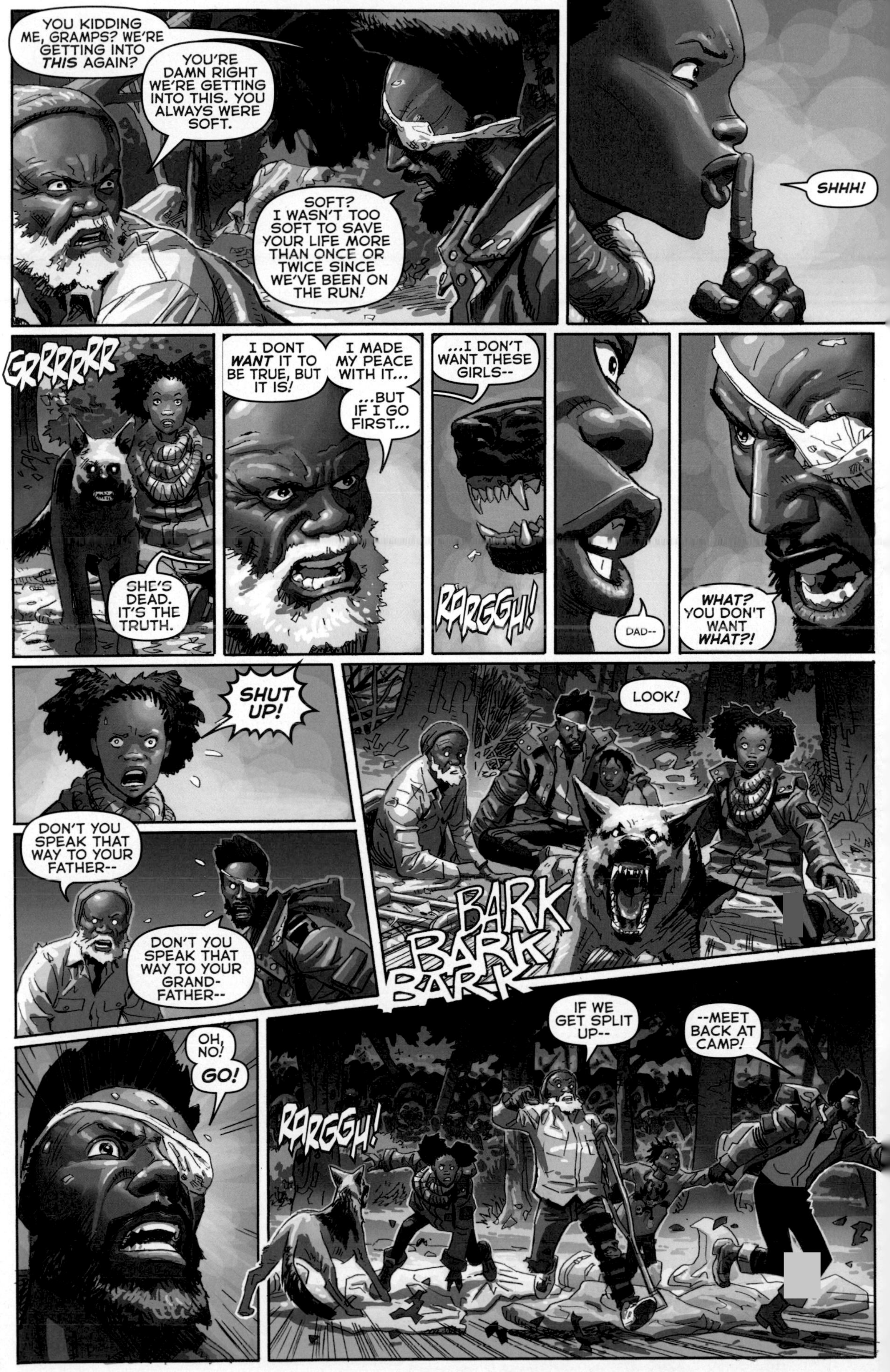

YOU KIDDING ME, GRAMPS? WE'RE GETTING INTO THIS AGAIN?
YOU'RE DAMN RIGHT WE'RE GETTING INTO THIS. YOU ALWAYS WERE SOFT.
SOFT? I WASN'T TOO SOFT TO SAVE YOUR LIFE MORE THAN ONCE OR TWICE SINCE WE'VE BEEN ON THE RUN!
SHHH!
GRRRRRR
SHE'S DEAD. IT'S THE TRUTH.
I DONT WANT IT TO BE TRUE, BUT IT IS!
I MADE MY PEACE WITH IT...
...BUT IF I GO FIRST...
...I DON'T WANT THESE GIRLS--
RARGGH!
DAD--
WHAT? YOU DON'T WANT WHAT?!
SHUT UP!
DON'T YOU SPEAK THAT WAY TO YOUR FATHER--
DON'T YOU SPEAK THAT WAY TO YOUR GRAND-FATHER--
LOOK!
BARK
BARK
BARK
OH, NO! GO!
RARGGH!
IF WE GET SPLIT UP--
--MEET BACK AT CAMP!

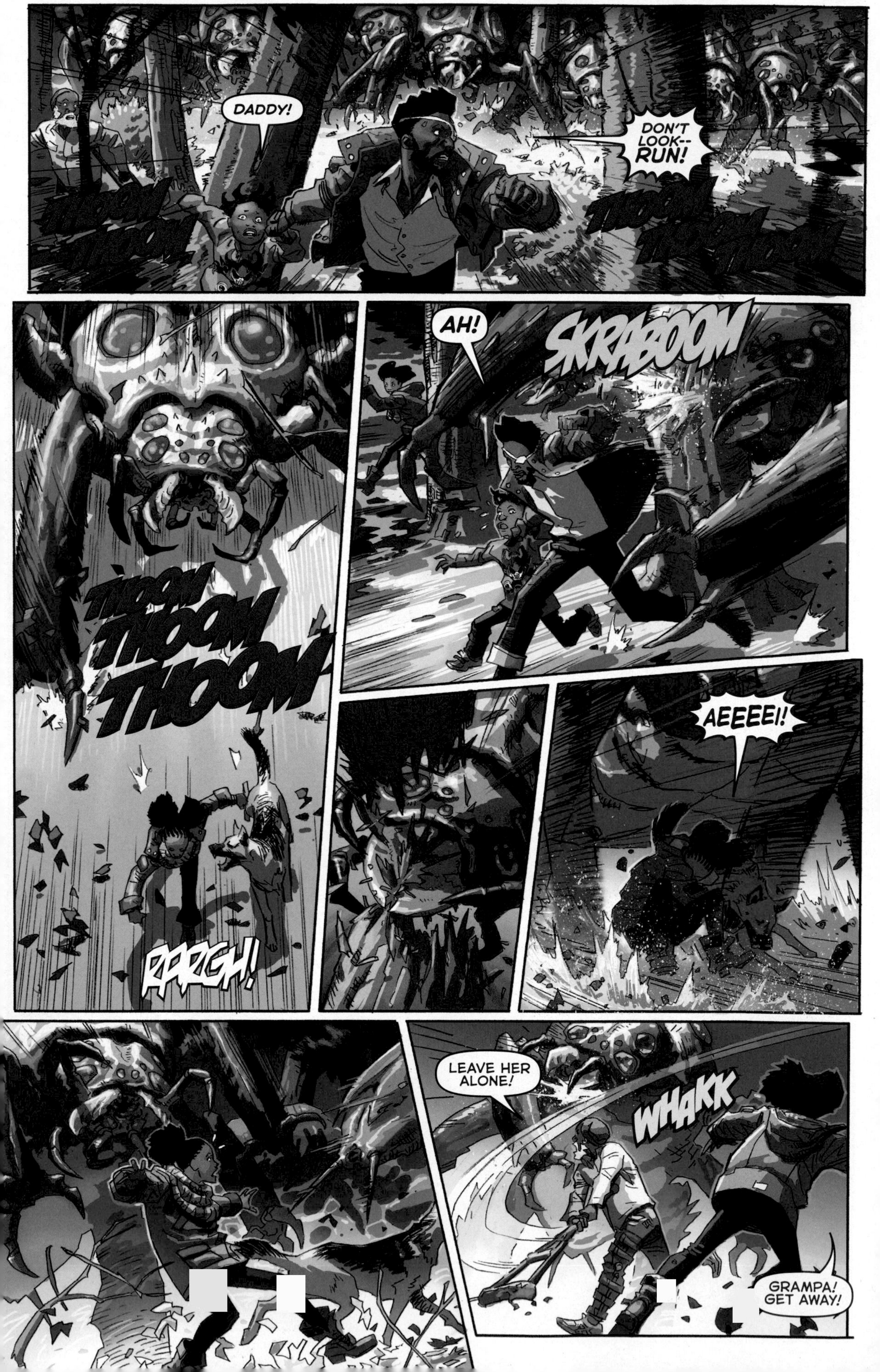
DADDY!
DON'T LOOK-- RUN!
THOOM THOOM
THOOM THOOM THOOM
THOOM THOOM THOOM
RRRGH!
AH!
SKRABOOM
AEEEEI!
LEAVE HER ALONE!
WHAKK
GRAMPA! GET AWAY!

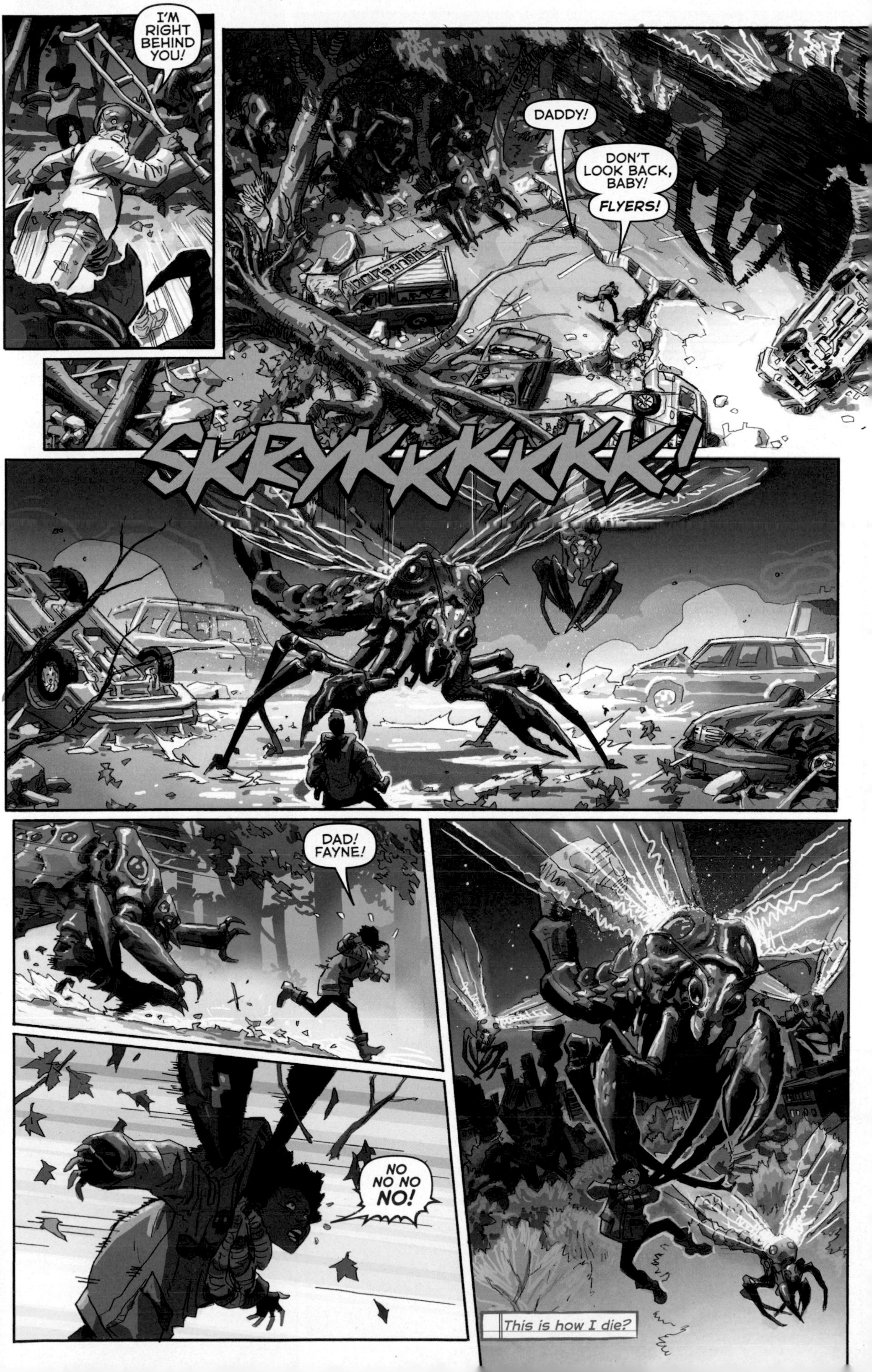
I'M RIGHT BEHIND YOU!
DADDY!
DON'T LOOK BACK, BABY!
FLYERS!
SKRYKKKKKK!
DAD! FAYNE!
NO NO NO NO!
This is how I die?

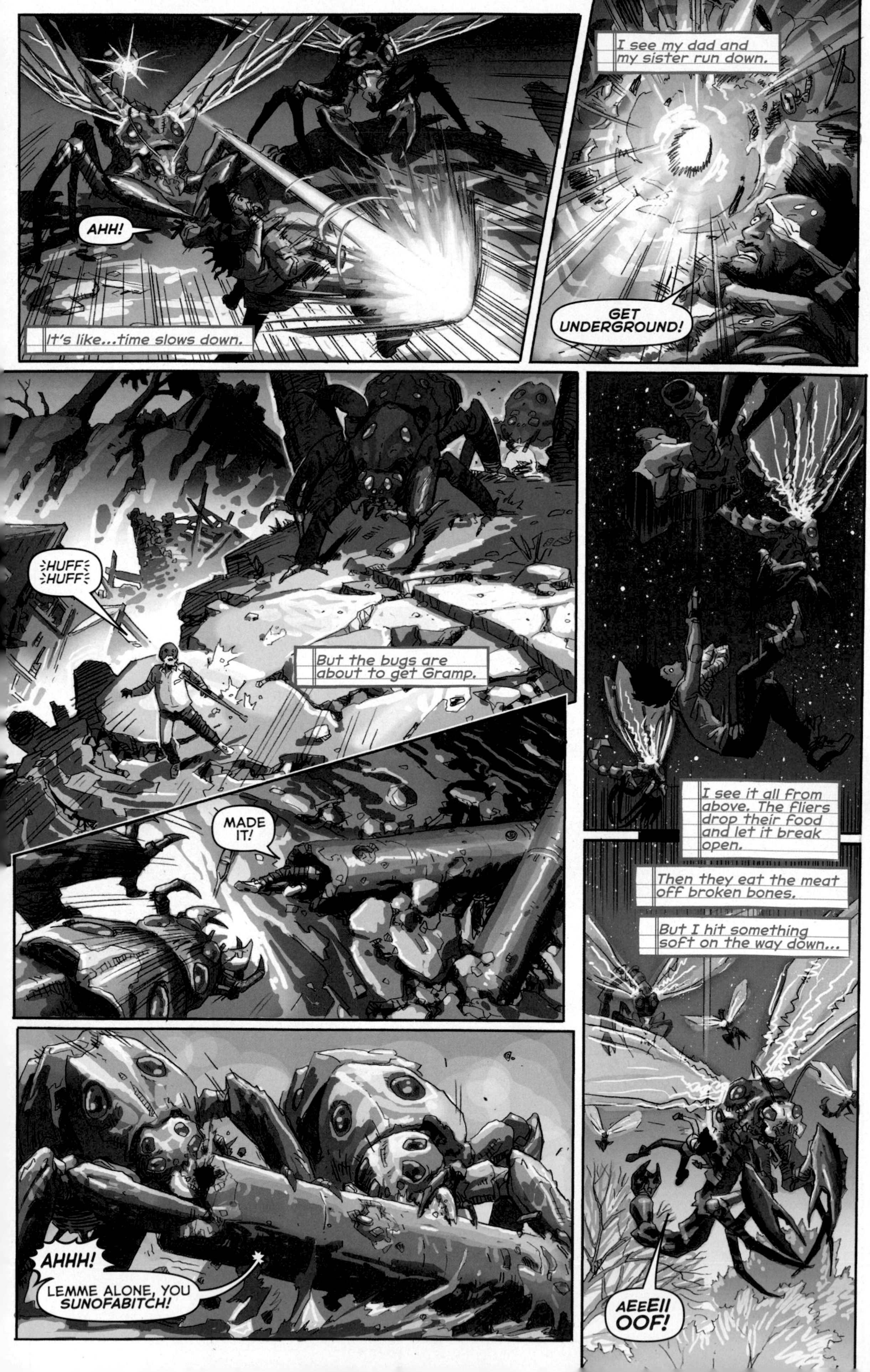
AHH!
It's like...time slows down.
I see my dad and my sister run down.
GET UNDERGROUND!
HUFF HUFF
But the bugs are about to get Gramp.
MADE IT!
AHHH!
LEMME ALONE, YOU SUNOFABITCH!
I see it all from above. The fliers drop their food and let it break open.
Then they eat the meat off broken bones.
But I hit something soft on the way down...
AEEEII OOF!

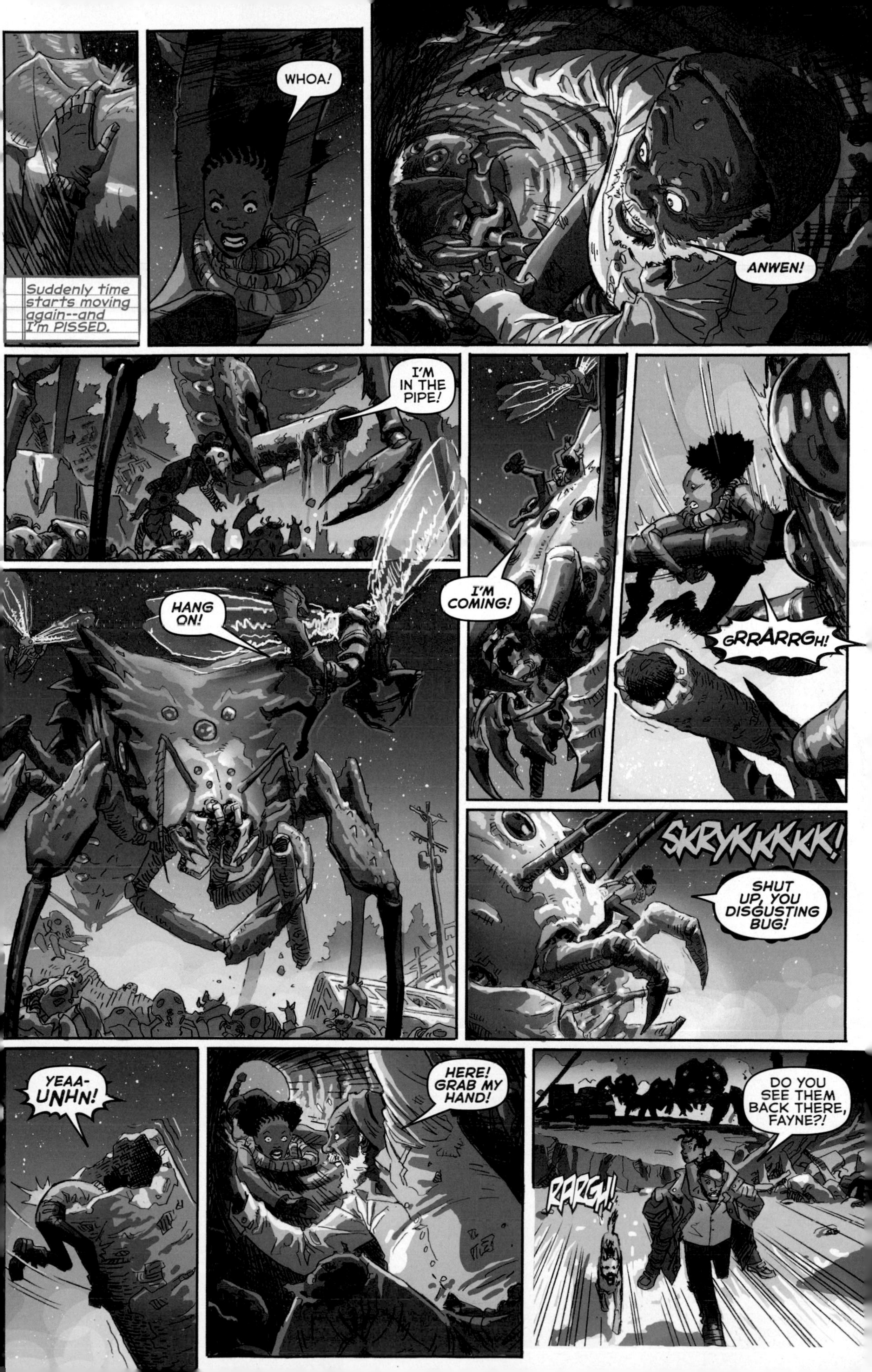
Suddenly time starts moving again--and I'm PISSED.
WHOA!
ANWEN!
I'M IN THE PIPE!
HANG ON!
I'M COMING!
GRRARRGH!
SKRYKKKKK!
SHUT UP, YOU DISGUSTING BUG!
YEAA-UNHN!
HERE! GRAB MY HAND!
DO YOU SEE THEM BACK THERE, FAYNE?!
RARGH!

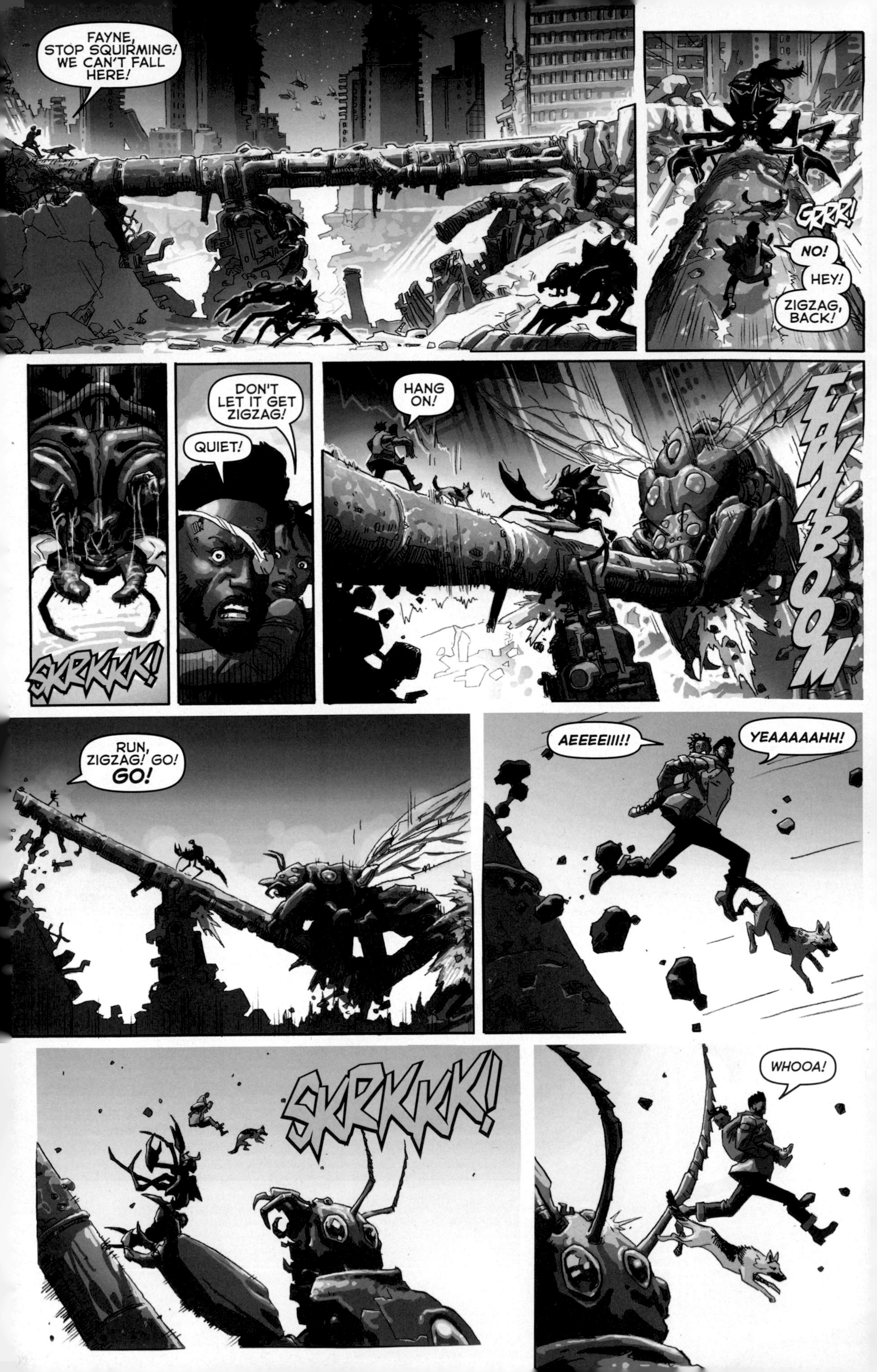

FAYNE, STOP SQUIRMING! WE CAN'T FALL HERE!
GRRR!
NO!
HEY!
ZIGZAG, BACK!
SKRKKK!
DON'T LET IT GET ZIGZAG!
QUIET!
HANG ON!
THWABOOM
RUN, ZIGZAG! GO! GO!
AEEEEIII!!
YEAAAAAHH!
SKRKKK!
WHOOA!

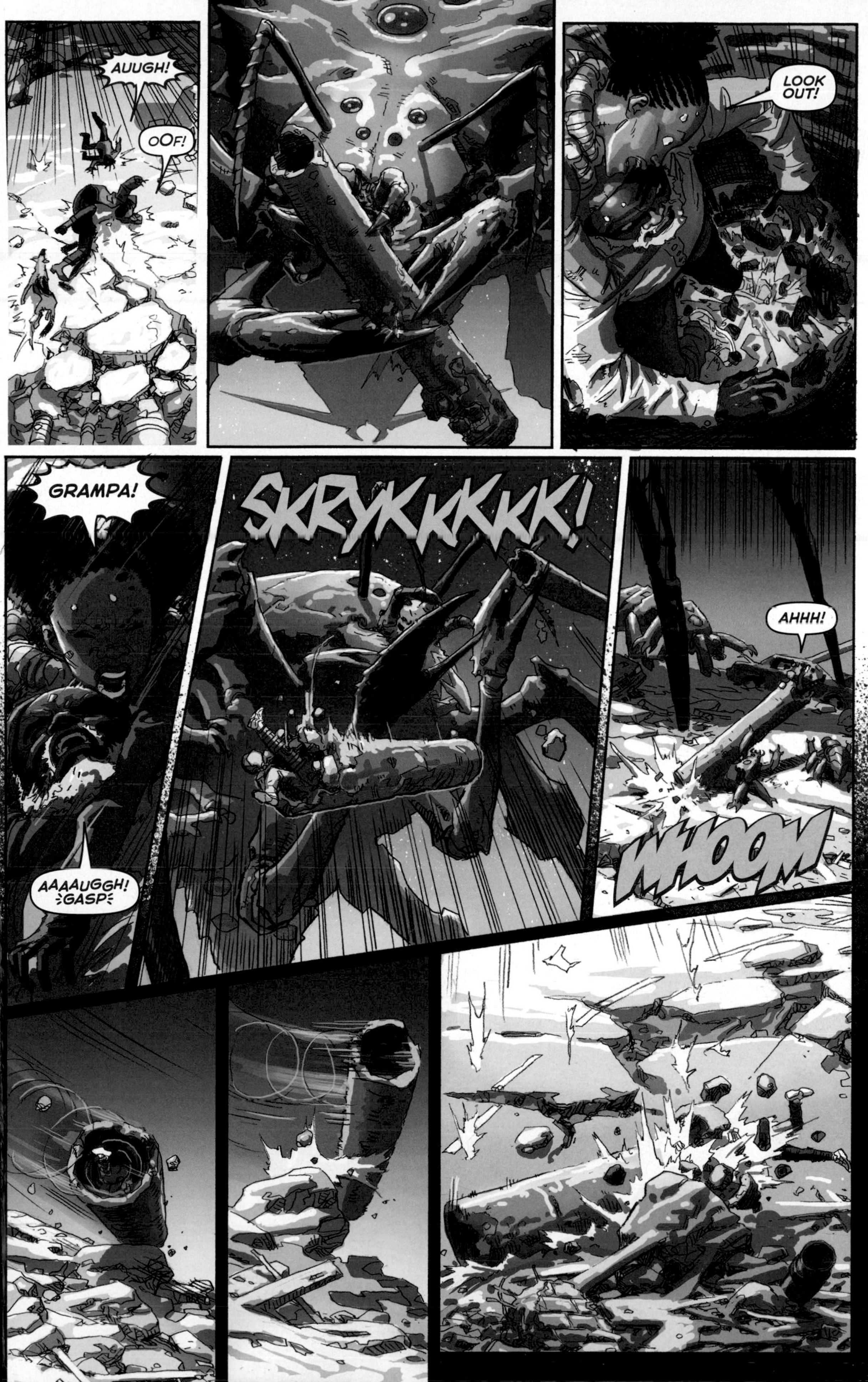
AUUGH!
OOF!
LOOK OUT!
GRAMPA!
AAAAUGGH! GASP
SKRYKKKKK!
AHHH!
WHOOM

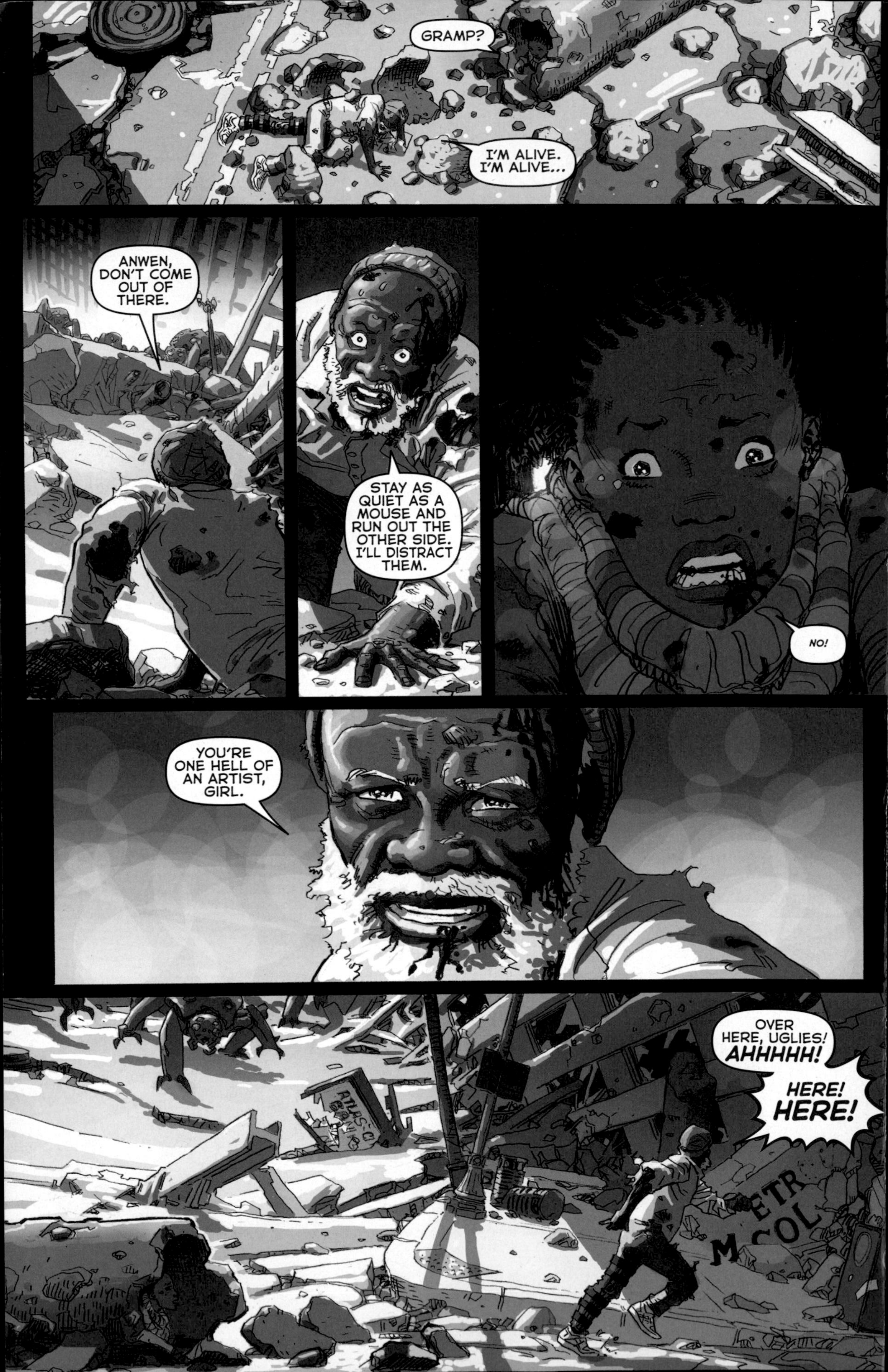
GRAMP?
I'M ALIVE. I'M ALIVE...
ANWEN, DON'T COME OUT OF THERE.
STAY AS QUIET AS A MOUSE AND RUN OUT THE OTHER SIDE. I'LL DISTRACT THEM.
NO!
YOU'RE ONE HELL OF AN ARTIST, GIRL.
OVER HERE, UGLIES! AHHHHH!
HERE! HERE!

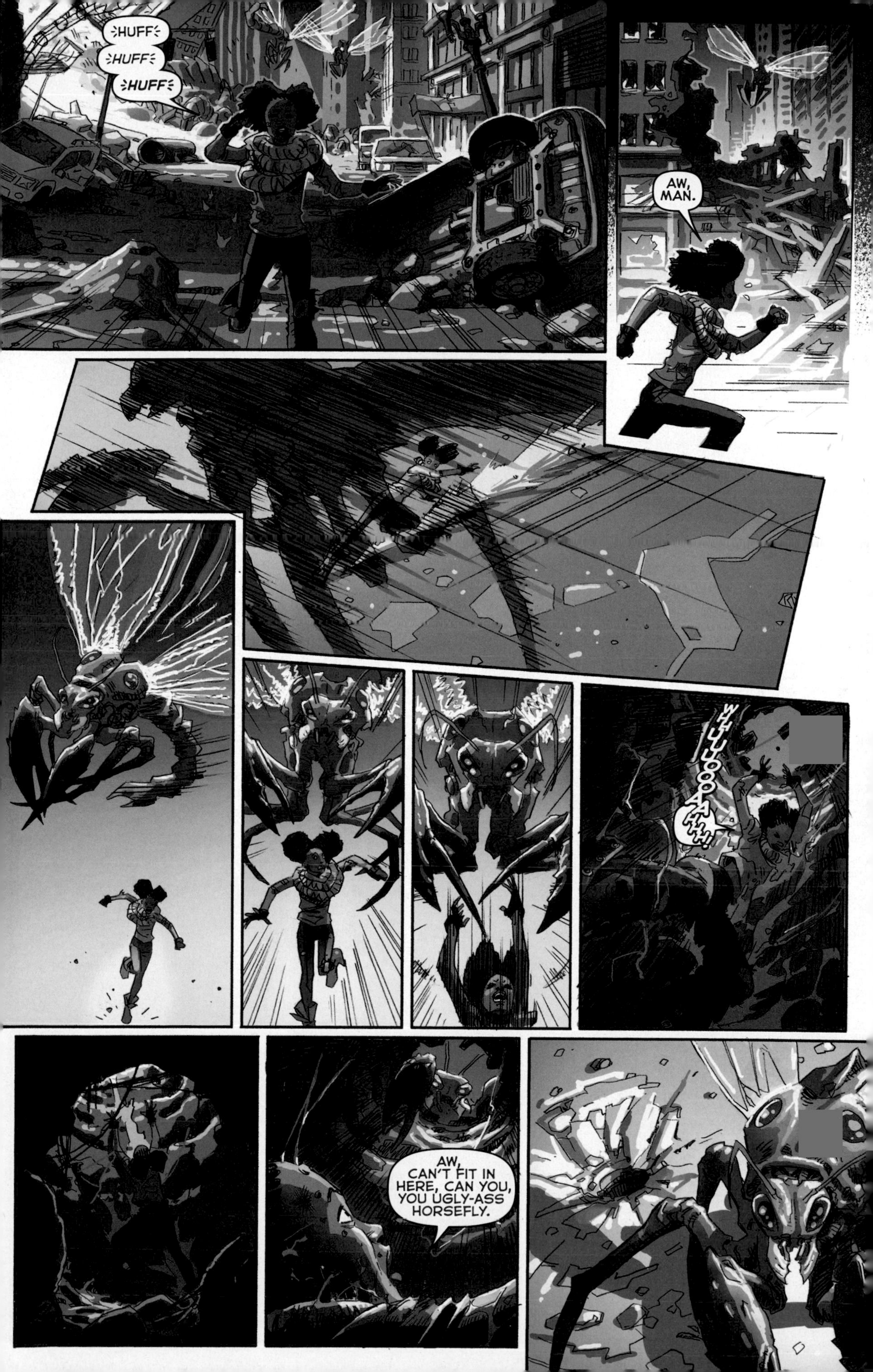
HUFF
HUFF
HUFF
AW, MAN.
WHUUUOOOAAHH!
AW, CAN'T FIT IN HERE, CAN YOU, YOU UGLY-ASS HORSEFLY.

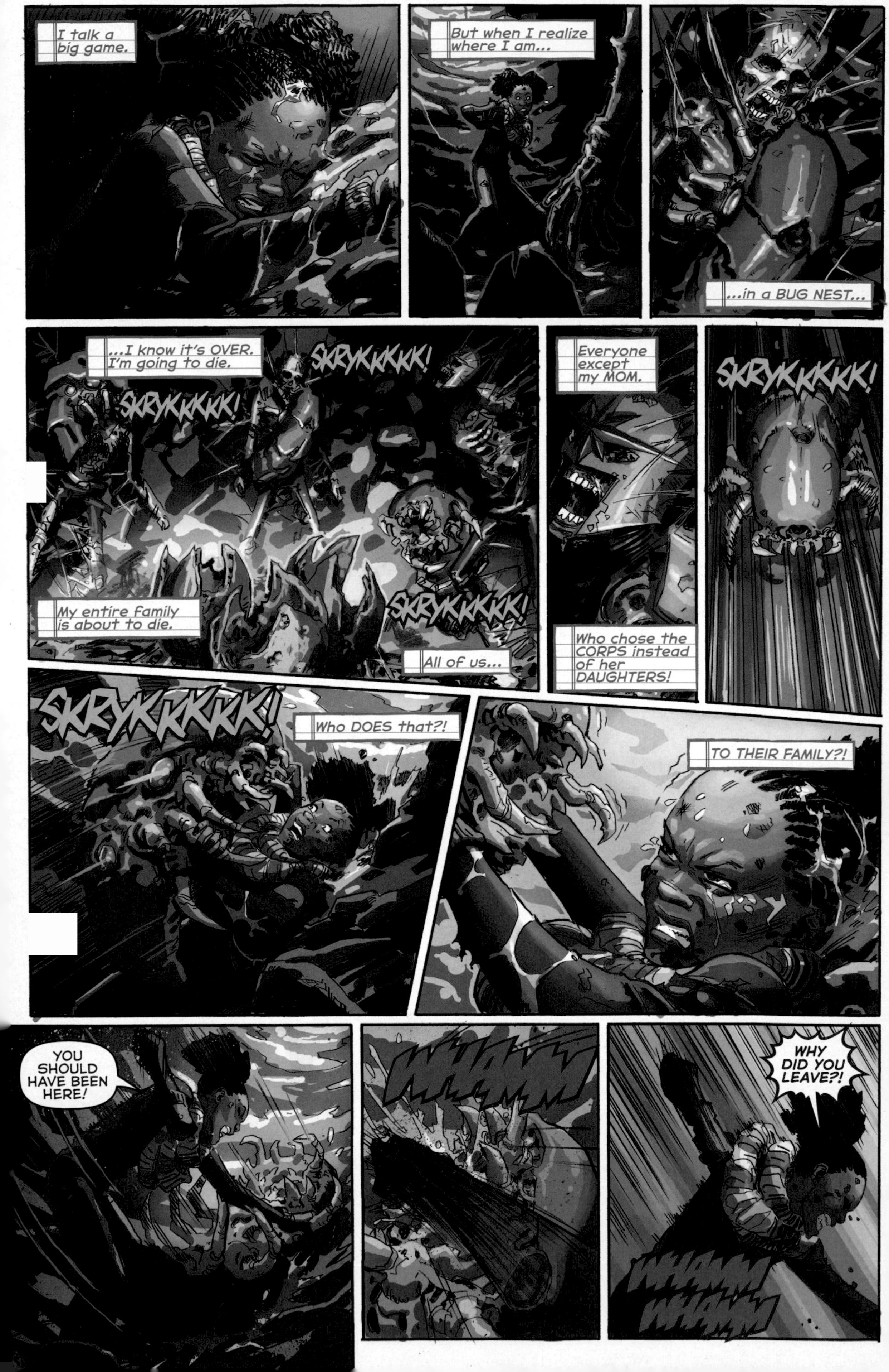
I talk a big game.
But when I realize where I am...
...in a BUG NEST...
...I know it's OVER. I'm going to die.
SKRYKKKKK!
SKRYKKKKK!
My entire family is about to die.
SKRYKKKKK!
All of us...
Everyone except my MOM.
Who chose the CORPS instead of her DAUGHTERS!
SKRYKKKKK!
SKRYKKKKK!
Who DOES that?!
TO THEIR FAMILY?!
YOU SHOULD HAVE BEEN HERE!
WHAM
WHY DID YOU LEAVE?!
WHAM
WHAM

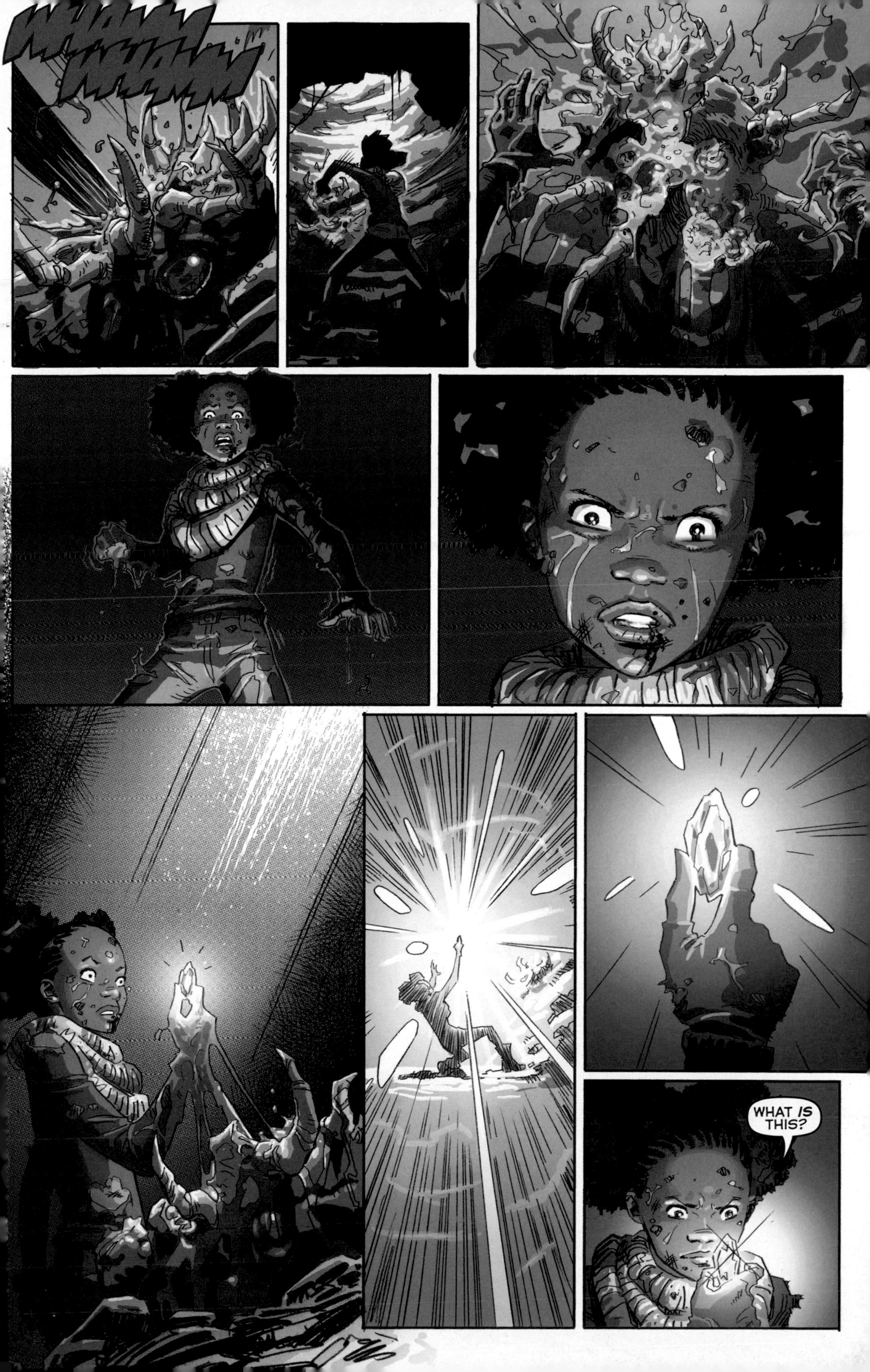
WHAT *IS* THIS?

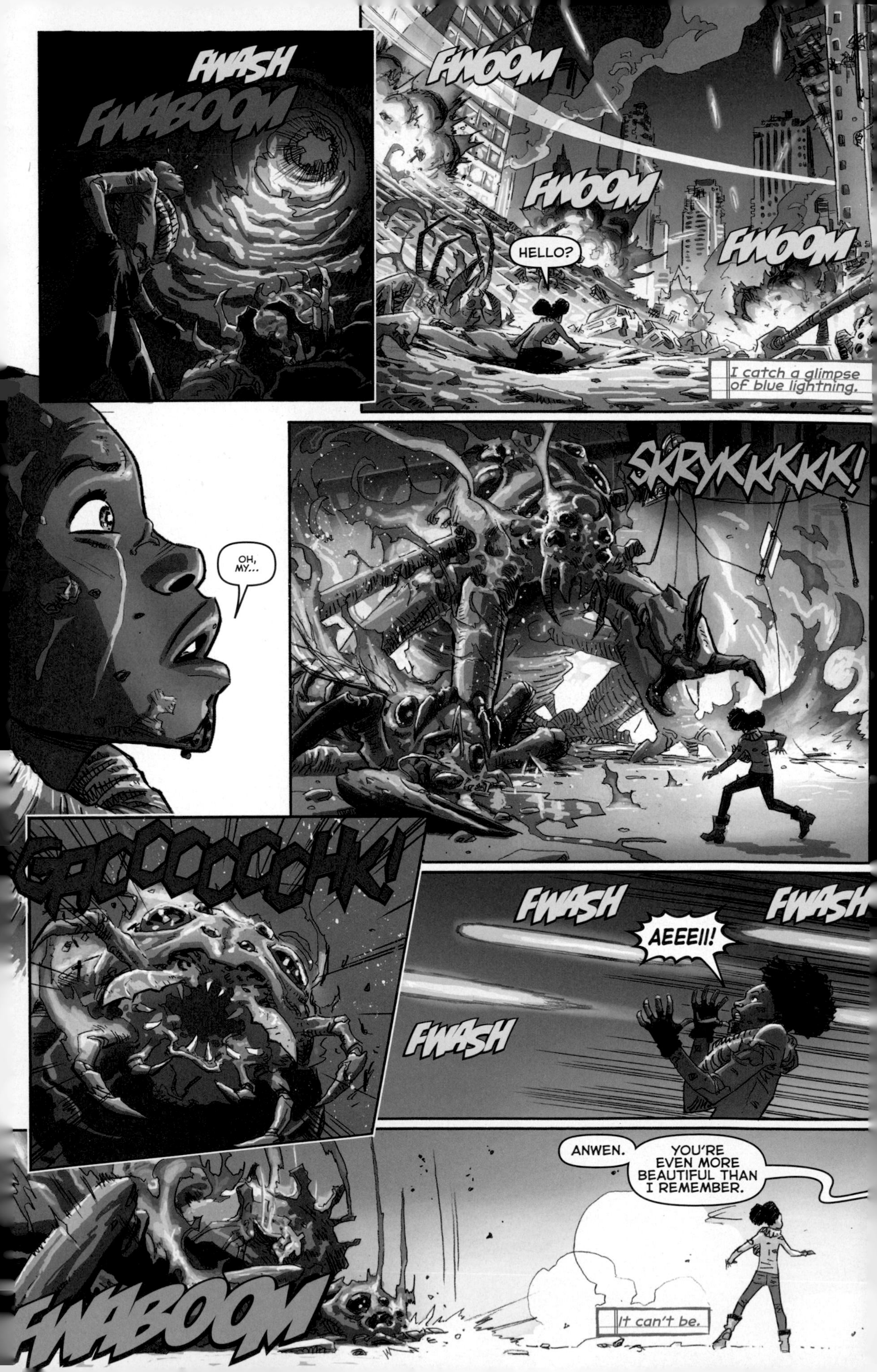
FWASH
FWABOOM
FWOOM
FWOOM
HELLO?
FWOOM
I catch a glimpse of blue lightning.
OH, MY...
SKRYKKKKK!
GRCCCCCCCHK!
FWASH
FWASH
AEEEII!
FWASH
FWABOOM
ANWEN.
YOU'RE EVEN MORE BEAUTIFUL THAN I REMEMBER.
It can't be.

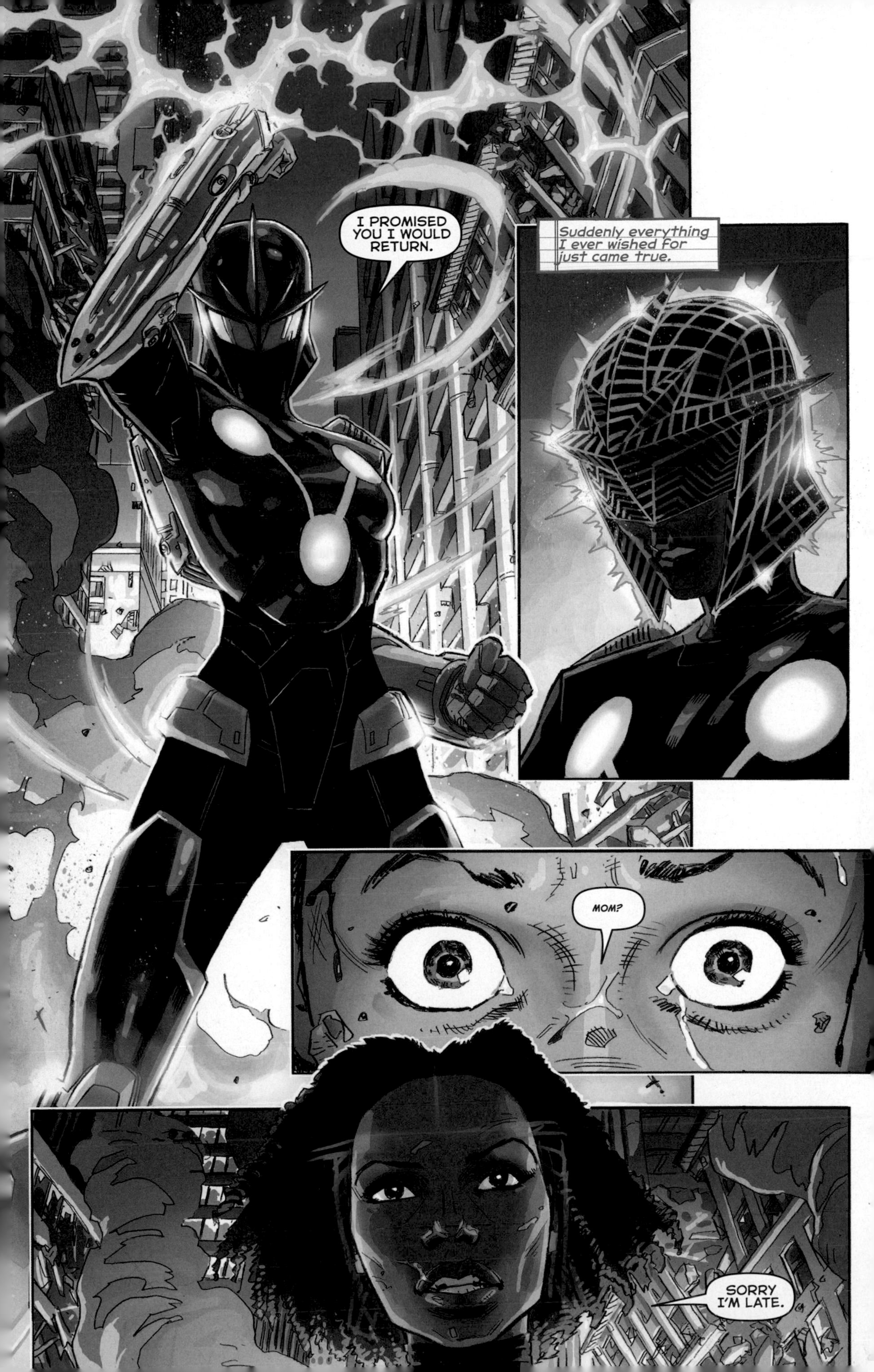
I PROMISED YOU I WOULD RETURN.
Suddenly everything I ever wished for just came true.
MOM?
SORRY I'M LATE.

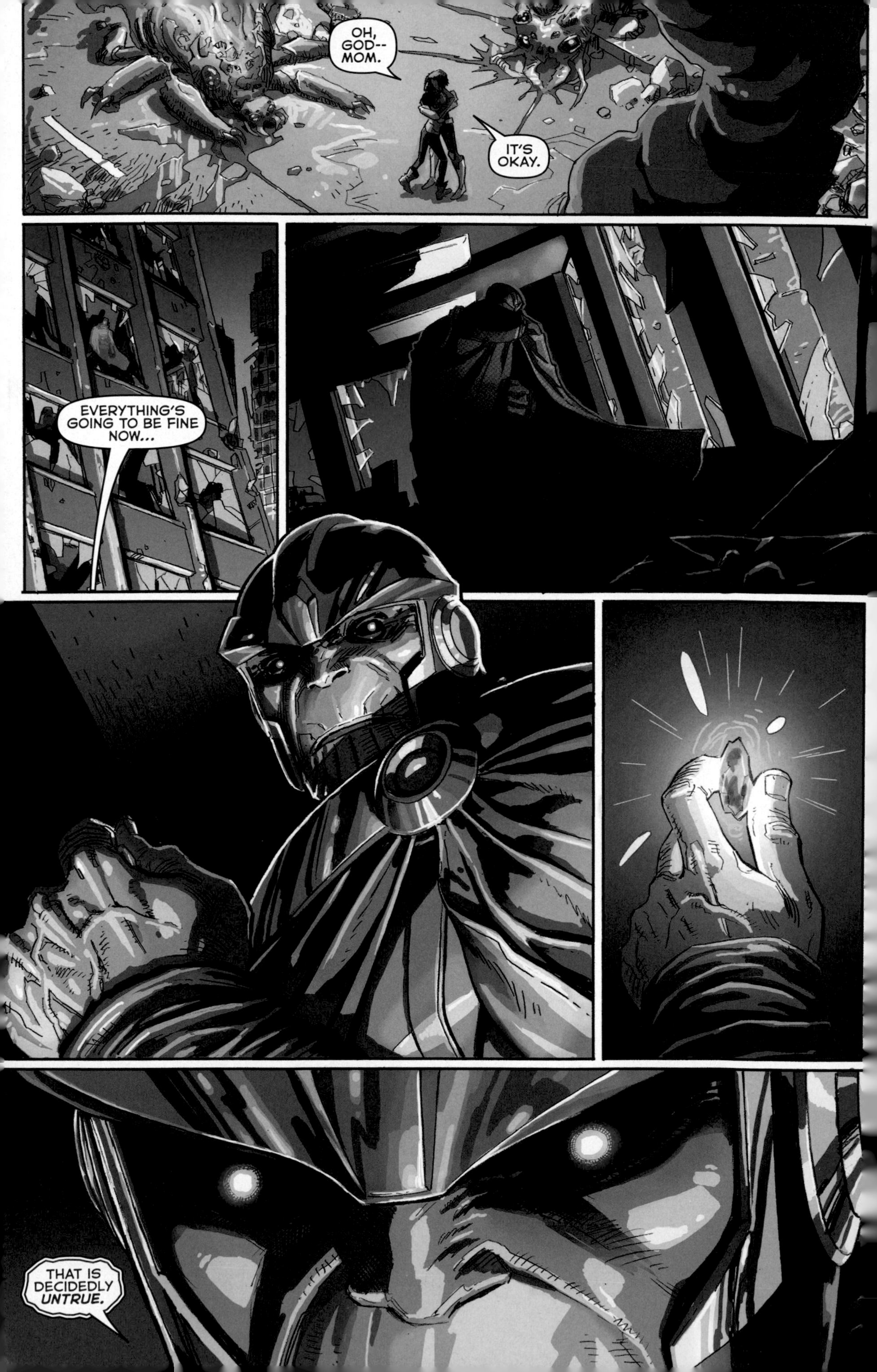
OH, GOD-- MOM.
IT'S OKAY.
EVERYTHING'S GOING TO BE FINE NOW...
THAT IS DECIDEDLY *UNTRUE.*

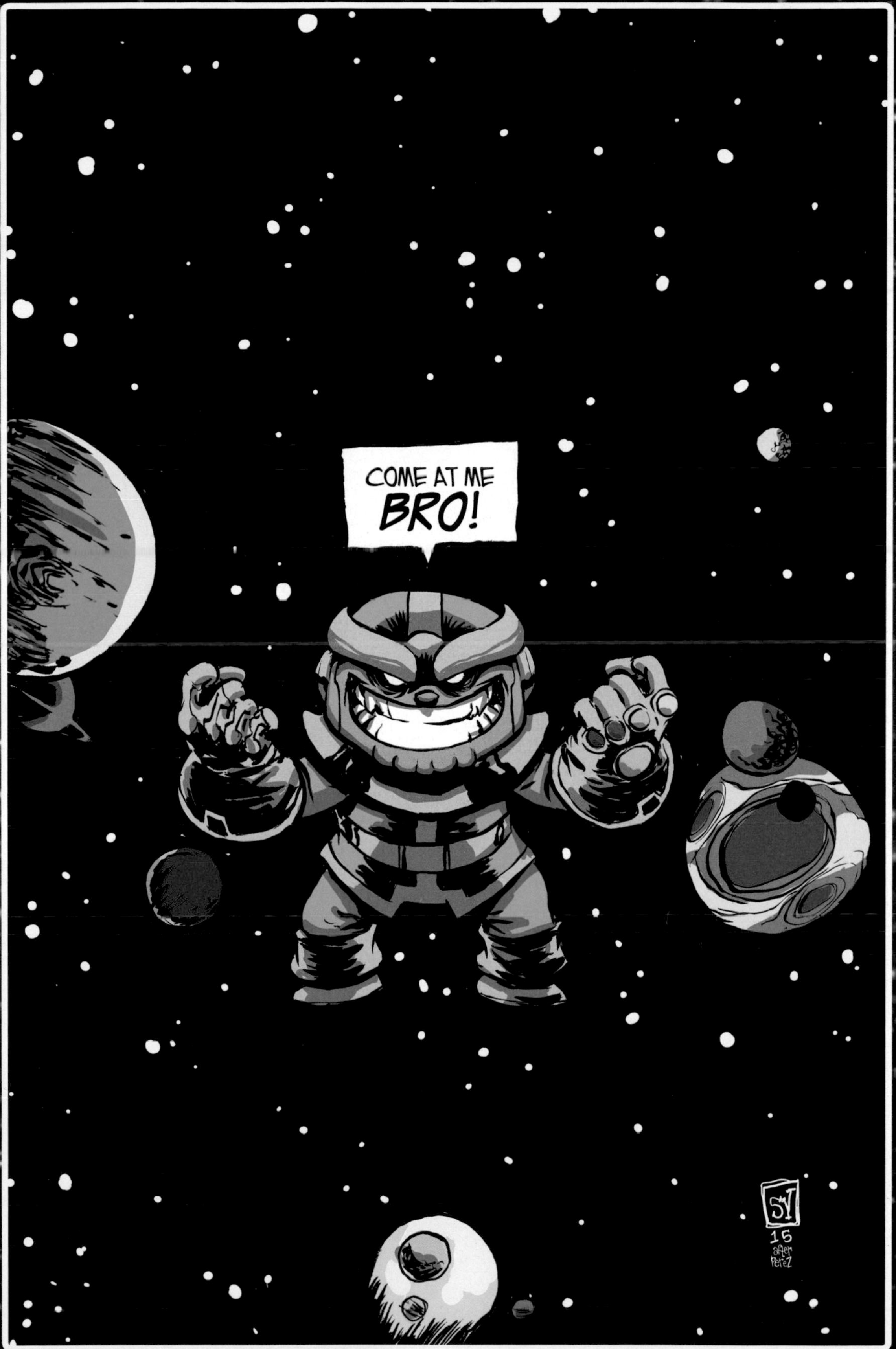
COME AT ME BRO!

INFINITY GAUNTLET 1
VARIANT COVER BY SKOTTIE YOUNG

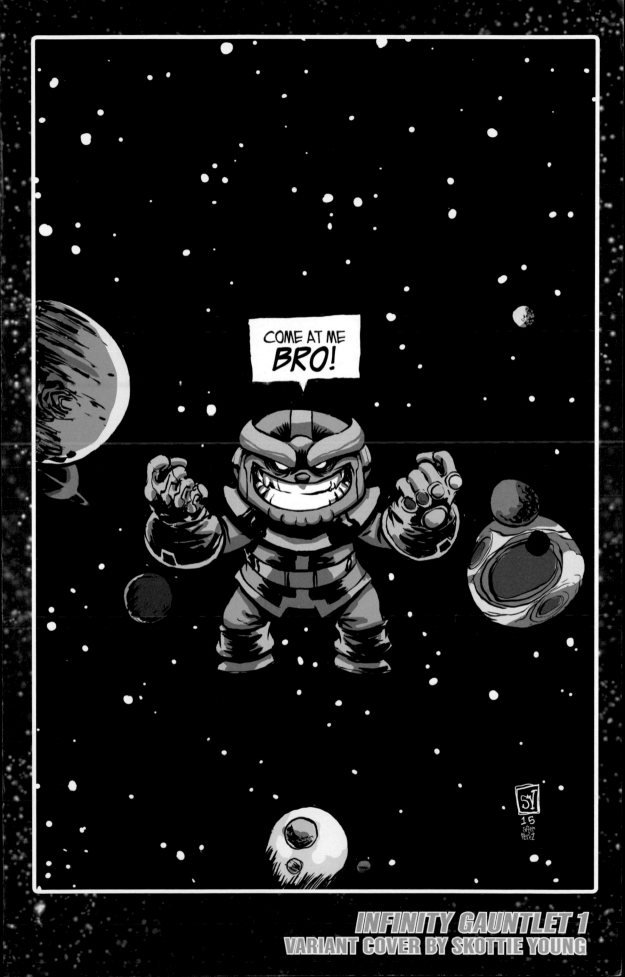

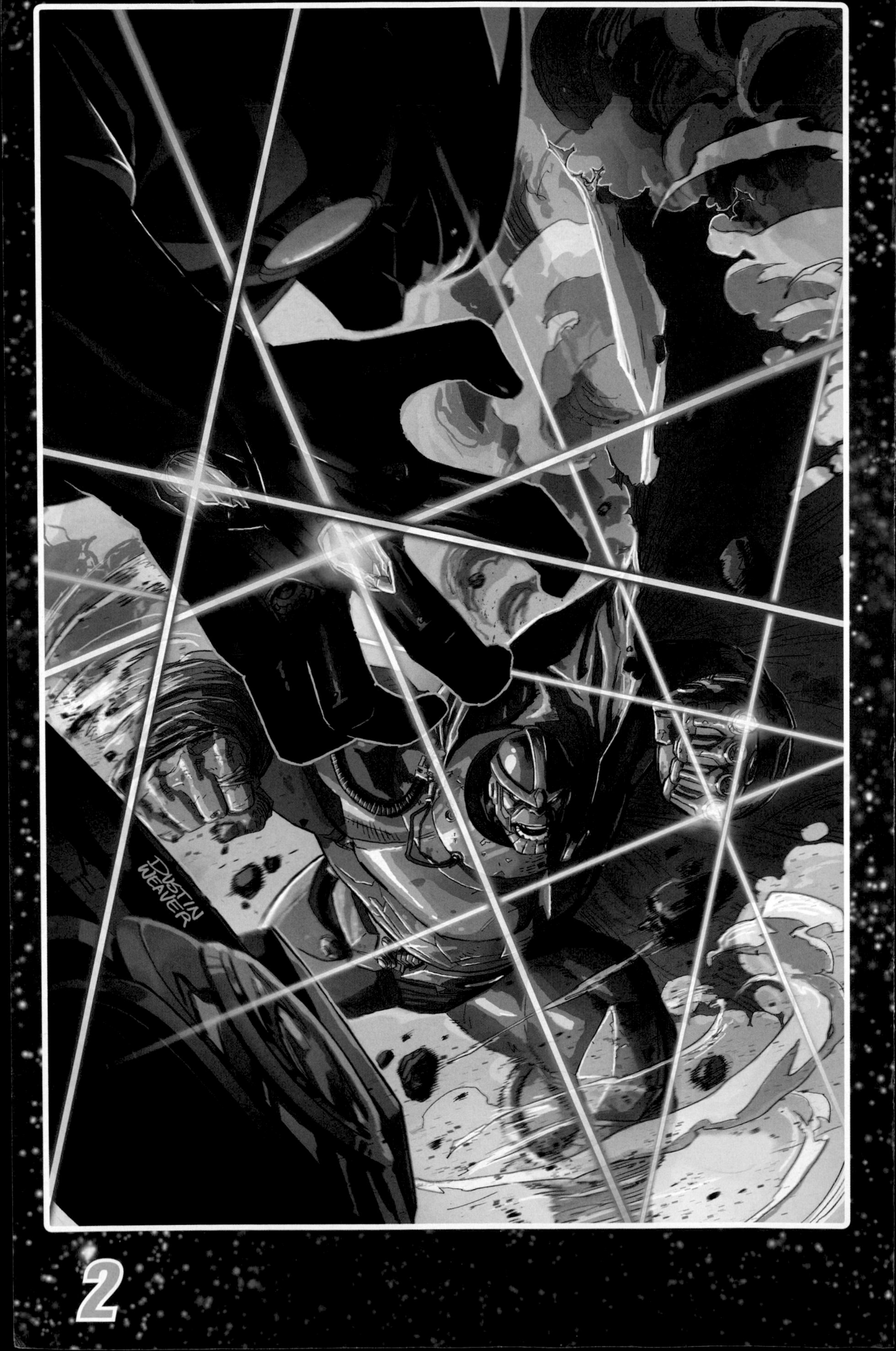
DUSTIN
WEAVER

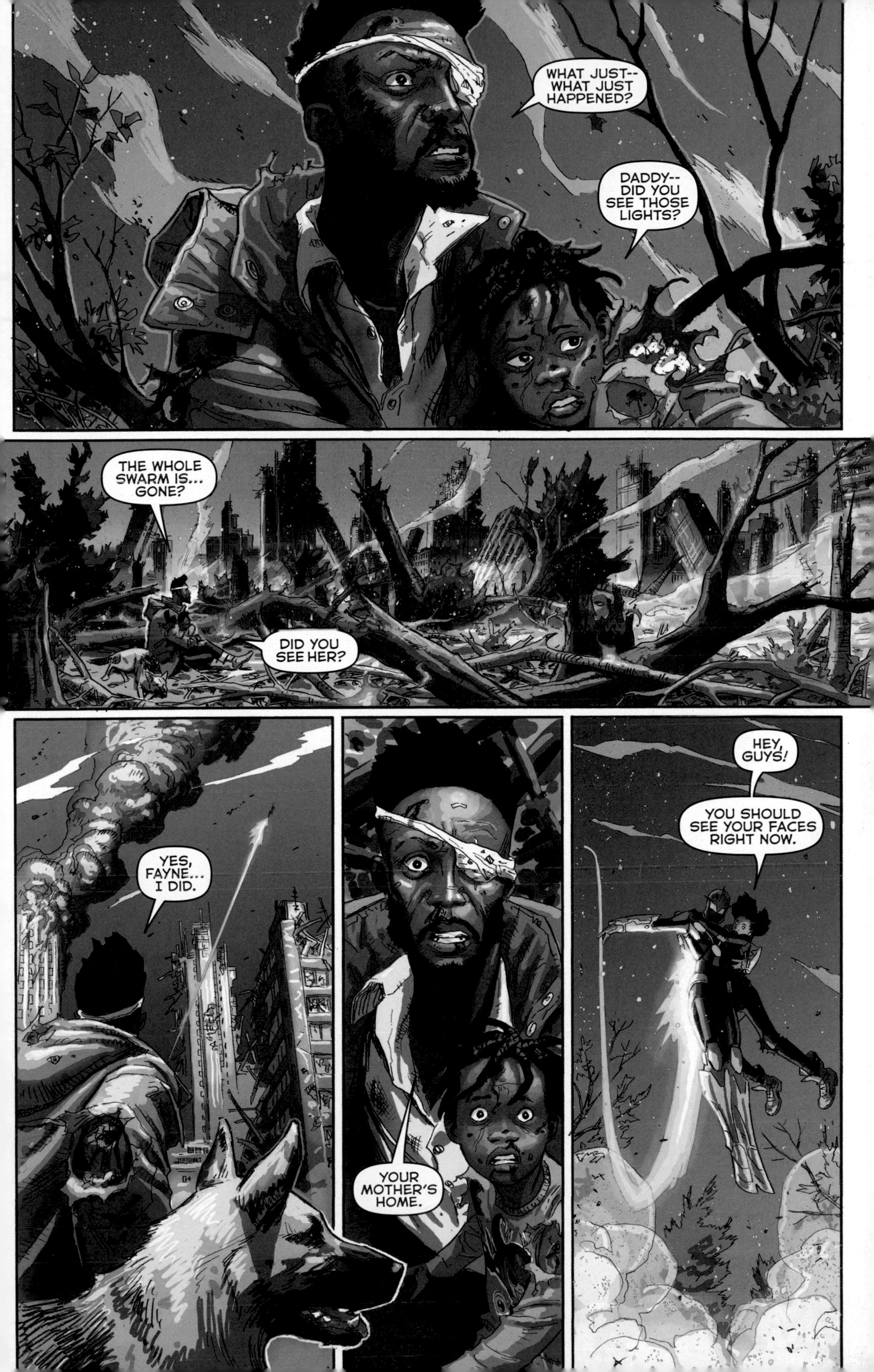
WHAT JUST-- WHAT JUST HAPPENED?
DADDY-- DID YOU SEE THOSE LIGHTS?
THE WHOLE SWARM IS... GONE?
DID YOU SEE HER?
YES, FAYNE... I DID.
YOUR MOTHER'S HOME.
HEY, GUYS!
YOU SHOULD SEE YOUR FACES RIGHT NOW.

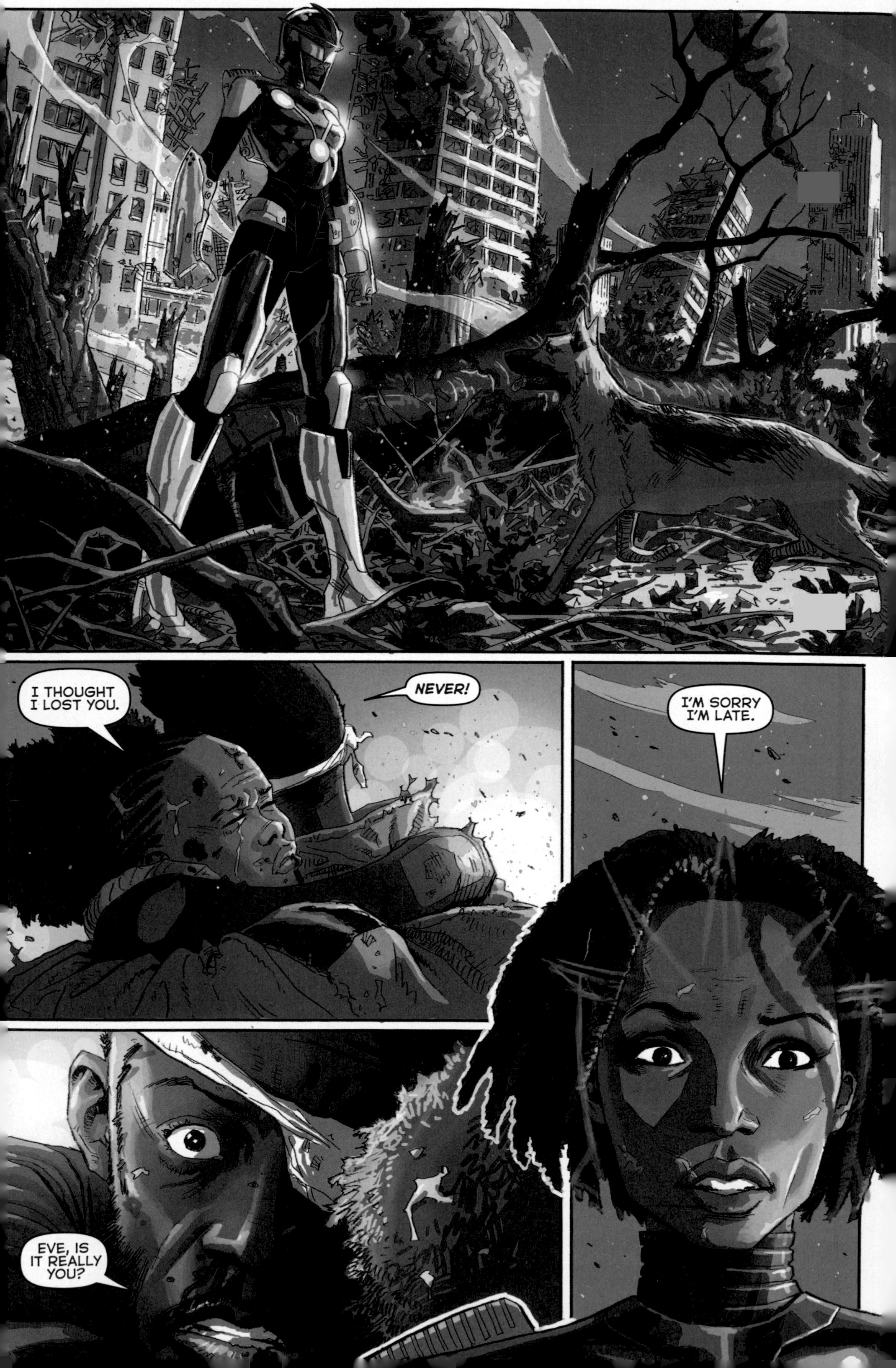
I THOUGHT I LOST YOU.
NEVER!
I'M SORRY I'M LATE.
EVE, IS IT REALLY YOU?

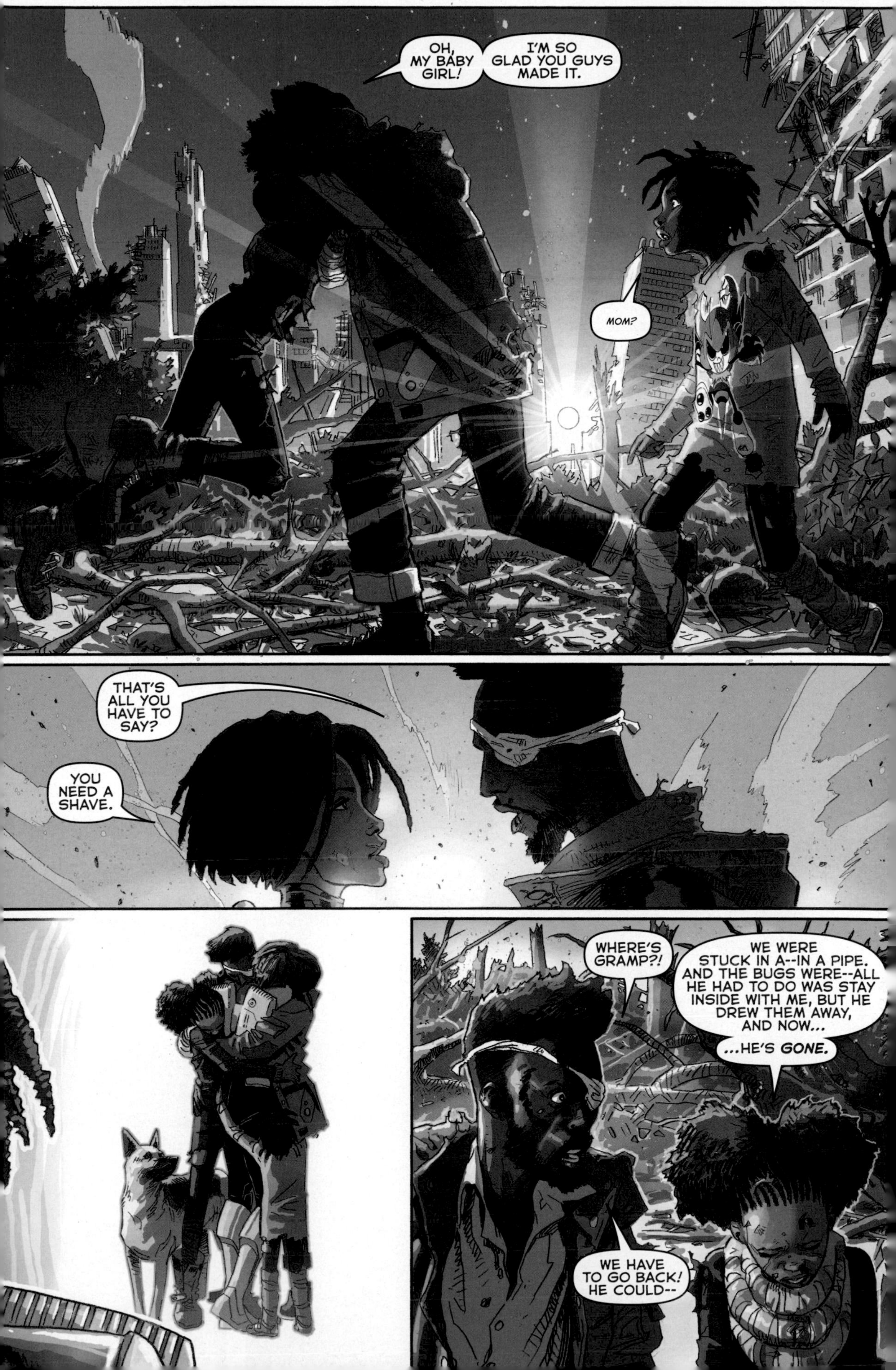
OH, MY BABY GIRL!
I'M SO GLAD YOU GUYS MADE IT.
MOM?
THAT'S ALL YOU HAVE TO SAY?
YOU NEED A SHAVE.
WHERE'S GRAMP?!
WE WERE STUCK IN A--IN A PIPE. AND THE BUGS WERE--ALL HE HAD TO DO WAS STAY INSIDE WITH ME, BUT HE DREW THEM AWAY, AND NOW...
...HE'S GONE.
WE HAVE TO GO BACK! HE COULD--

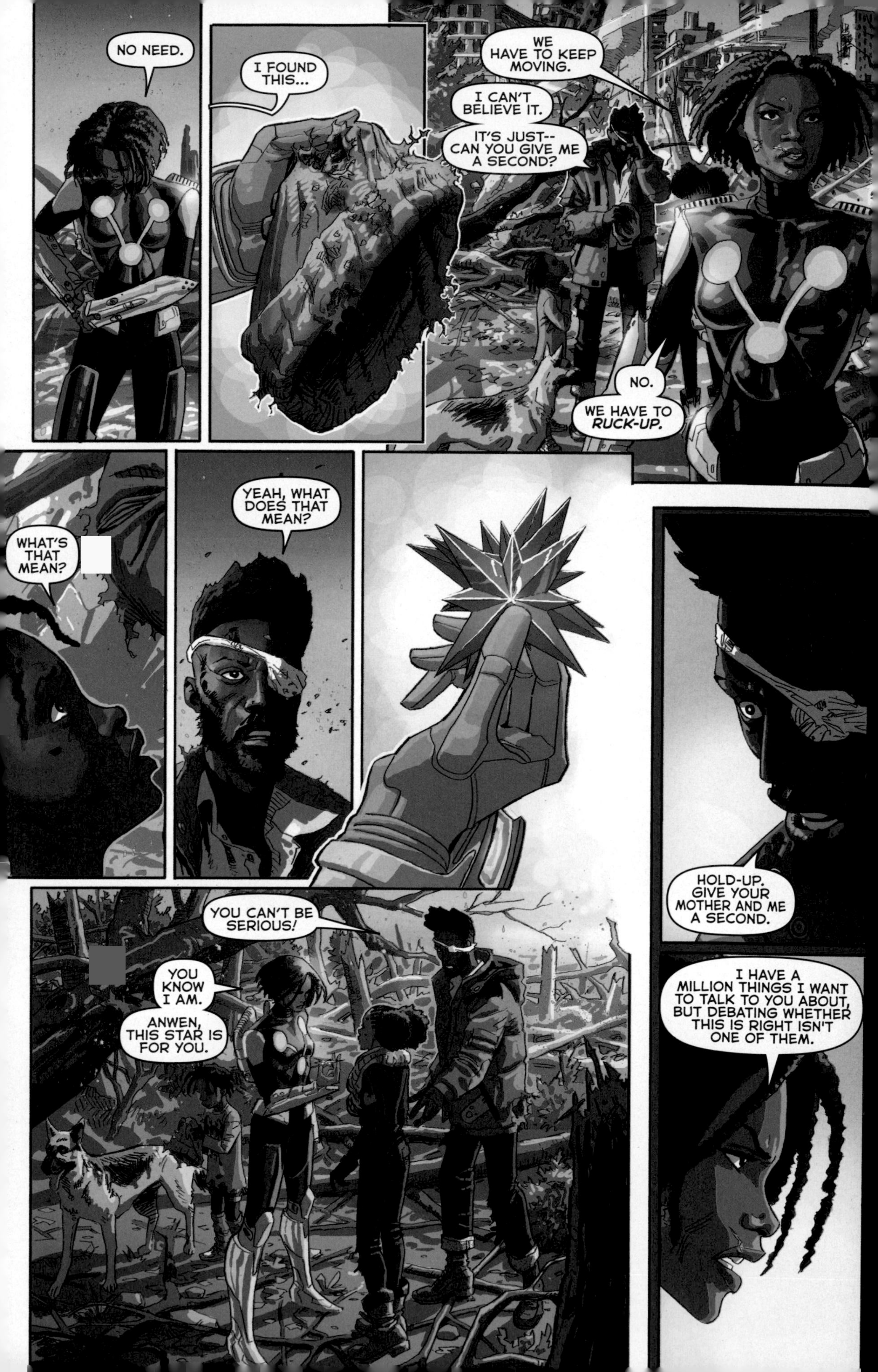
NO NEED.
I FOUND THIS...
WE HAVE TO KEEP MOVING.
I CAN'T BELIEVE IT.
IT'S JUST-- CAN YOU GIVE ME A SECOND?
NO.
WE HAVE TO *RUCK-UP.*
WHAT'S THAT MEAN?
YEAH, WHAT DOES THAT MEAN?
HOLD-UP. GIVE YOUR MOTHER AND ME A SECOND.
YOU CAN'T BE SERIOUS!
YOU KNOW I AM.
ANWEN, THIS STAR IS FOR YOU.
I HAVE A MILLION THINGS I WANT TO TALK TO YOU ABOUT, BUT DEBATING WHETHER THIS IS RIGHT ISN'T ONE OF THEM.

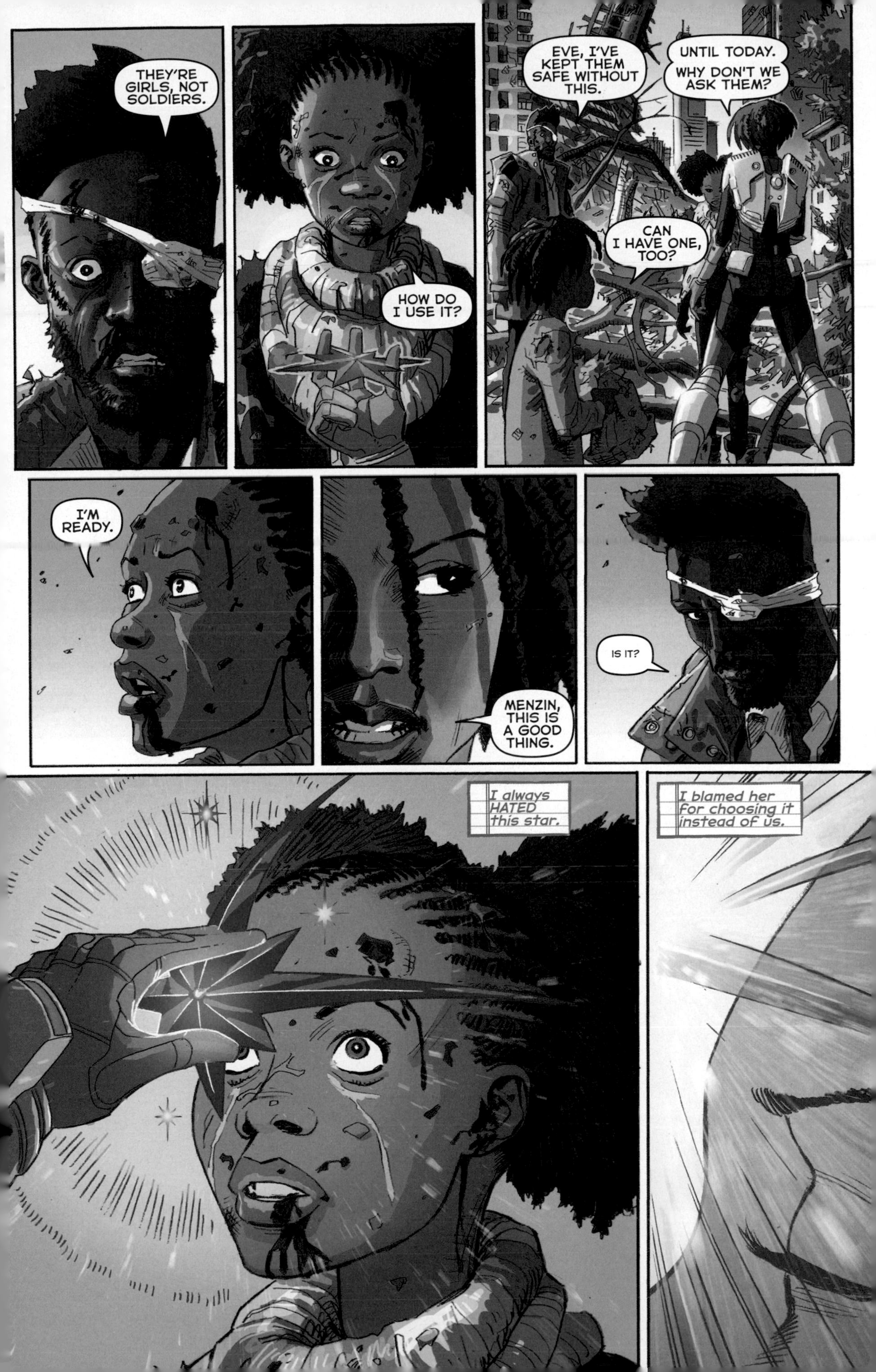
THEY'RE GIRLS, NOT SOLDIERS.
HOW DO I USE IT?
EVE, I'VE KEPT THEM SAFE WITHOUT THIS.
UNTIL TODAY. WHY DON'T WE ASK THEM?
CAN I HAVE ONE, TOO?
I'M READY.
MENZIN, THIS IS A GOOD THING.
IS IT?
I always HATED this star.
I blamed her for choosing it instead of us.

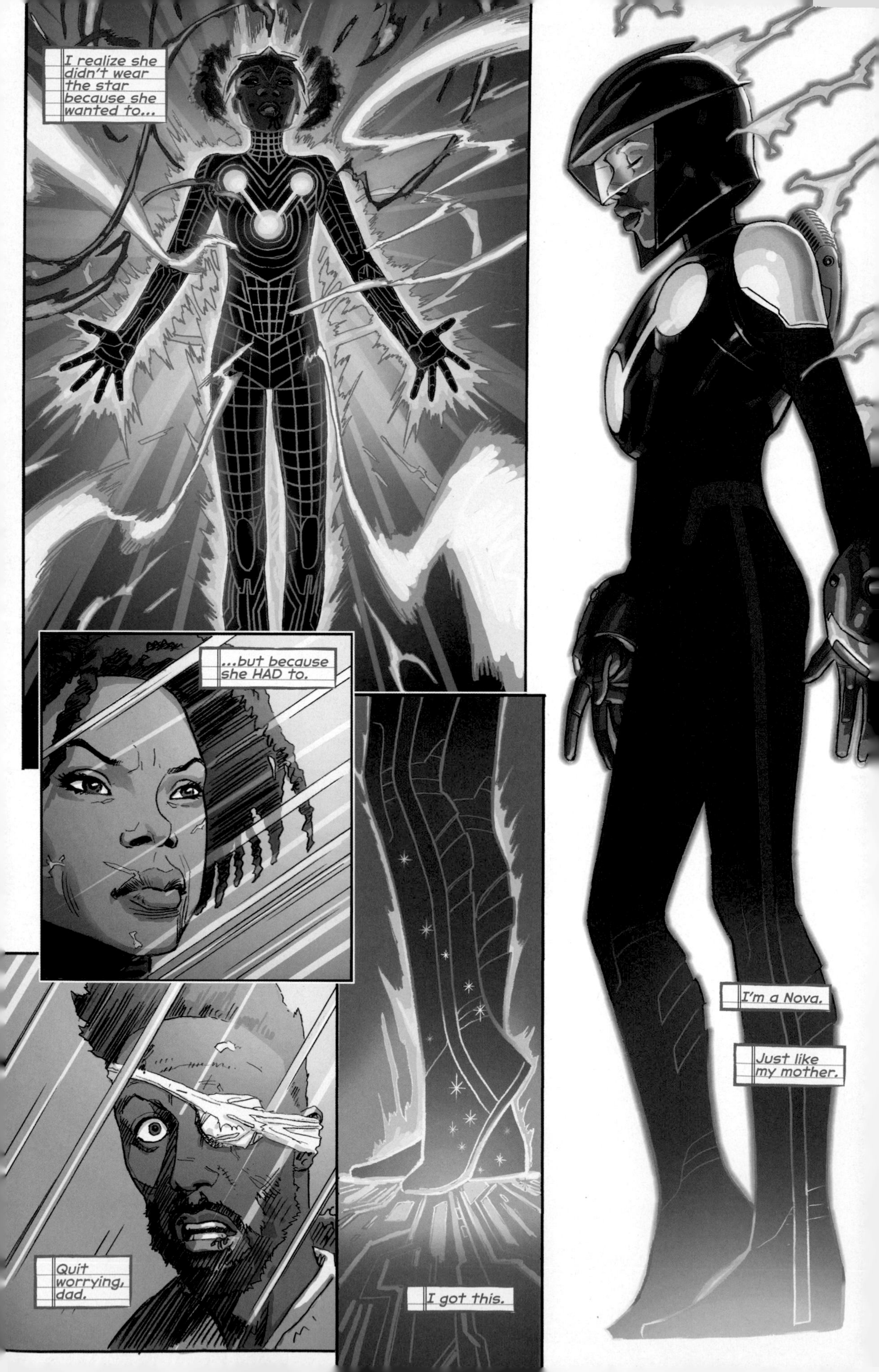
I realize she didn't wear the star because she wanted to...
...but because she HAD to.
Quit worrying, dad.
I got this.
I'm a Nova.
Just like my mother.

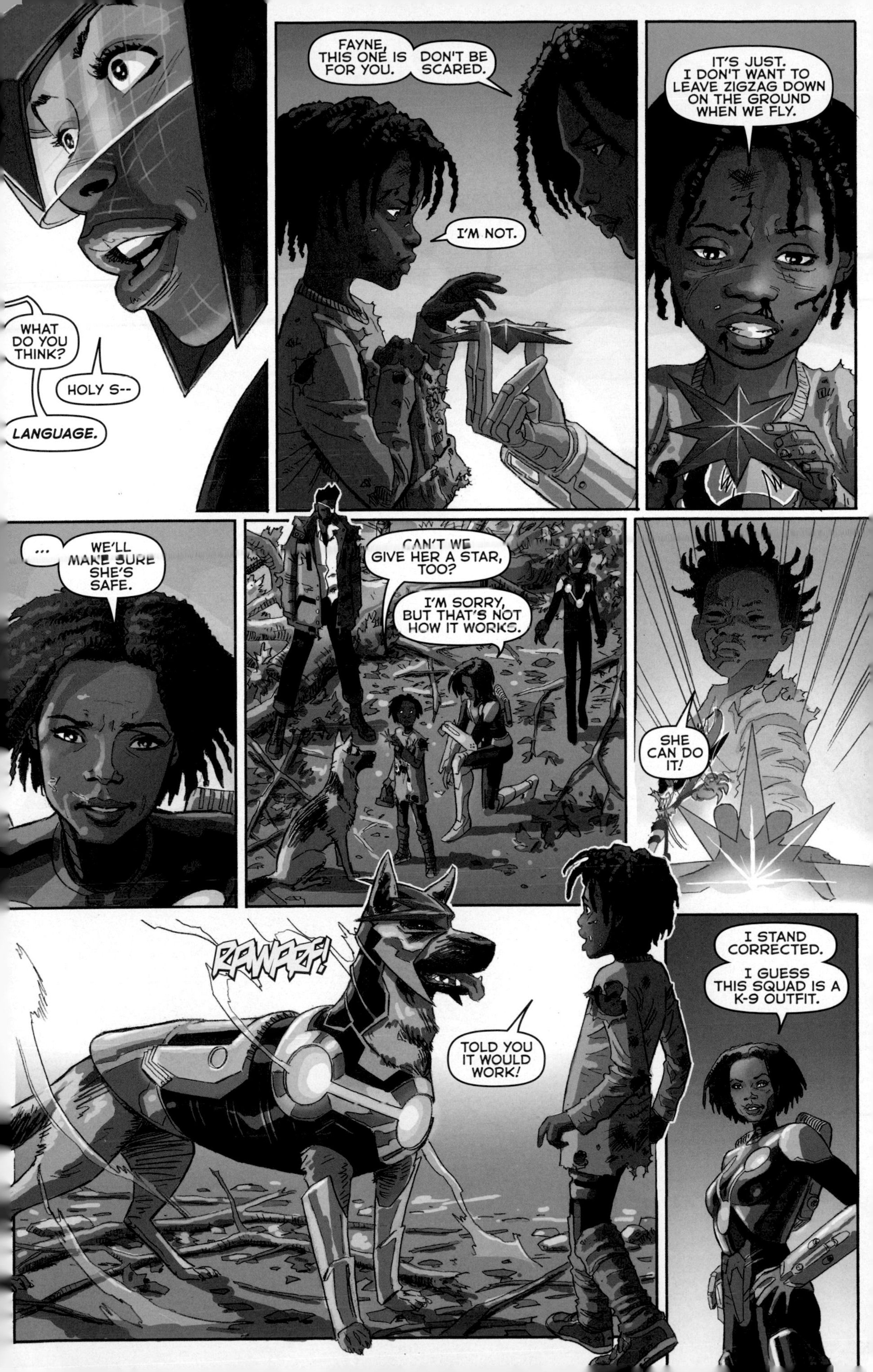
WHAT DO YOU THINK?
HOLY S--
LANGUAGE.
FAYNE, THIS ONE IS FOR YOU.
DON'T BE SCARED.
I'M NOT.
IT'S JUST. I DON'T WANT TO LEAVE ZIGZAG DOWN ON THE GROUND WHEN WE FLY.
...
WE'LL MAKE SURE SHE'S SAFE.
CAN'T WE GIVE HER A STAR, TOO?
I'M SORRY, BUT THAT'S NOT HOW IT WORKS.
SHE CAN DO IT!
RAWRF!
TOLD YOU IT WOULD WORK!
I STAND CORRECTED.
I GUESS THIS SQUAD IS A K-9 OUTFIT.

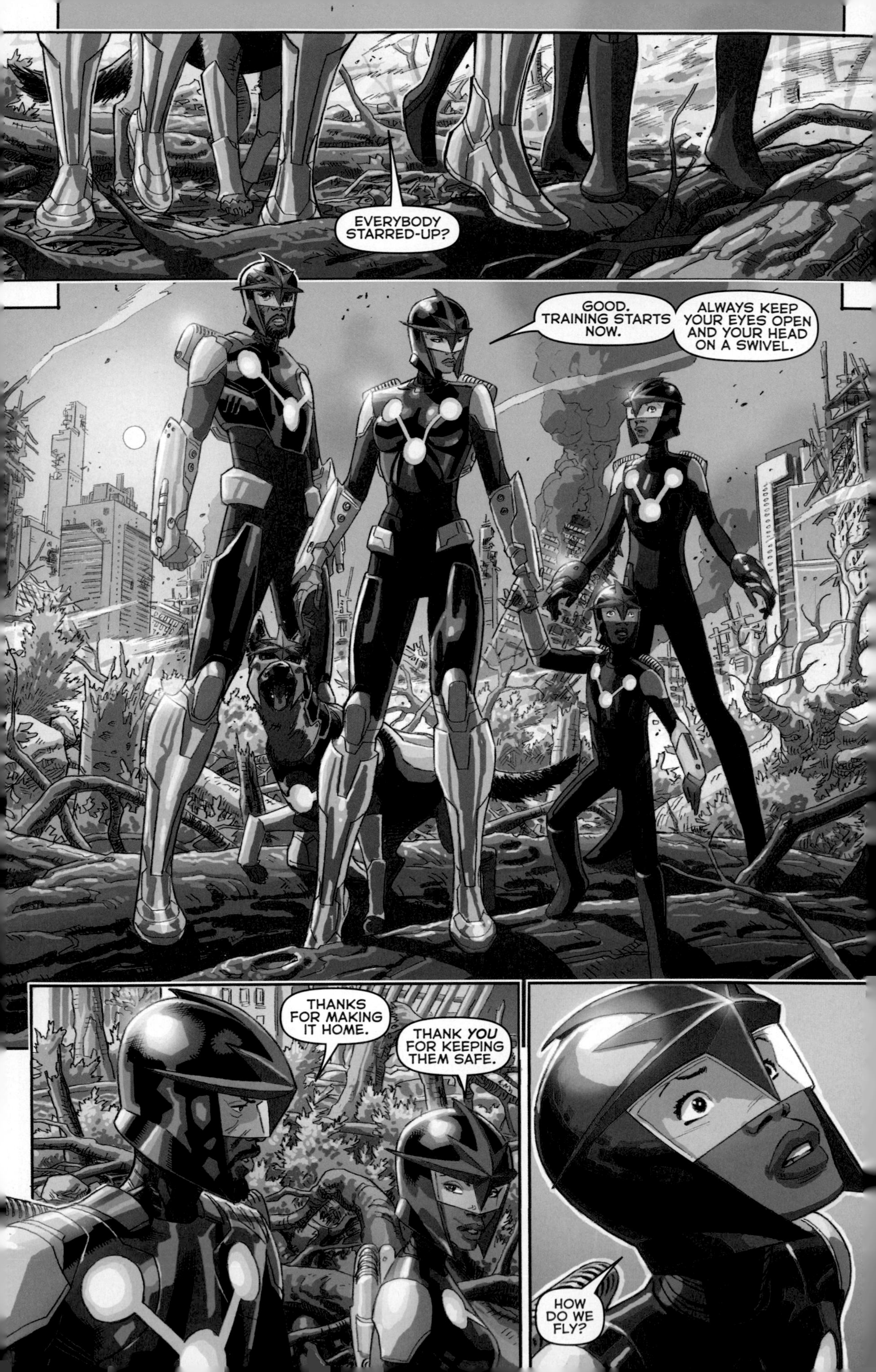
EVERYBODY STARRED-UP?
GOOD. TRAINING STARTS NOW.
ALWAYS KEEP YOUR EYES OPEN AND YOUR HEAD ON A SWIVEL.
THANKS FOR MAKING IT HOME.
THANK *YOU* FOR KEEPING THEM SAFE.
HOW DO WE FLY?

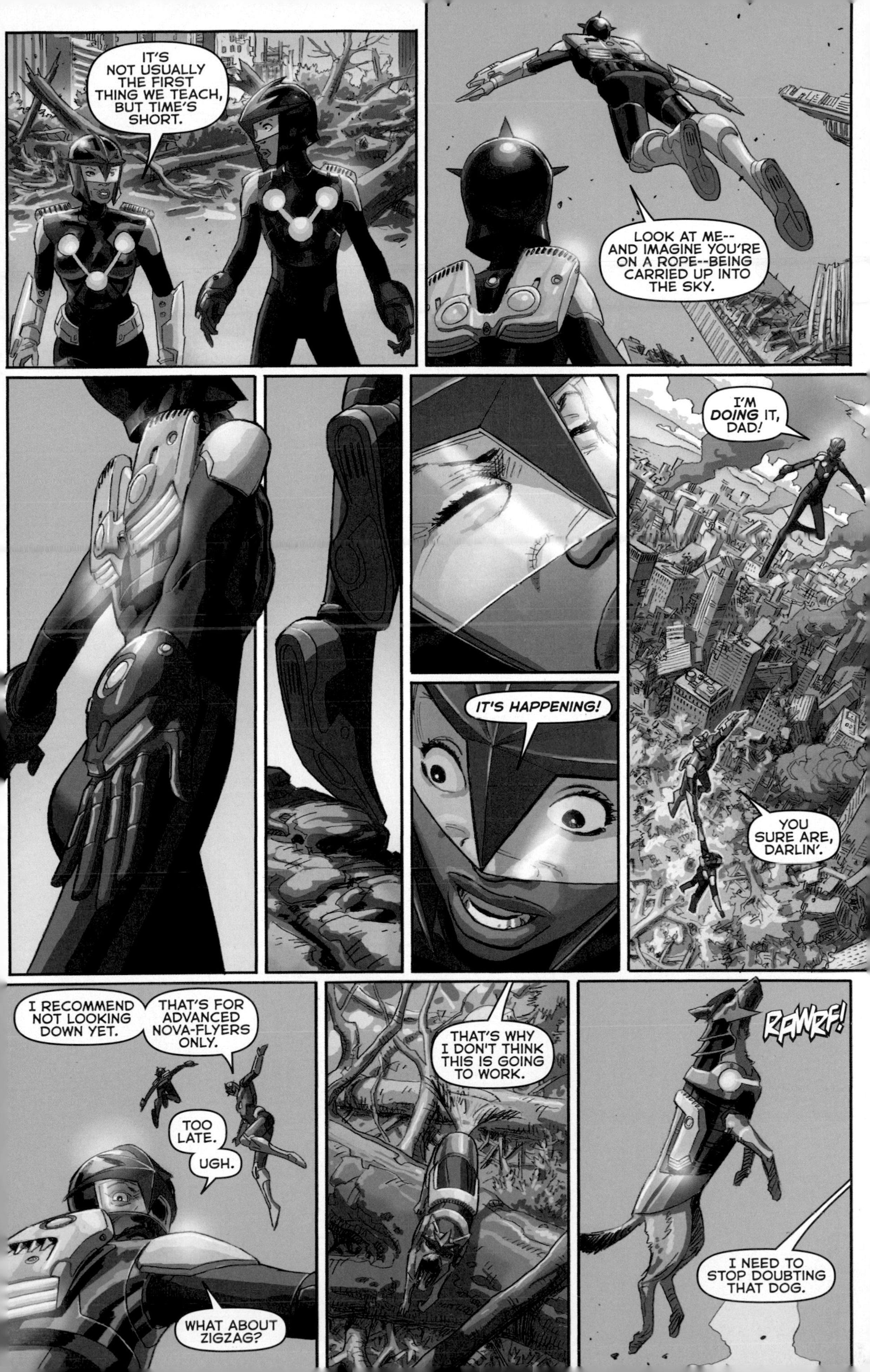
IT'S NOT USUALLY THE FIRST THING WE TEACH, BUT TIME'S SHORT.
LOOK AT ME-- AND IMAGINE YOU'RE ON A ROPE--BEING CARRIED UP INTO THE SKY.
IT'S HAPPENING!
I'M *DOING* IT, DAD!
YOU SURE ARE, DARLIN'.
I RECOMMEND NOT LOOKING DOWN YET.
THAT'S FOR ADVANCED NOVA-FLYERS ONLY.
TOO LATE.
UGH.
WHAT ABOUT ZIGZAG?
THAT'S WHY I DON'T THINK THIS IS GOING TO WORK.
RAWRF!
I NEED TO STOP DOUBTING THAT DOG.

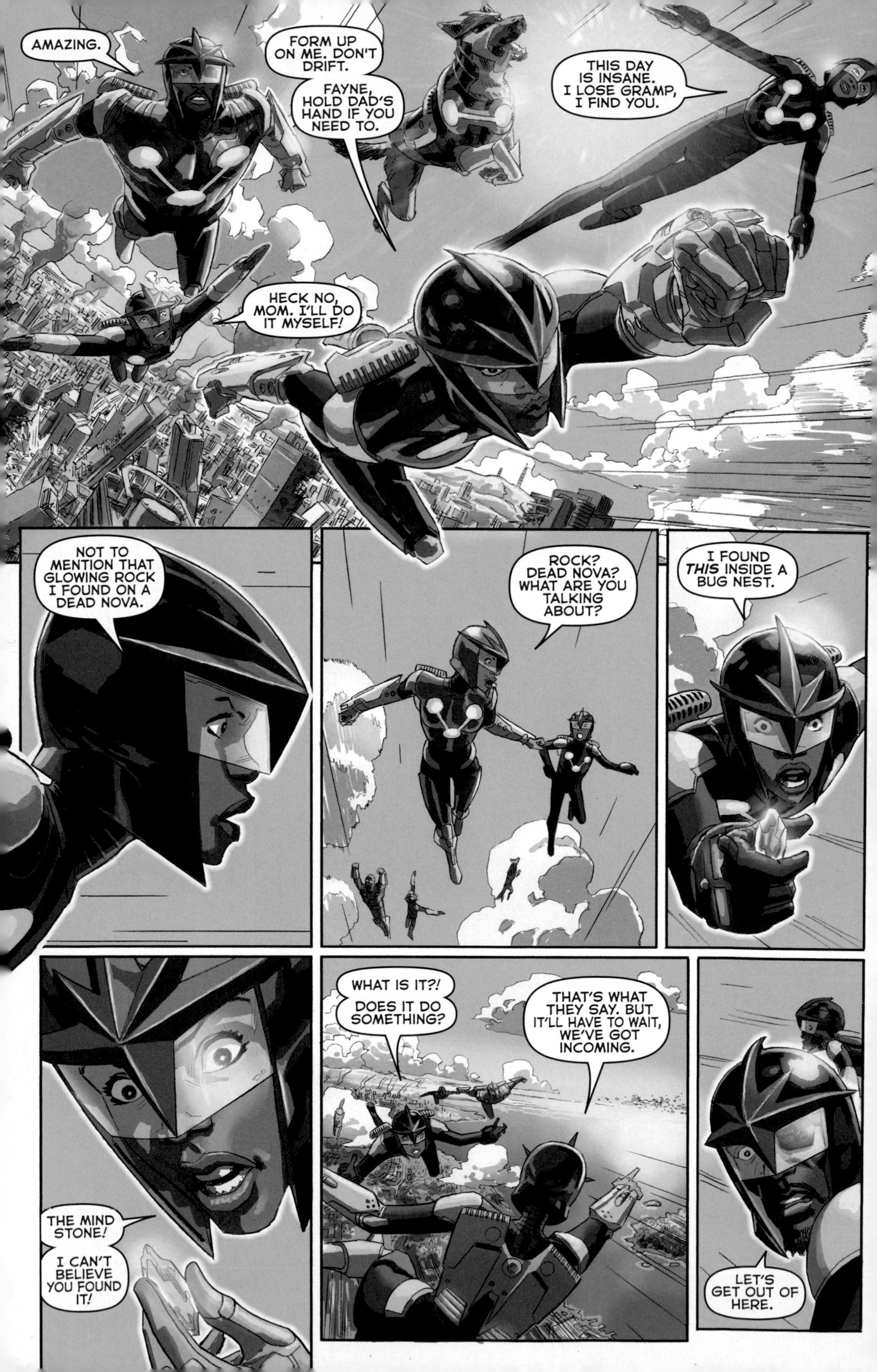
AMAZING.
FORM UP ON ME. DON'T DRIFT.
FAYNE, HOLD DAD'S HAND IF YOU NEED TO.
THIS DAY IS INSANE. I LOSE GRAMP, I FIND YOU.
HECK NO, MOM. I'LL DO IT MYSELF!
NOT TO MENTION THAT GLOWING ROCK I FOUND ON A DEAD NOVA.
ROCK? DEAD NOVA? WHAT ARE YOU TALKING ABOUT?
I FOUND *THIS* INSIDE A BUG NEST.
THE MIND STONE!
I CAN'T BELIEVE YOU FOUND IT!
WHAT IS IT?!
DOES IT DO SOMETHING?
THAT'S WHAT THEY SAY. BUT IT'LL HAVE TO WAIT, WE'VE GOT INCOMING.
LET'S GET OUT OF HERE.

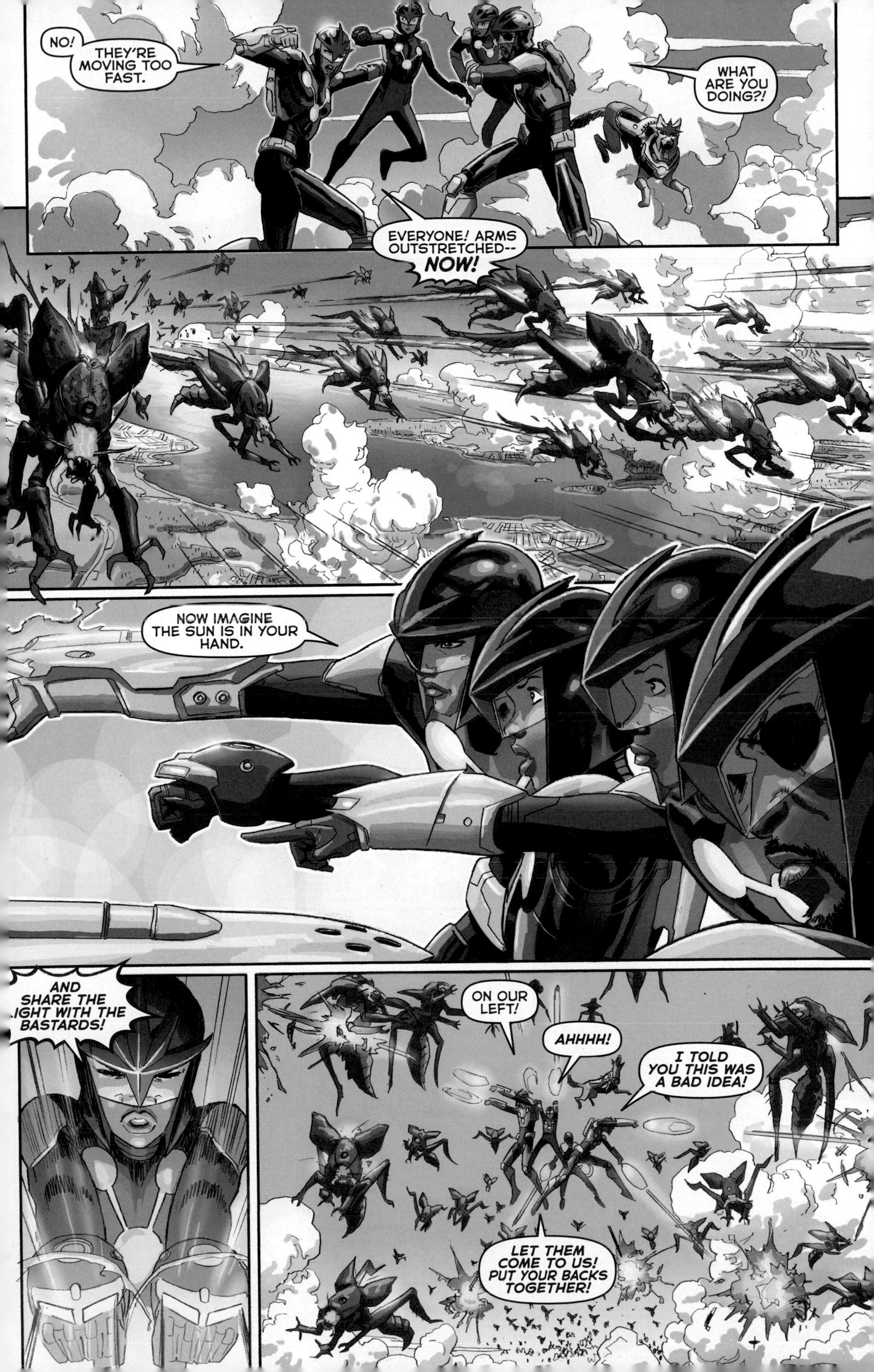
NO!
THEY'RE MOVING TOO FAST.
WHAT ARE YOU DOING?!
EVERYONE! ARMS OUTSTRETCHED-- NOW!
NOW IMAGINE THE SUN IS IN YOUR HAND.
AND SHARE THE LIGHT WITH THE BASTARDS!
ON OUR LEFT!
AHHHH!
I TOLD YOU THIS WAS A BAD IDEA!
LET THEM COME TO US! PUT YOUR BACKS TOGETHER!

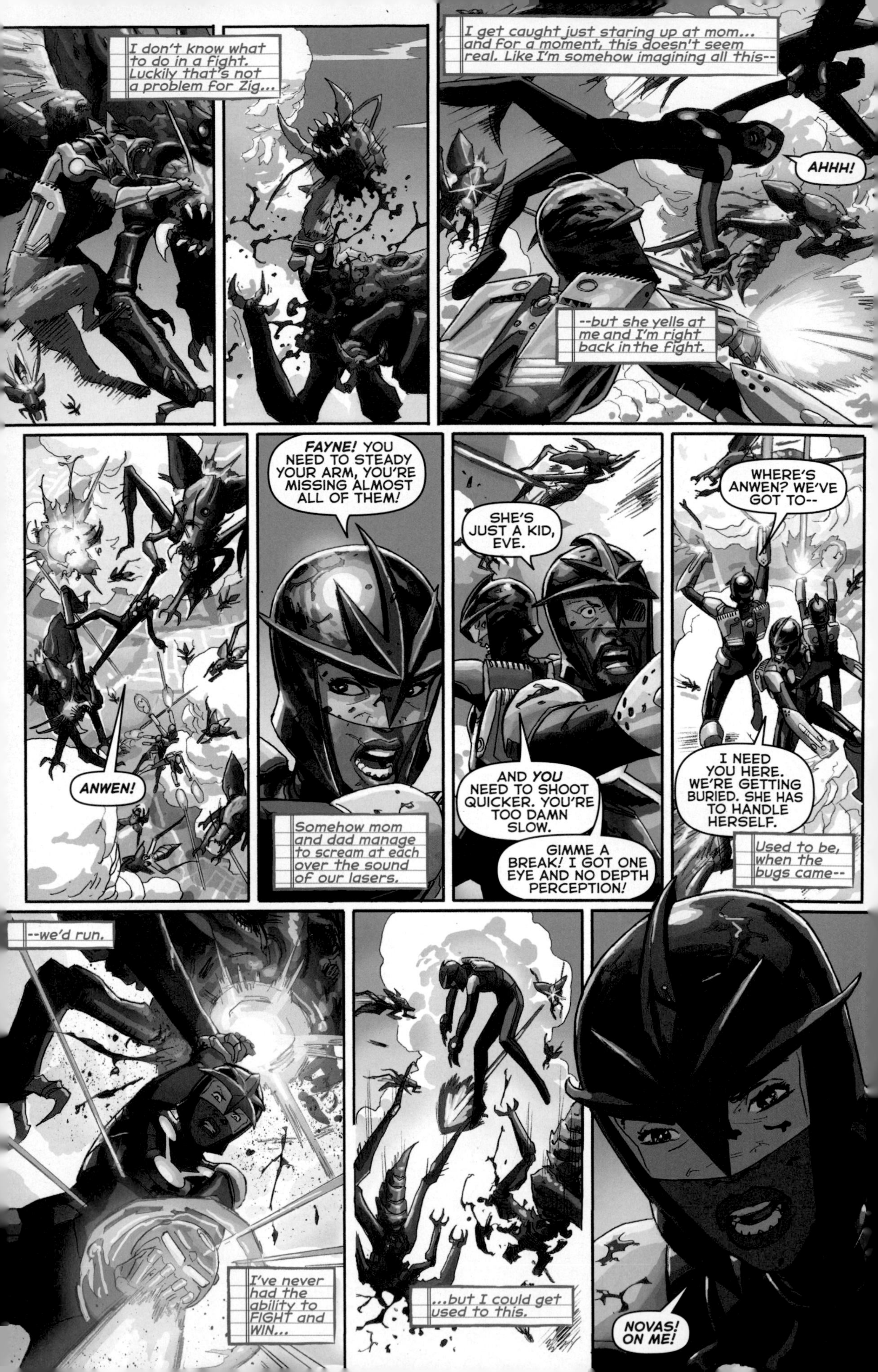
I don't know what to do in a fight. Luckily that's not a problem for Zig...
I get caught just staring up at mom... and for a moment, this doesn't seem real. Like I'm somehow imagining all this--
AHHH!
--but she yells at me and I'm right back in the fight.
ANWEN!
FAYNE! YOU NEED TO STEADY YOUR ARM, YOU'RE MISSING ALMOST ALL OF THEM!
Somehow mom and dad manage to scream at each over the sound of our lasers.
SHE'S JUST A KID, EVE.
AND YOU NEED TO SHOOT QUICKER. YOU'RE TOO DAMN SLOW.
GIMME A BREAK! I GOT ONE EYE AND NO DEPTH PERCEPTION!
WHERE'S ANWEN? WE'VE GOT TO--
I NEED YOU HERE. WE'RE GETTING BURIED. SHE HAS TO HANDLE HERSELF.
Used to be, when the bugs came--
--we'd run.
I've never had the ability to FIGHT and WIN...
...but I could get used to this.
NOVAS! ON ME!

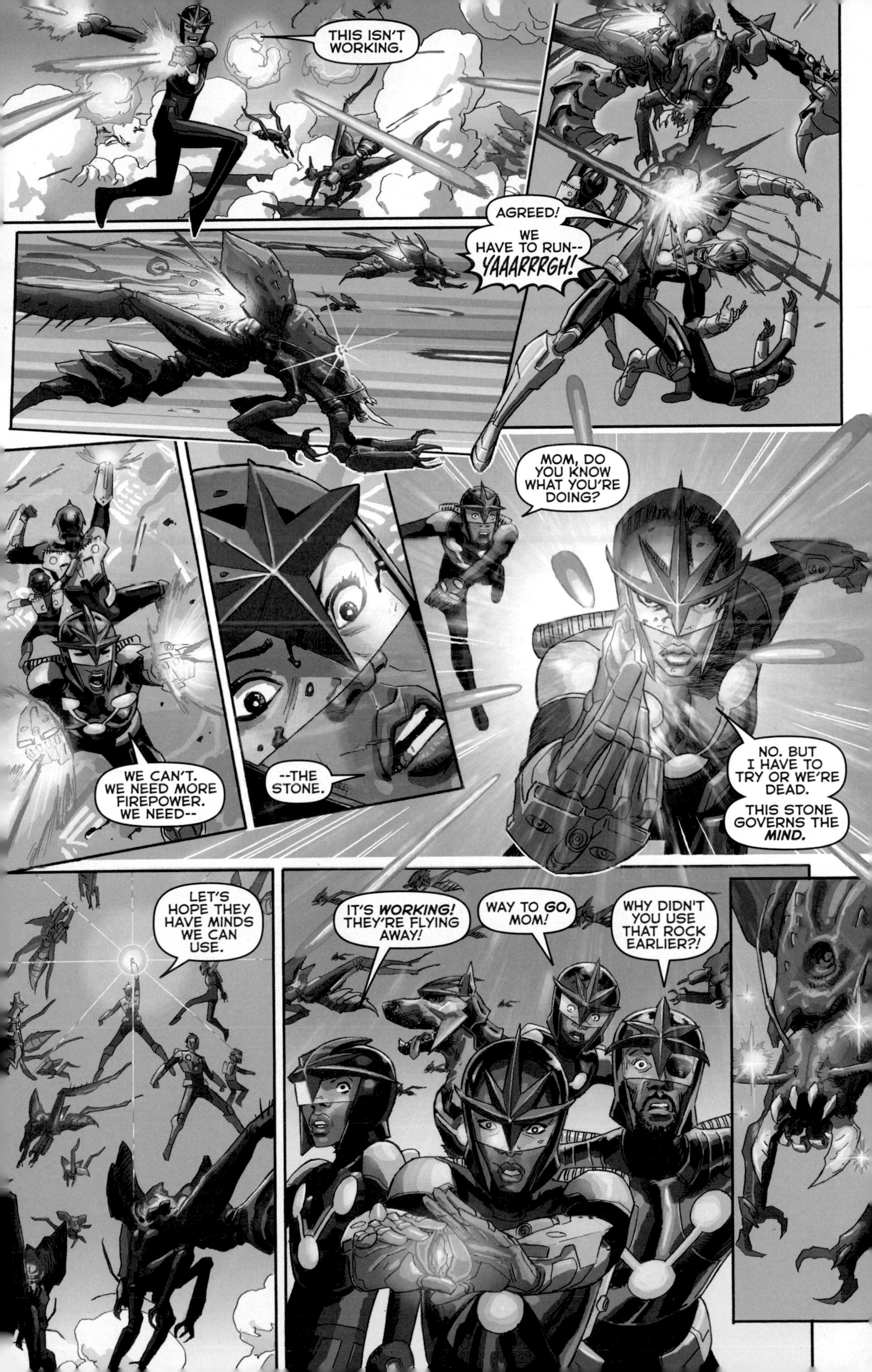
THIS ISN'T WORKING.
AGREED!
WE HAVE TO RUN--
YAAARRRGH!
WE CAN'T. WE NEED MORE FIREPOWER. WE NEED--
--THE STONE.
MOM, DO YOU KNOW WHAT YOU'RE DOING?
NO. BUT I HAVE TO TRY OR WE'RE DEAD.
THIS STONE GOVERNS THE *MIND.*
LET'S HOPE THEY HAVE MINDS WE CAN USE.
IT'S *WORKING!* THEY'RE FLYING AWAY!
WAY TO *GO,* MOM!
WHY DIDN'T YOU USE THAT ROCK EARLIER?!

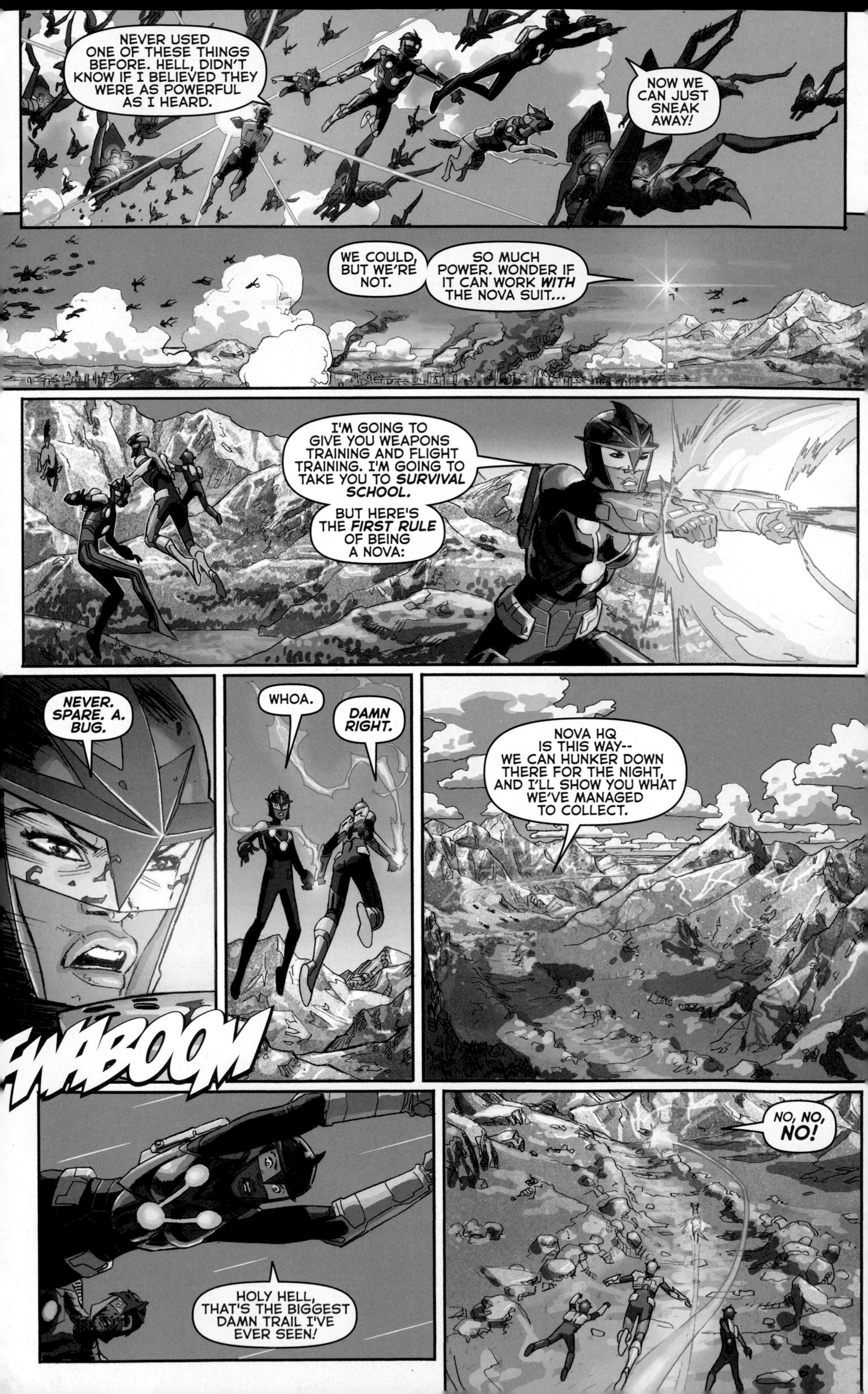
NEVER USED ONE OF THESE THINGS BEFORE. HELL, DIDN'T KNOW IF I BELIEVED THEY WERE AS POWERFUL AS I HEARD.
NOW WE CAN JUST SNEAK AWAY!
WE COULD, BUT WE'RE NOT.
SO MUCH POWER. WONDER IF IT CAN WORK WITH THE NOVA SUIT...
I'M GOING TO GIVE YOU WEAPONS TRAINING AND FLIGHT TRAINING. I'M GOING TO TAKE YOU TO SURVIVAL SCHOOL.
BUT HERE'S THE FIRST RULE OF BEING A NOVA:
NEVER. SPARE. A. BUG.
WHOA.
DAMN RIGHT.
NOVA HQ IS THIS WAY-- WE CAN HUNKER DOWN THERE FOR THE NIGHT, AND I'LL SHOW YOU WHAT WE'VE MANAGED TO COLLECT.
FWABOOM
HOLY HELL, THAT'S THE BIGGEST DAMN TRAIL I'VE EVER SEEN!
NO, NO, NO!

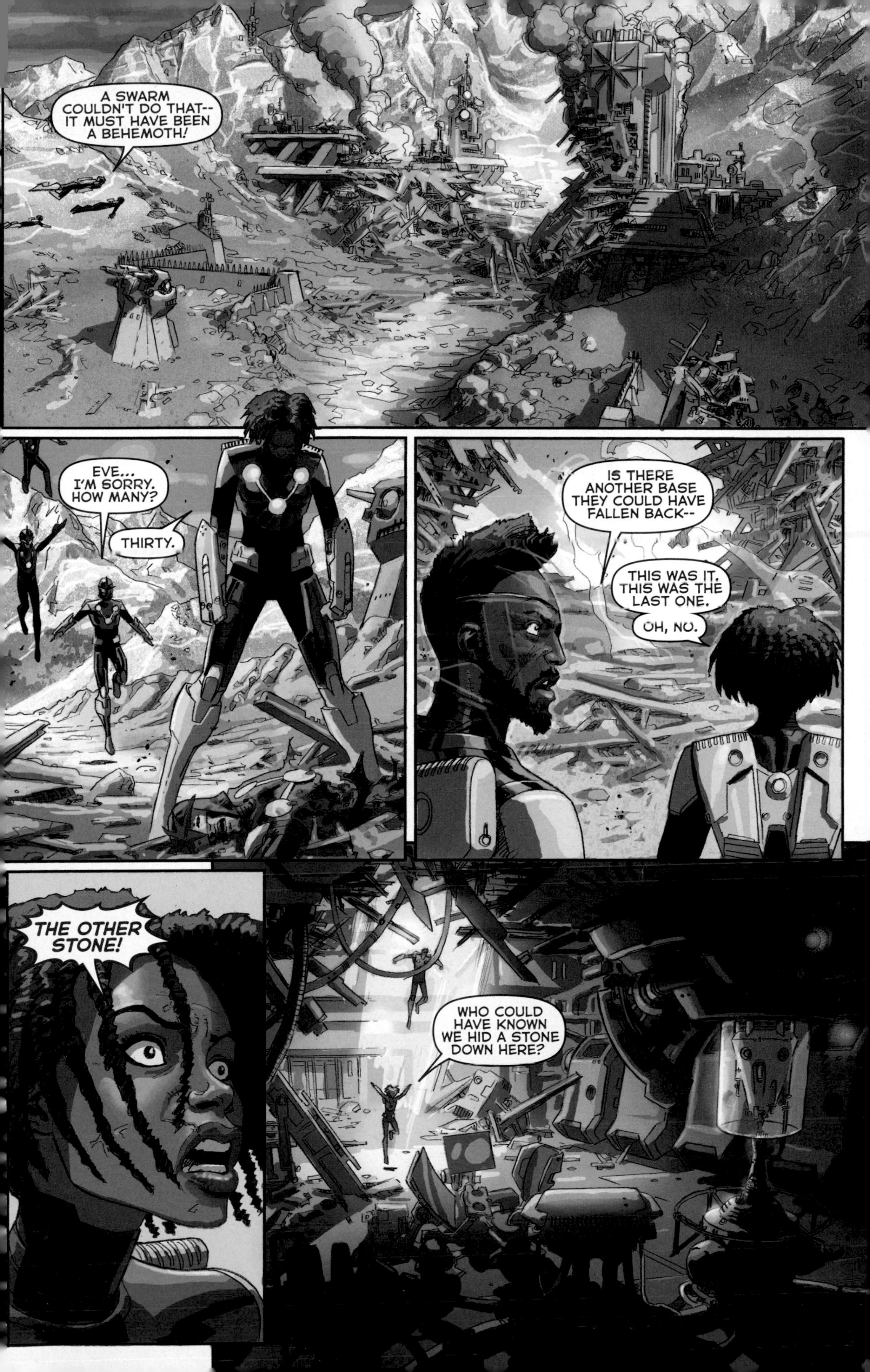
A SWARM COULDN'T DO THAT-- IT MUST HAVE BEEN A BEHEMOTH!
EVE... I'M SORRY. HOW MANY?
THIRTY.
IS THERE ANOTHER BASE THEY COULD HAVE FALLEN BACK--
THIS WAS IT. THIS WAS THE LAST ONE.
OH, NO.
THE OTHER STONE!
WHO COULD HAVE KNOWN WE HID A STONE DOWN HERE?

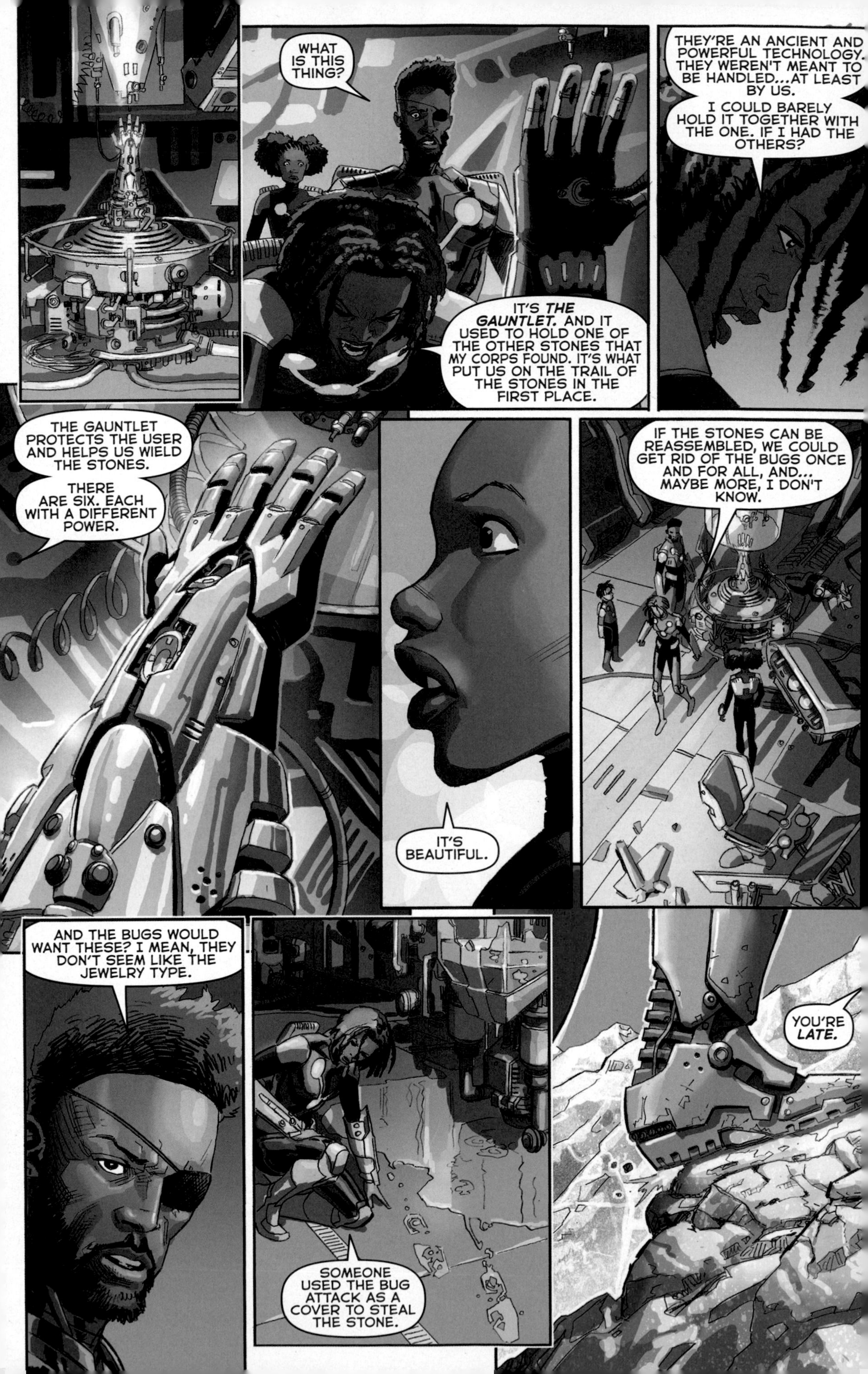
WHAT IS THIS THING?
IT'S *THE GAUNTLET.* AND IT USED TO HOLD ONE OF THE OTHER STONES THAT MY CORPS FOUND. IT'S WHAT PUT US ON THE TRAIL OF THE STONES IN THE FIRST PLACE.
THEY'RE AN ANCIENT AND POWERFUL TECHNOLOGY. THEY WEREN'T MEANT TO BE HANDLED...AT LEAST BY US.
I COULD BARELY HOLD IT TOGETHER WITH THE ONE. IF I HAD THE OTHERS?
THE GAUNTLET PROTECTS THE USER AND HELPS US WIELD THE STONES.
THERE ARE SIX. EACH WITH A DIFFERENT POWER.
IT'S BEAUTIFUL.
IF THE STONES CAN BE REASSEMBLED, WE COULD GET RID OF THE BUGS ONCE AND FOR ALL, AND... MAYBE MORE, I DON'T KNOW.
AND THE BUGS WOULD WANT THESE? I MEAN, THEY DON'T SEEM LIKE THE JEWELRY TYPE.
SOMEONE USED THE BUG ATTACK AS A COVER TO STEAL THE STONE.
YOU'RE *LATE.*

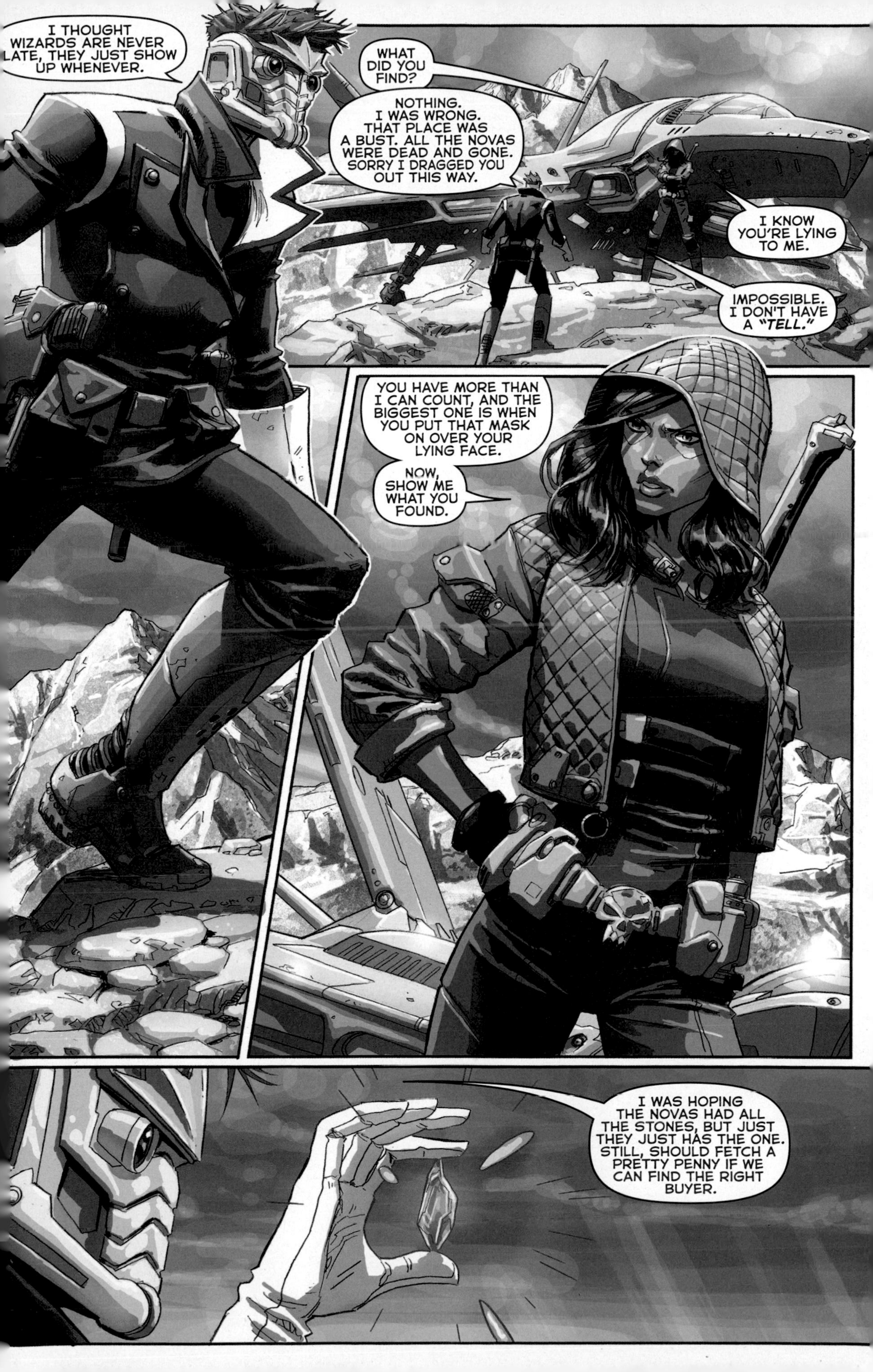

I THOUGHT WIZARDS ARE NEVER LATE, THEY JUST SHOW UP WHENEVER.
WHAT DID YOU FIND?
NOTHING. I WAS WRONG. THAT PLACE WAS A BUST. ALL THE NOVAS WERE DEAD AND GONE. SORRY I DRAGGED YOU OUT THIS WAY.
I KNOW YOU'RE LYING TO ME.
IMPOSSIBLE. I DON'T HAVE A "TELL."
YOU HAVE MORE THAN I CAN COUNT, AND THE BIGGEST ONE IS WHEN YOU PUT THAT MASK ON OVER YOUR LYING FACE.
NOW, SHOW ME WHAT YOU FOUND.
I WAS HOPING THE NOVAS HAD ALL THE STONES, BUT JUST THEY JUST HAS THE ONE. STILL, SHOULD FETCH A PRETTY PENNY IF WE CAN FIND THE RIGHT BUYER.

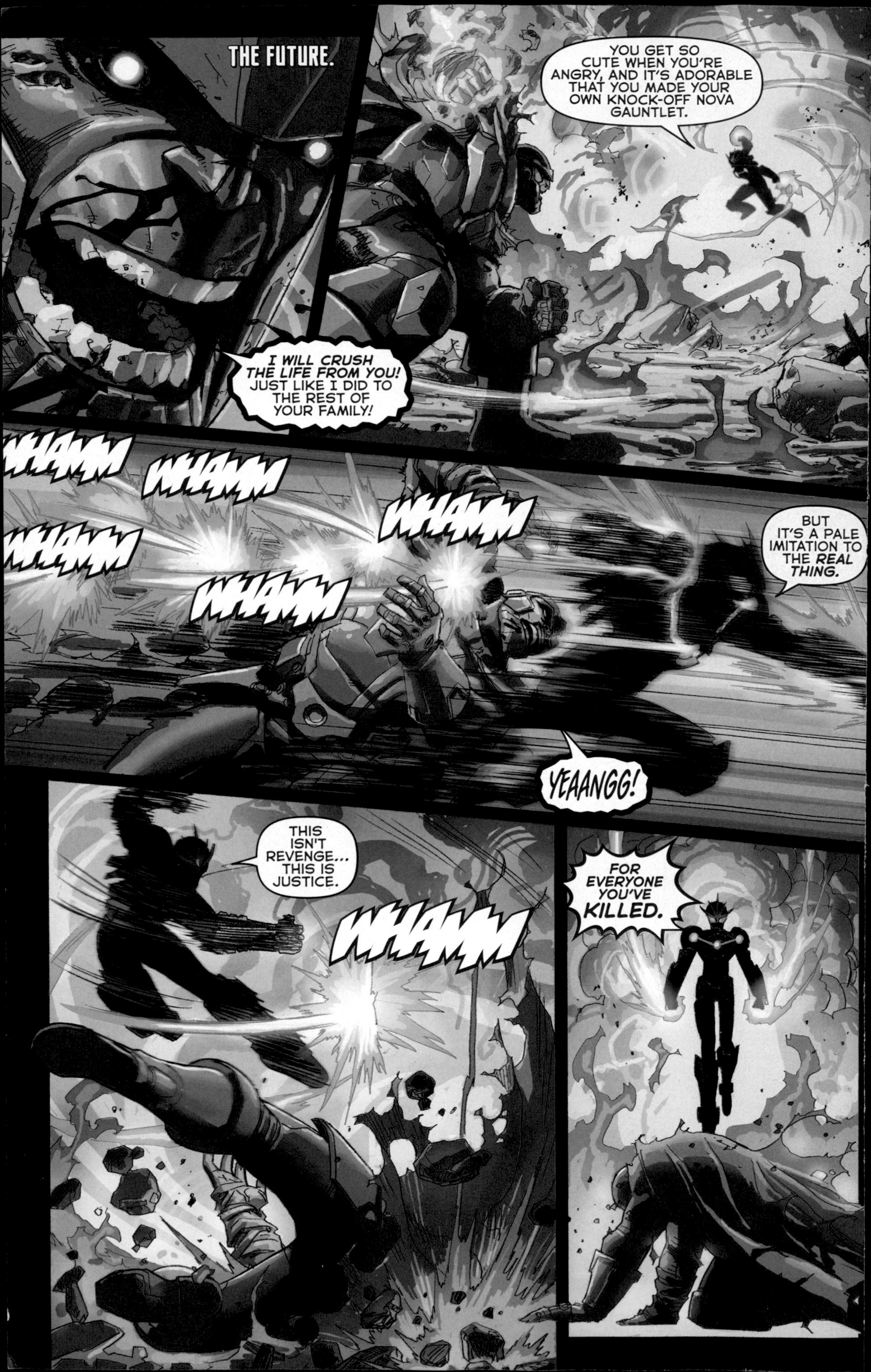
THE FUTURE.
YOU GET SO CUTE WHEN YOU'RE ANGRY, AND IT'S ADORABLE THAT YOU MADE YOUR OWN KNOCK-OFF NOVA GAUNTLET.
I WILL CRUSH THE LIFE FROM YOU! JUST LIKE I DID TO THE REST OF YOUR FAMILY!
WHAMM
WHAMM
WHAMM
WHAMM
WHAMM
BUT IT'S A PALE IMITATION TO THE REAL THING.
YEAANGG!
THIS ISN'T REVENGE... THIS IS JUSTICE.
WHAMM
FOR EVERYONE YOU'VE KILLED.

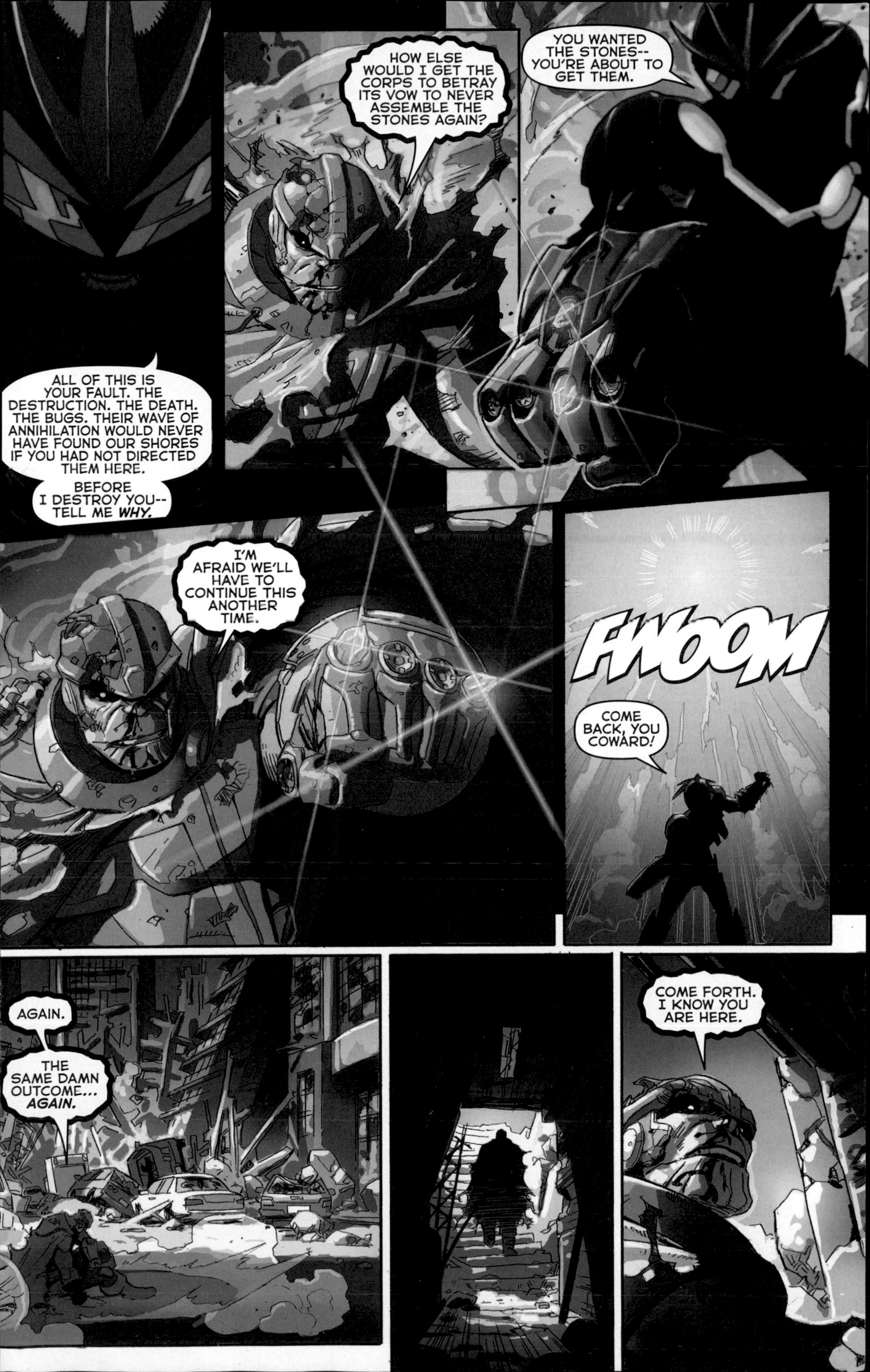
HOW ELSE WOULD I GET THE CORPS TO BETRAY ITS VOW TO NEVER ASSEMBLE THE STONES AGAIN?
YOU WANTED THE STONES-- YOU'RE ABOUT TO GET THEM.
ALL OF THIS IS YOUR FAULT. THE DESTRUCTION. THE DEATH. THE BUGS. THEIR WAVE OF ANNIHILATION WOULD NEVER HAVE FOUND OUR SHORES IF YOU HAD NOT DIRECTED THEM HERE.
BEFORE I DESTROY YOU-- TELL ME WHY.
I'M AFRAID WE'LL HAVE TO CONTINUE THIS ANOTHER TIME.
FWOOM
COME BACK, YOU COWARD!
AGAIN.
THE SAME DAMN OUTCOME... AGAIN.
COME FORTH. I KNOW YOU ARE HERE.

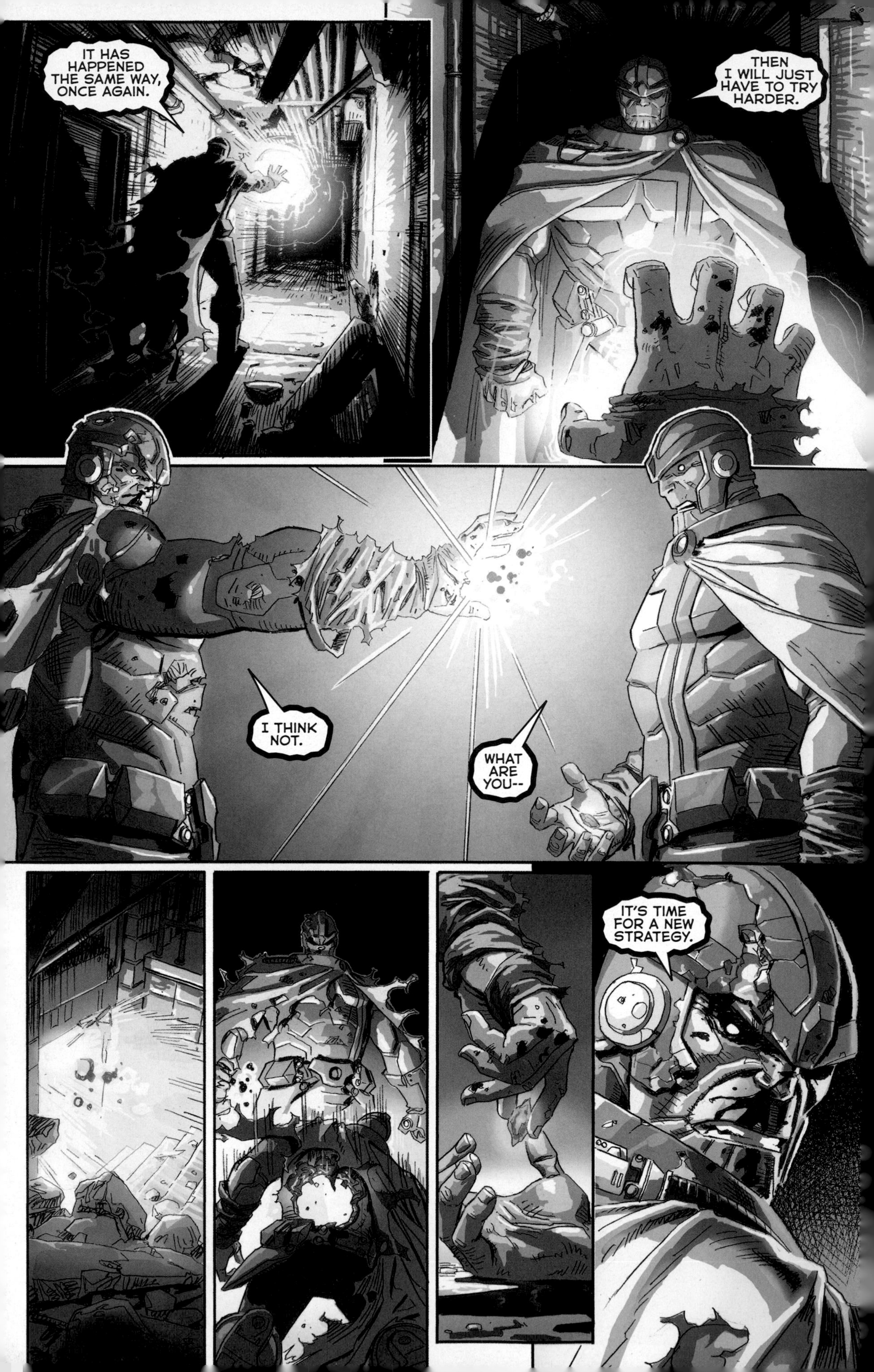
IT HAS HAPPENED THE SAME WAY, ONCE AGAIN.
THEN I WILL JUST HAVE TO TRY HARDER.
I THINK NOT.
WHAT ARE YOU--
IT'S TIME FOR A NEW STRATEGY.

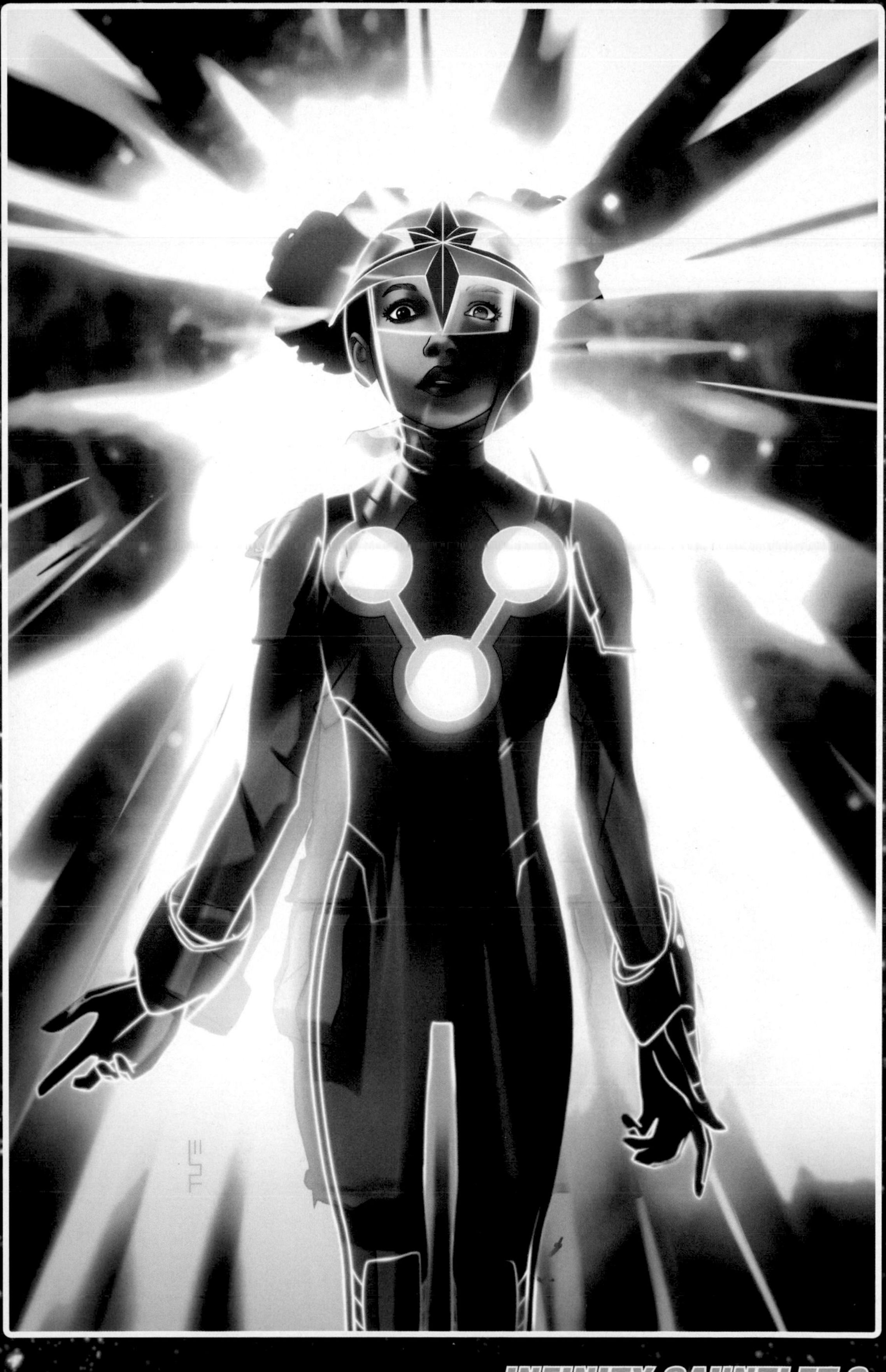

INFINITY GAUNTLET 2
VARIANT COVER BY W. SCOTT FORBES

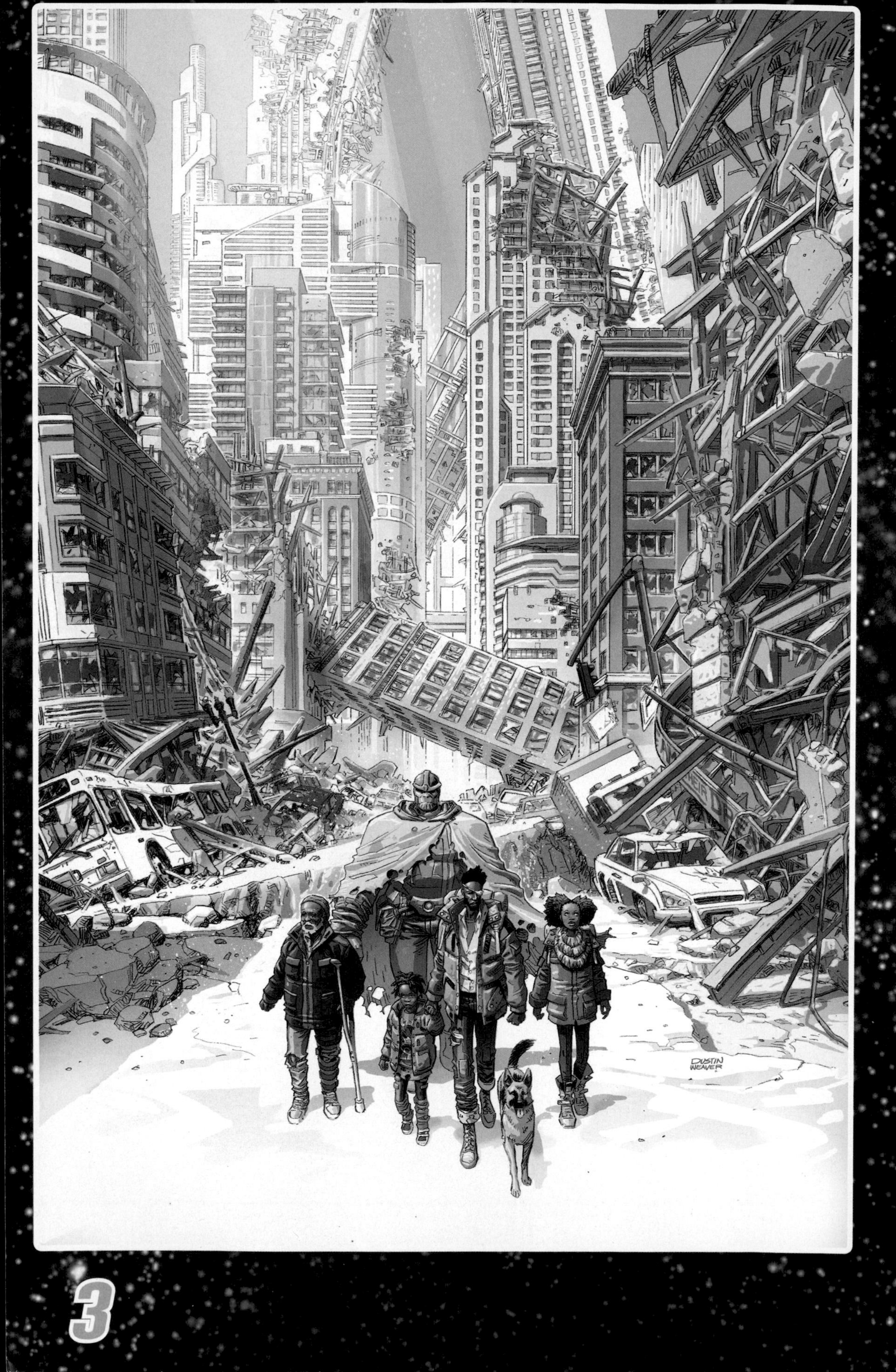
DUSTIN WEAVER

3

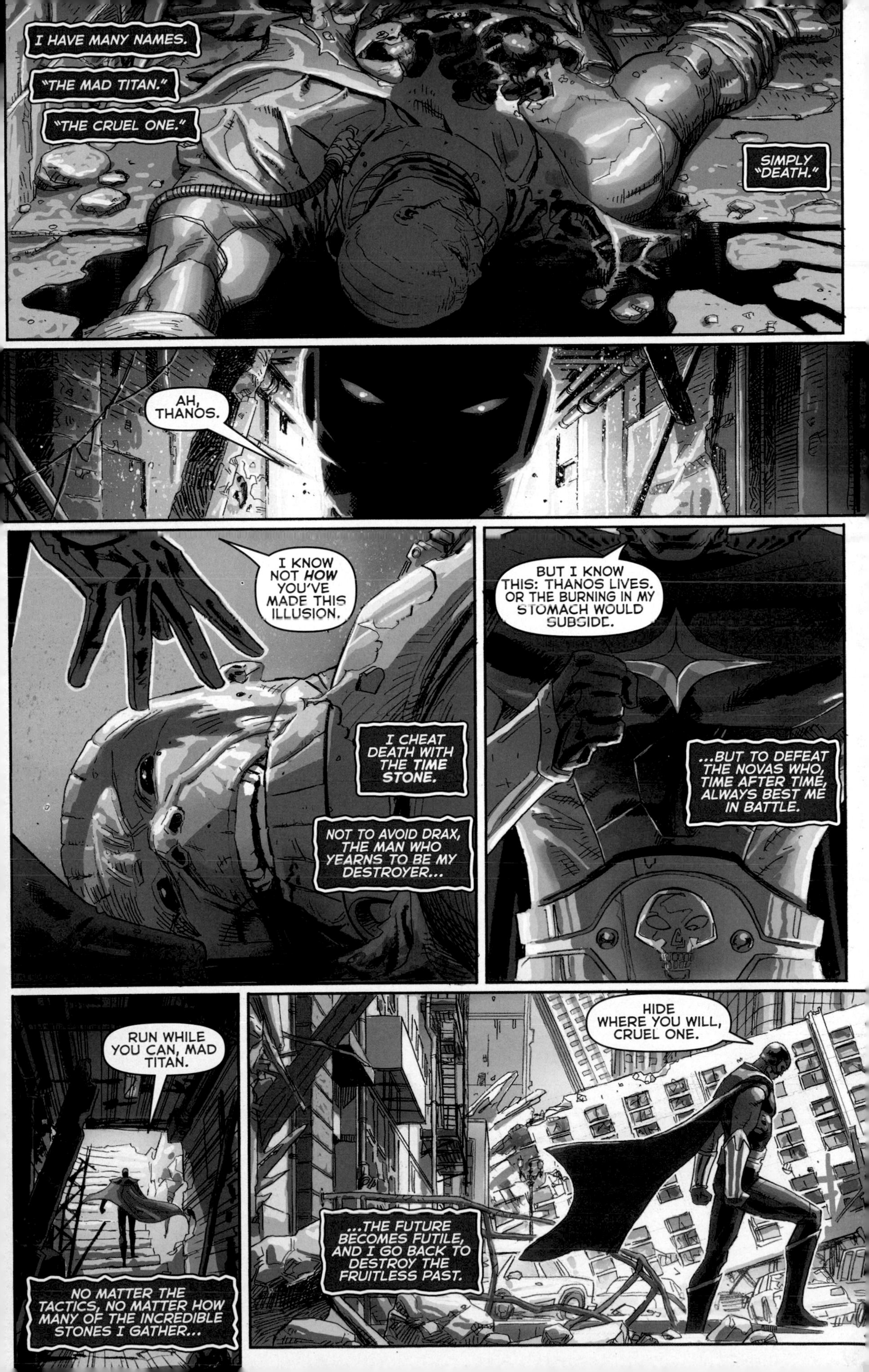
I HAVE MANY NAMES.
"THE MAD TITAN."
"THE CRUEL ONE."
SIMPLY "DEATH."
AH, THANOS.
I KNOW NOT HOW YOU'VE MADE THIS ILLUSION.
I CHEAT DEATH WITH THE TIME STONE.
NOT TO AVOID DRAX, THE MAN WHO YEARNS TO BE MY DESTROYER...
BUT I KNOW THIS: THANOS LIVES. OR THE BURNING IN MY STOMACH WOULD SUBSIDE.
...BUT TO DEFEAT THE NOVAS WHO, TIME AFTER TIME, ALWAYS BEST ME IN BATTLE.
RUN WHILE YOU CAN, MAD TITAN.
NO MATTER THE TACTICS, NO MATTER HOW MANY OF THE INCREDIBLE STONES I GATHER...
HIDE WHERE YOU WILL, CRUEL ONE.
...THE FUTURE BECOMES FUTILE, AND I GO BACK TO DESTROY THE FRUITLESS PAST.

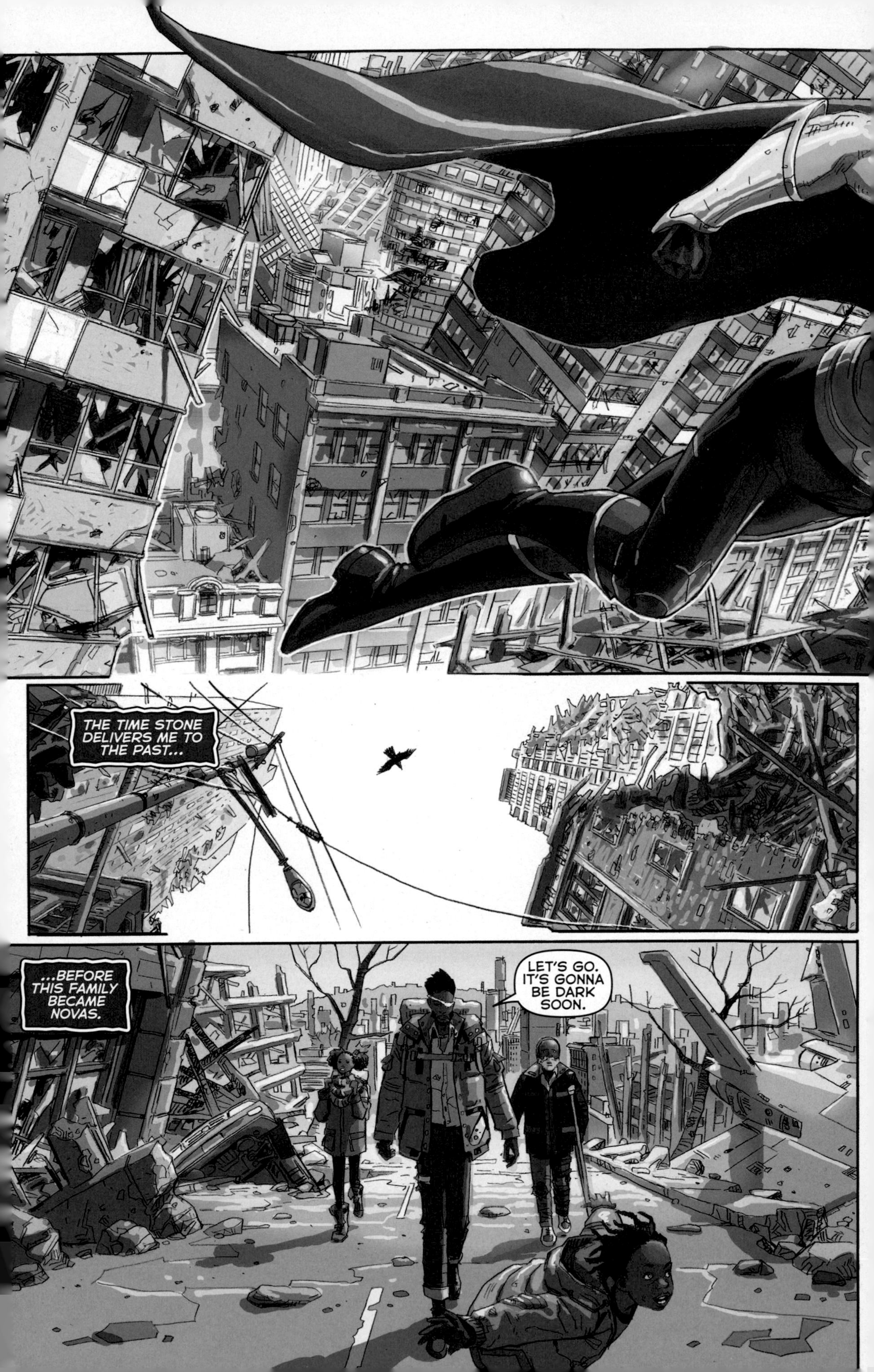
THE TIME STONE DELIVERS ME TO THE PAST...
...BEFORE THIS FAMILY BECAME NOVAS.
LET'S GO. IT'S GONNA BE DARK SOON.

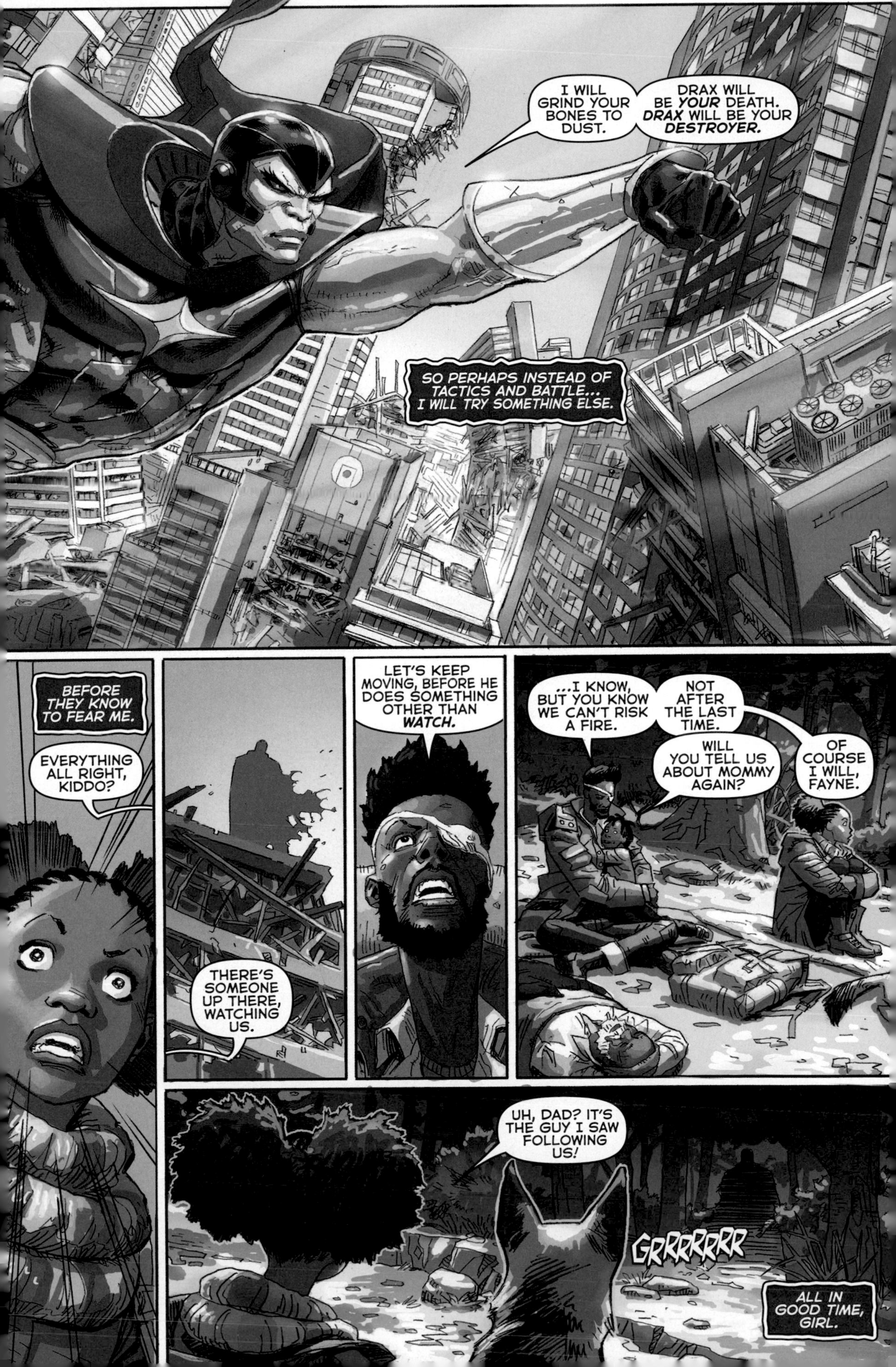
I WILL GRIND YOUR BONES TO DUST.
DRAX WILL BE YOUR DEATH. DRAX WILL BE YOUR DESTROYER.
SO PERHAPS INSTEAD OF TACTICS AND BATTLE... I WILL TRY SOMETHING ELSE.
BEFORE THEY KNOW TO FEAR ME.
EVERYTHING ALL RIGHT, KIDDO?
THERE'S SOMEONE UP THERE, WATCHING US.
LET'S KEEP MOVING, BEFORE HE DOES SOMETHING OTHER THAN WATCH.
...I KNOW, BUT YOU KNOW WE CAN'T RISK A FIRE.
NOT AFTER THE LAST TIME.
WILL YOU TELL US ABOUT MOMMY AGAIN?
OF COURSE I WILL, FAYNE.
UH, DAD? IT'S THE GUY I SAW FOLLOWING US!
GRRRRRRR
ALL IN GOOD TIME, GIRL.

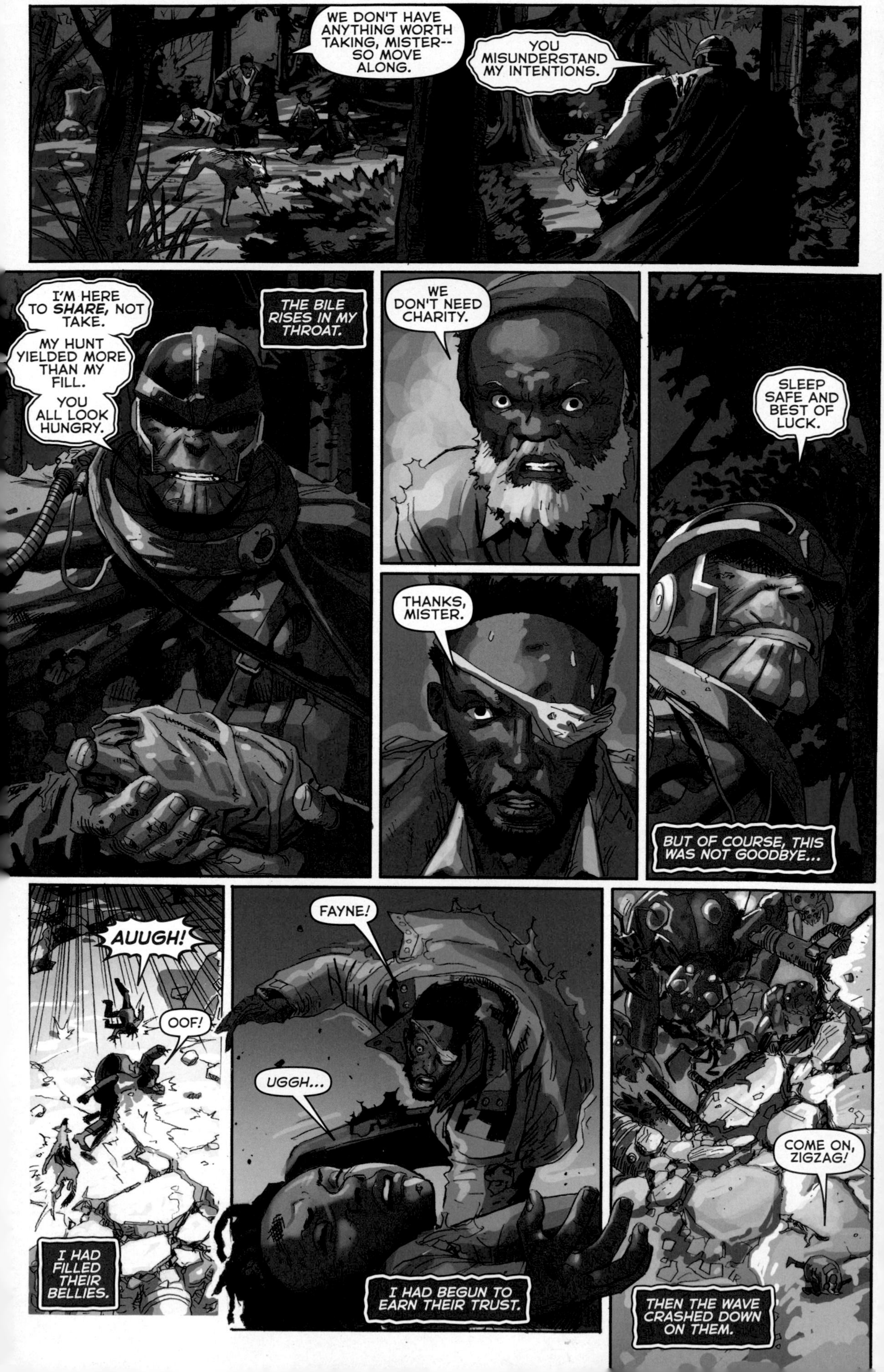
WE DON'T HAVE ANYTHING WORTH TAKING, MISTER-- SO MOVE ALONG.
YOU MISUNDERSTAND MY INTENTIONS.
I'M HERE TO SHARE, NOT TAKE.
MY HUNT YIELDED MORE THAN MY FILL.
YOU ALL LOOK HUNGRY.
THE BILE RISES IN MY THROAT.
WE DON'T NEED CHARITY.
THANKS, MISTER.
SLEEP SAFE AND BEST OF LUCK.
BUT OF COURSE, THIS WAS NOT GOODBYE...
AUUGH!
OOF!
I HAD FILLED THEIR BELLIES.
FAYNE!
UGGH...
I HAD BEGUN TO EARN THEIR TRUST.
COME ON, ZIGZAG!
THEN THE WAVE CRASHED DOWN ON THEM.

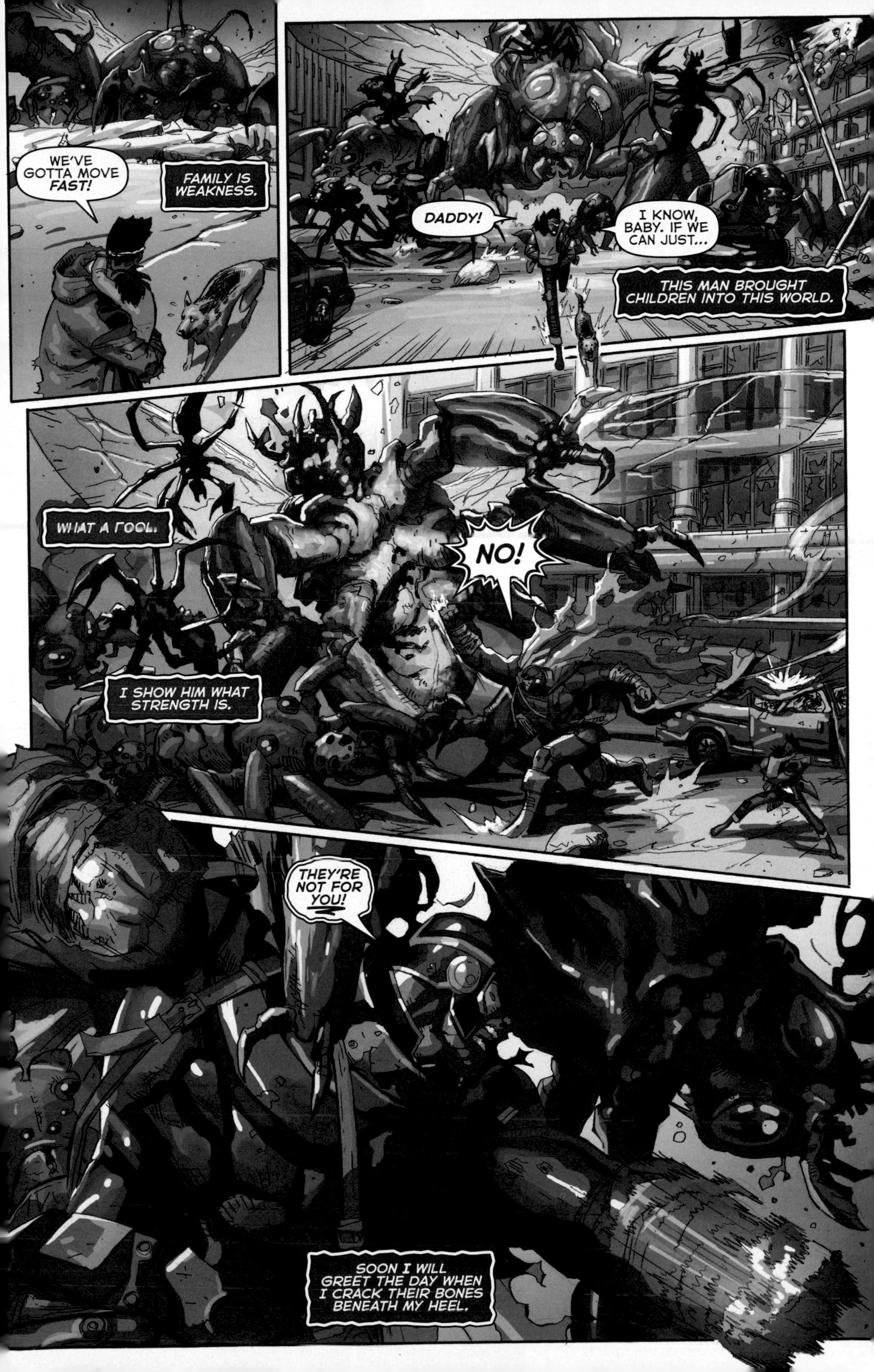
WE'VE GOTTA MOVE FAST!
FAMILY IS WEAKNESS.
DADDY!
I KNOW, BABY. IF WE CAN JUST...
THIS MAN BROUGHT CHILDREN INTO THIS WORLD.
WHAT A FOOL.
NO!
I SHOW HIM WHAT STRENGTH IS.
THEY'RE NOT FOR YOU!
SOON I WILL GREET THE DAY WHEN I CRACK THEIR BONES BENEATH MY HEEL.

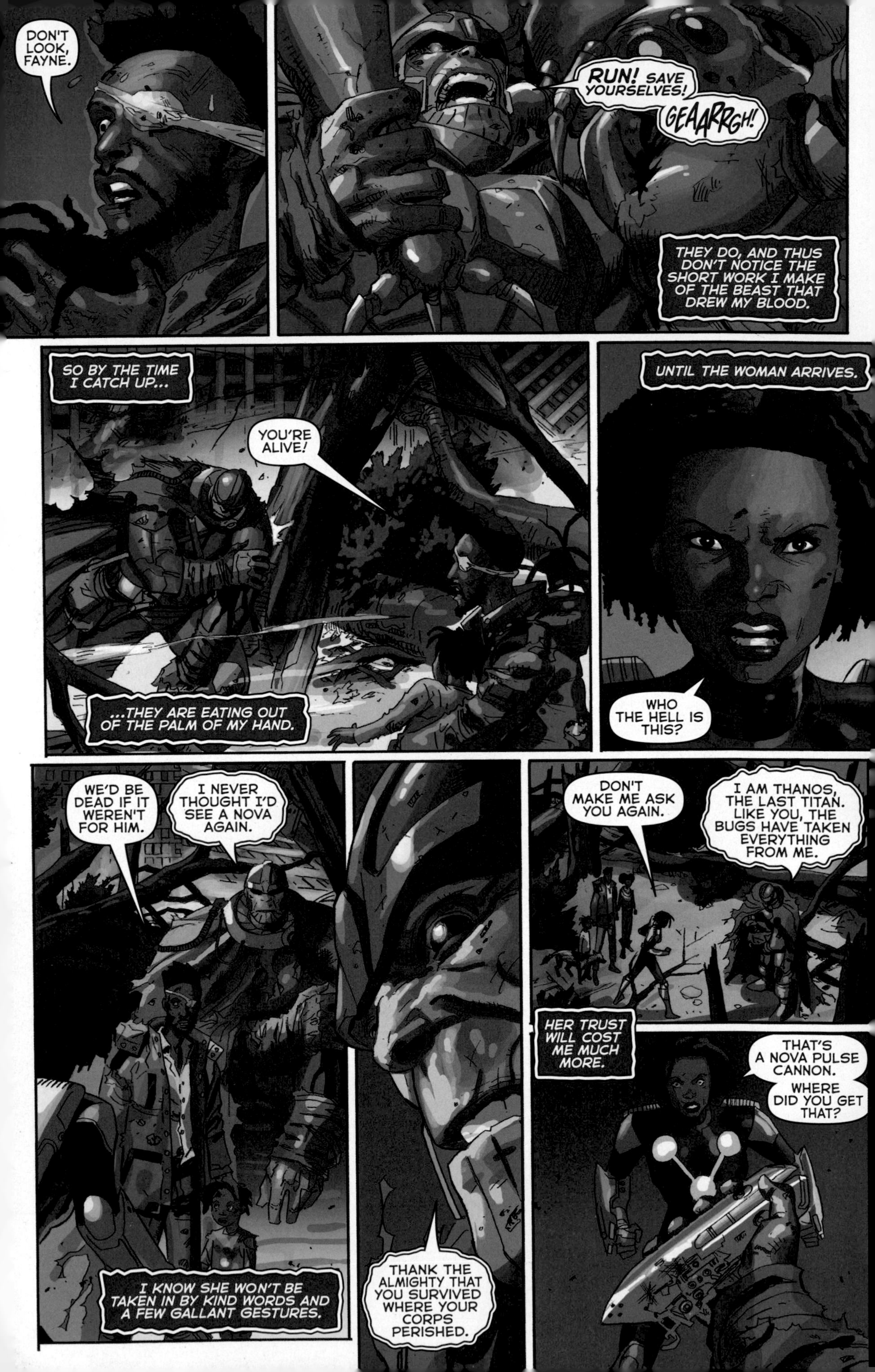
DON'T LOOK, FAYNE.
RUN! SAVE YOURSELVES!
GEAARRGH!
THEY DO, AND THUS DON'T NOTICE THE SHORT WORK I MAKE OF THE BEAST THAT DREW MY BLOOD.
SO BY THE TIME I CATCH UP...
YOU'RE ALIVE!
...THEY ARE EATING OUT OF THE PALM OF MY HAND.
UNTIL THE WOMAN ARRIVES.
WHO THE HELL IS THIS?
WE'D BE DEAD IF IT WEREN'T FOR HIM.
I NEVER THOUGHT I'D SEE A NOVA AGAIN.
I KNOW SHE WON'T BE TAKEN IN BY KIND WORDS AND A FEW GALLANT GESTURES.
THANK THE ALMIGHTY THAT YOU SURVIVED WHERE YOUR CORPS PERISHED.
DON'T MAKE ME ASK YOU AGAIN.
I AM THANOS, THE LAST TITAN. LIKE YOU, THE BUGS HAVE TAKEN EVERYTHING FROM ME.
HER TRUST WILL COST ME MUCH MORE.
THAT'S A NOVA PULSE CANNON. WHERE DID YOU GET THAT?

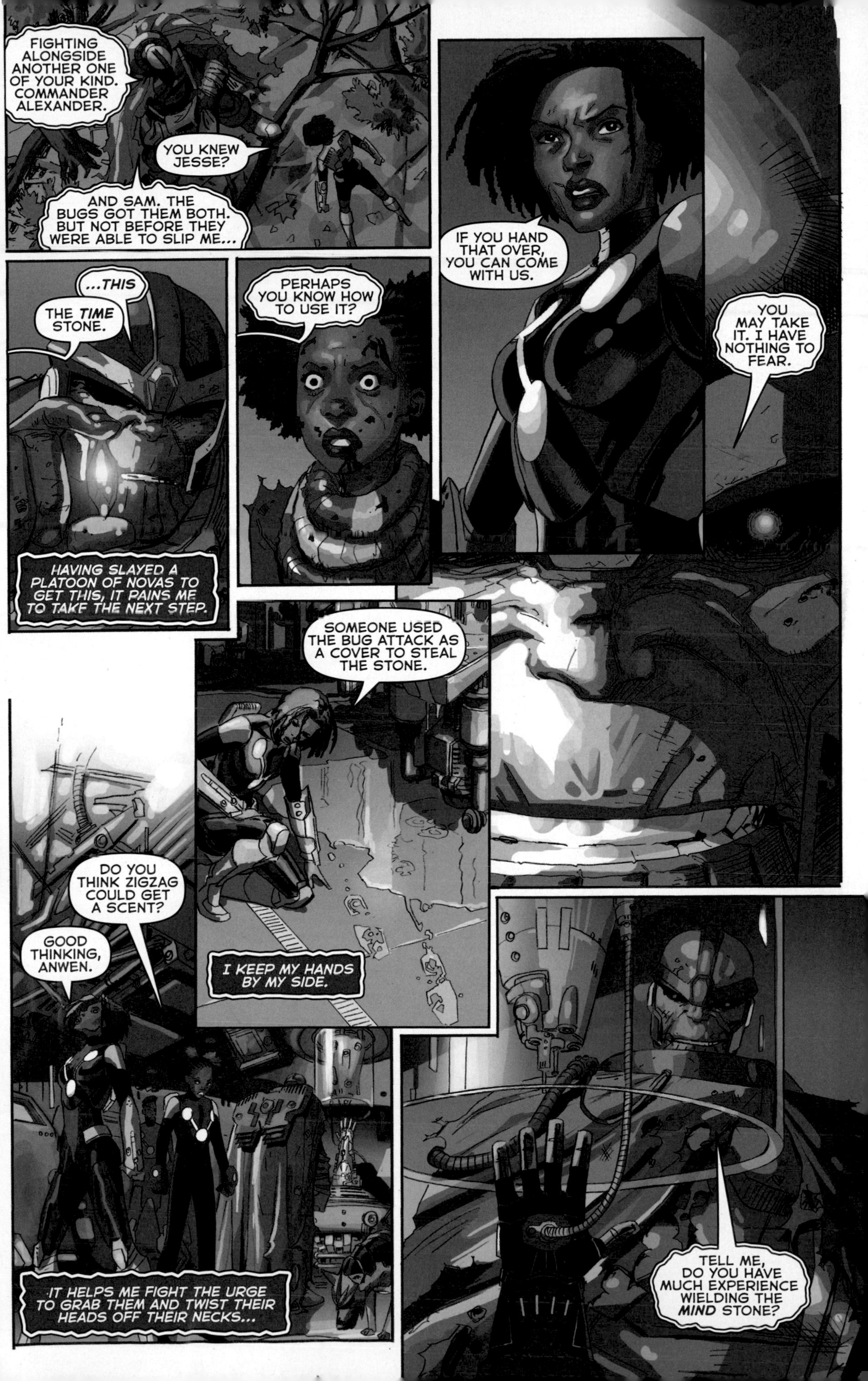

FIGHTING ALONGSIDE ANOTHER ONE OF YOUR KIND. COMMANDER ALEXANDER.
YOU KNEW JESSE?
AND SAM. THE BUGS GOT THEM BOTH. BUT NOT BEFORE THEY WERE ABLE TO SLIP ME...
IF YOU HAND THAT OVER, YOU CAN COME WITH US.
...THIS
THE *TIME* STONE.
PERHAPS YOU KNOW HOW TO USE IT?
YOU MAY TAKE IT. I HAVE NOTHING TO FEAR.
HAVING SLAYED A PLATOON OF NOVAS TO GET THIS, IT PAINS ME TO TAKE THE NEXT STEP.
SOMEONE USED THE BUG ATTACK AS A COVER TO STEAL THE STONE.
I KEEP MY HANDS BY MY SIDE.
DO YOU THINK ZIGZAG COULD GET A SCENT?
GOOD THINKING, ANWEN.
IT HELPS ME FIGHT THE URGE TO GRAB THEM AND TWIST THEIR HEADS OFF THEIR NECKS...
TELL ME, DO YOU HAVE MUCH EXPERIENCE WIELDING THE *MIND* STONE?

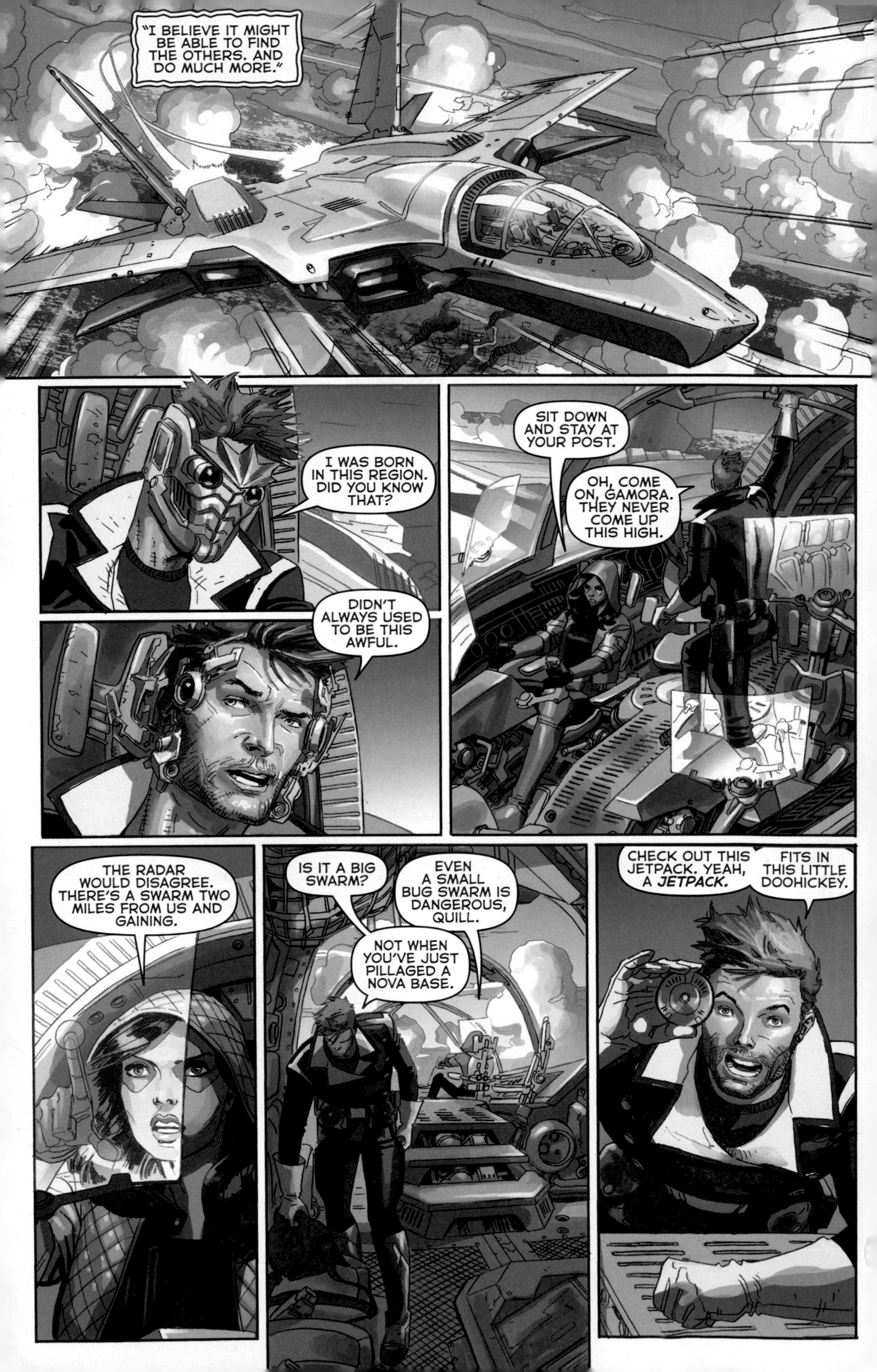
"I BELIEVE IT MIGHT BE ABLE TO FIND THE OTHERS. AND DO MUCH MORE."
I WAS BORN IN THIS REGION. DID YOU KNOW THAT?
DIDN'T ALWAYS USED TO BE THIS AWFUL.
SIT DOWN AND STAY AT YOUR POST.
OH, COME ON, GAMORA. THEY NEVER COME UP THIS HIGH.
THE RADAR WOULD DISAGREE. THERE'S A SWARM TWO MILES FROM US AND GAINING.
IS IT A BIG SWARM?
EVEN A SMALL BUG SWARM IS DANGEROUS, QUILL.
NOT WHEN YOU'VE JUST PILLAGED A NOVA BASE.
CHECK OUT THIS JETPACK. YEAH, A *JETPACK.*
FITS IN THIS LITTLE DOOHICKEY.

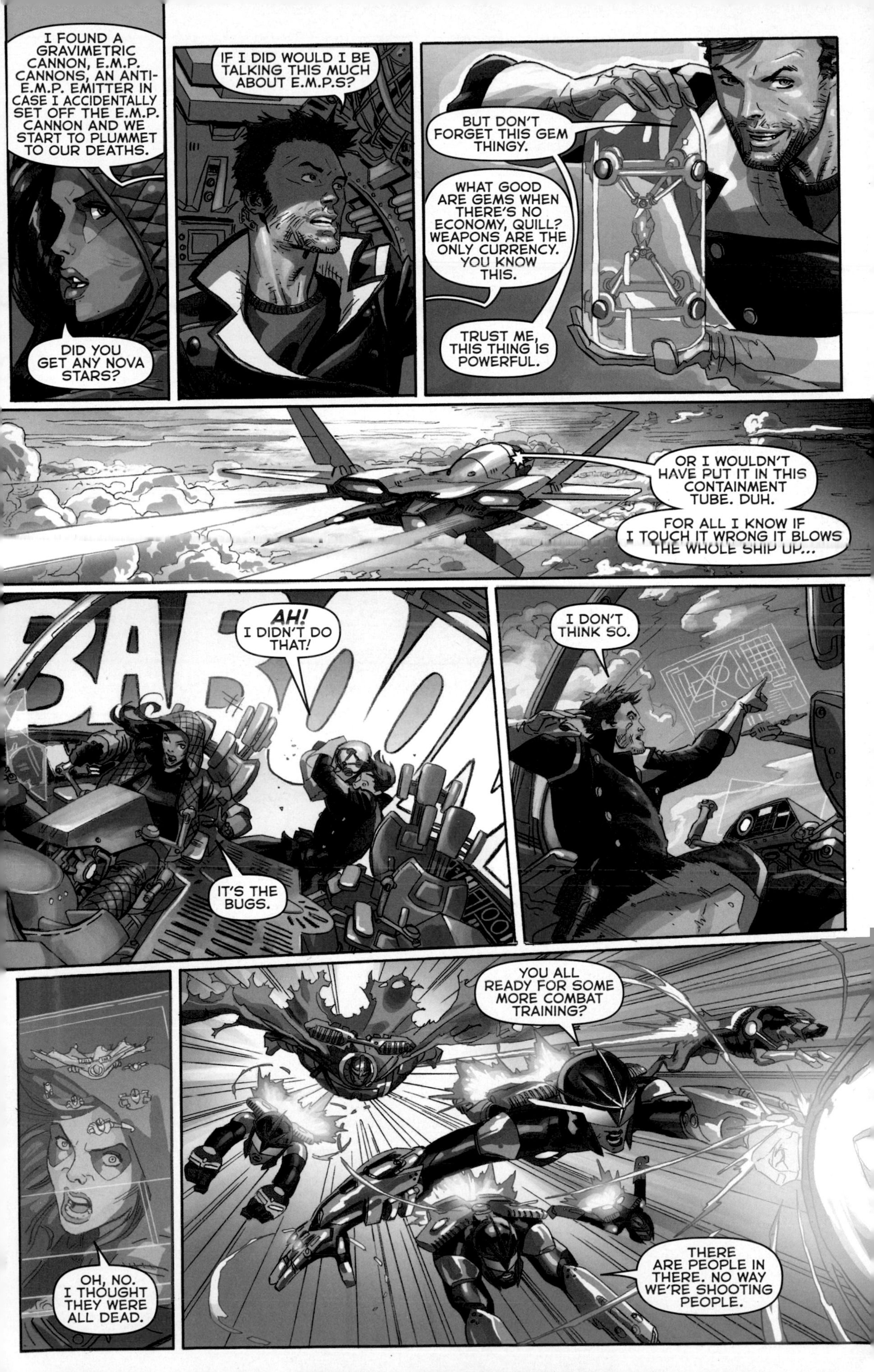
I FOUND A GRAVIMETRIC CANNON, E.M.P. CANNONS, AN ANTI-E.M.P. EMITTER IN CASE I ACCIDENTALLY SET OFF THE E.M.P. CANNON AND WE START TO PLUMMET TO OUR DEATHS.
DID YOU GET ANY NOVA STARS?
IF I DID WOULD I BE TALKING THIS MUCH ABOUT E.M.P.S?
BUT DON'T FORGET THIS GEM THINGY.
WHAT GOOD ARE GEMS WHEN THERE'S NO ECONOMY, QUILL? WEAPONS ARE THE ONLY CURRENCY. YOU KNOW THIS.
TRUST ME, THIS THING IS POWERFUL.
OR I WOULDN'T HAVE PUT IT IN THIS CONTAINMENT TUBE. DUH.
FOR ALL I KNOW IF I TOUCH IT WRONG IT BLOWS THE WHOLE SHIP UP...
AH! I DIDN'T DO THAT!
IT'S THE BUGS.
I DON'T THINK SO.
OH, NO. I THOUGHT THEY WERE ALL DEAD.
YOU ALL READY FOR SOME MORE COMBAT TRAINING?
THERE ARE PEOPLE IN THERE. NO WAY WE'RE SHOOTING PEOPLE.

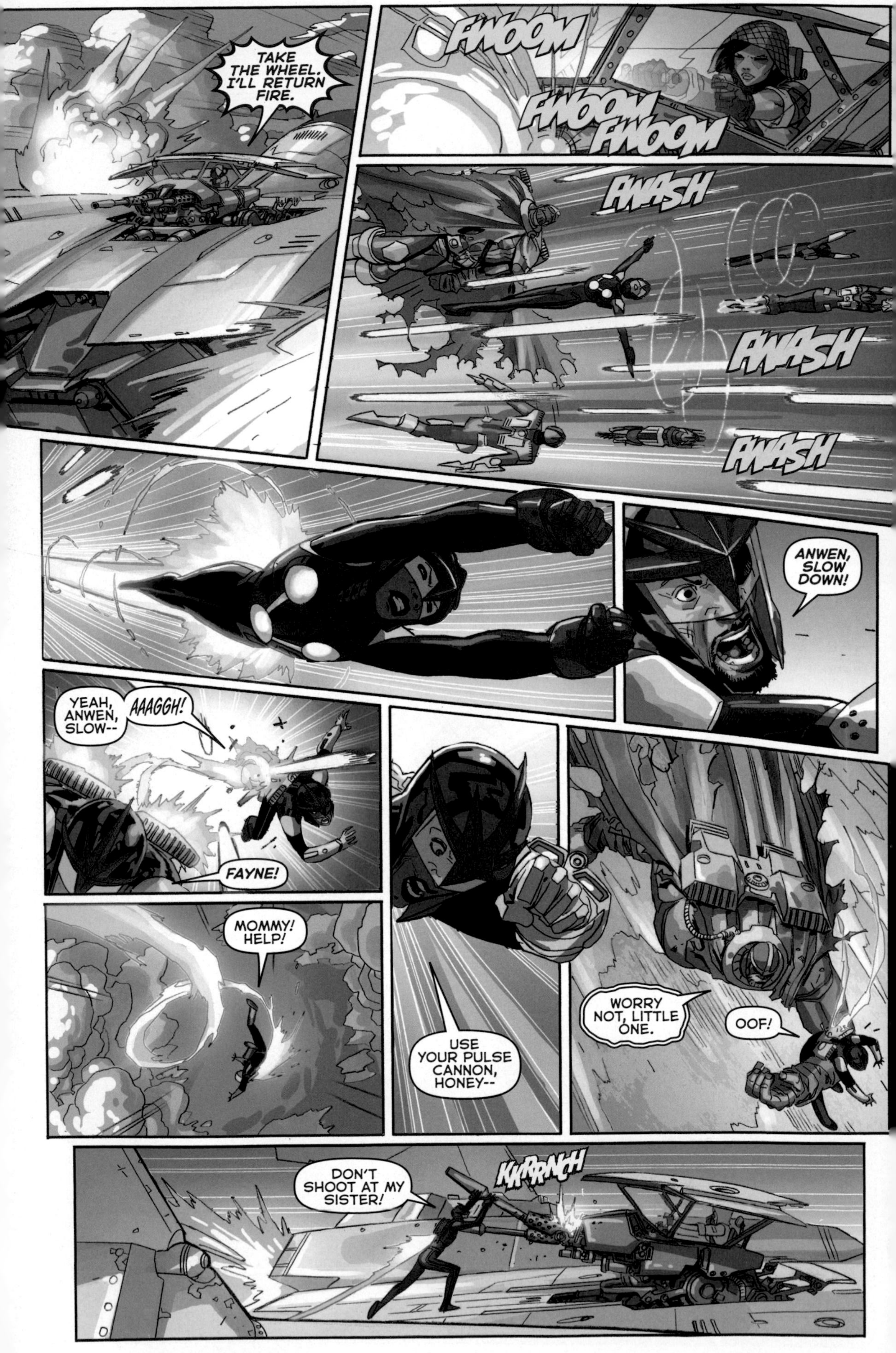
TAKE THE WHEEL. I'LL RETURN FIRE.
FWOOM
FWOOM
FWOOM
FWASH
FWASH
FWASH
ANWEN, SLOW DOWN!
YEAH, ANWEN, SLOW--
AAAGGH!
FAYNE!
MOMMY! HELP!
USE YOUR PULSE CANNON, HONEY--
WORRY NOT, LITTLE ONE.
OOF!
DON'T SHOOT AT MY SISTER!
KKRRNCH

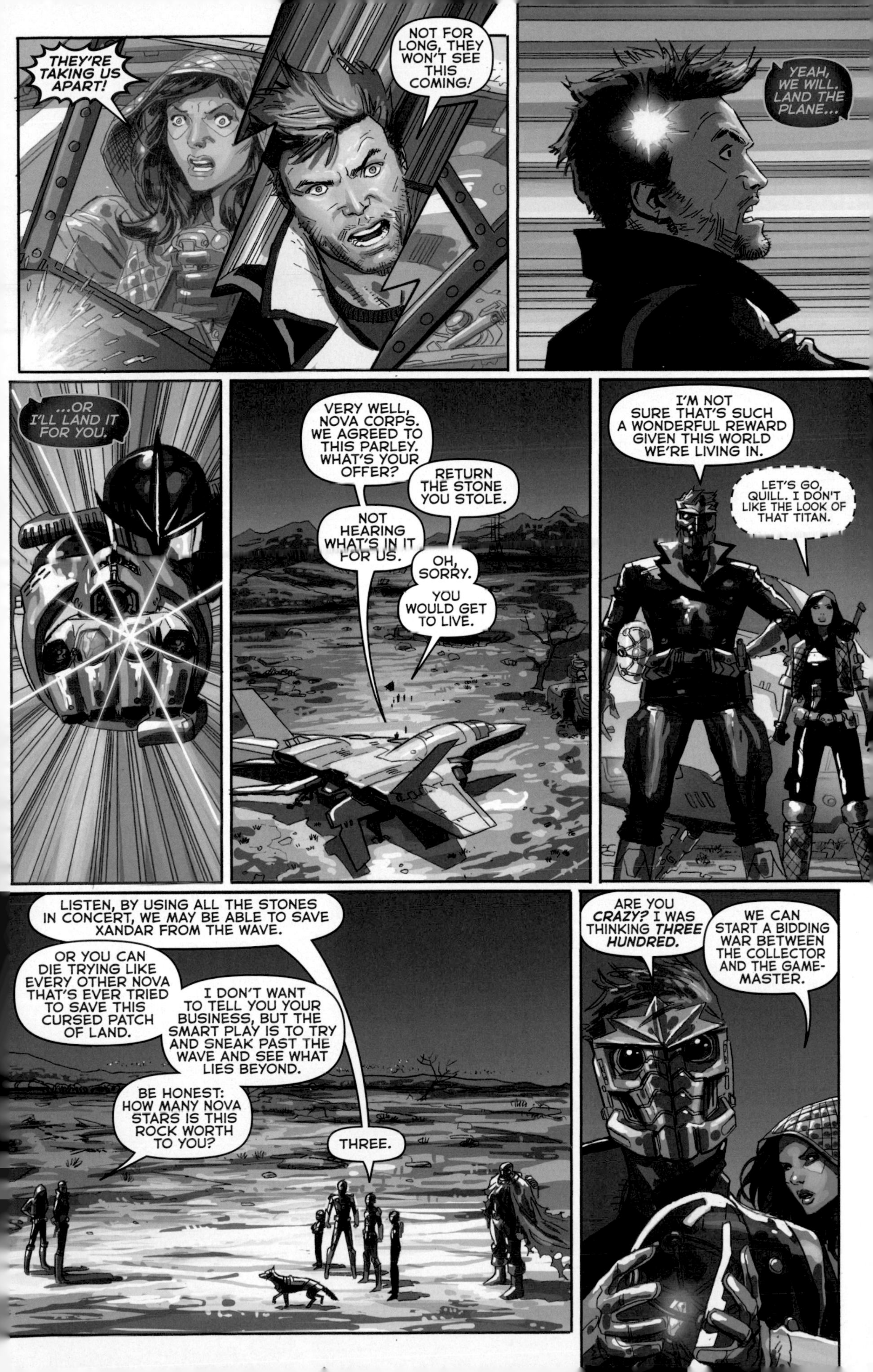
THEY'RE TAKING US APART!
NOT FOR LONG, THEY WON'T SEE THIS COMING!
YEAH, WE WILL. LAND THE PLANE...
...OR I'LL LAND IT FOR YOU.
VERY WELL, NOVA CORPS. WE AGREED TO THIS PARLEY. WHAT'S YOUR OFFER?
RETURN THE STONE YOU STOLE.
NOT HEARING WHAT'S IN IT FOR US.
OH, SORRY.
YOU WOULD GET TO LIVE.
I'M NOT SURE THAT'S SUCH A WONDERFUL REWARD GIVEN THIS WORLD WE'RE LIVING IN.
LET'S GO, QUILL. I DON'T LIKE THE LOOK OF THAT TITAN.
LISTEN, BY USING ALL THE STONES IN CONCERT, WE MAY BE ABLE TO SAVE XANDAR FROM THE WAVE.
OR YOU CAN DIE TRYING LIKE EVERY OTHER NOVA THAT'S EVER TRIED TO SAVE THIS CURSED PATCH OF LAND.
I DON'T WANT TO TELL YOU YOUR BUSINESS, BUT THE SMART PLAY IS TO TRY AND SNEAK PAST THE WAVE AND SEE WHAT LIES BEYOND.
BE HONEST: HOW MANY NOVA STARS IS THIS ROCK WORTH TO YOU?
THREE.
ARE YOU *CRAZY?* I WAS THINKING *THREE HUNDRED.*
WE CAN START A BIDDING WAR BETWEEN THE COLLECTOR AND THE GAME-MASTER.

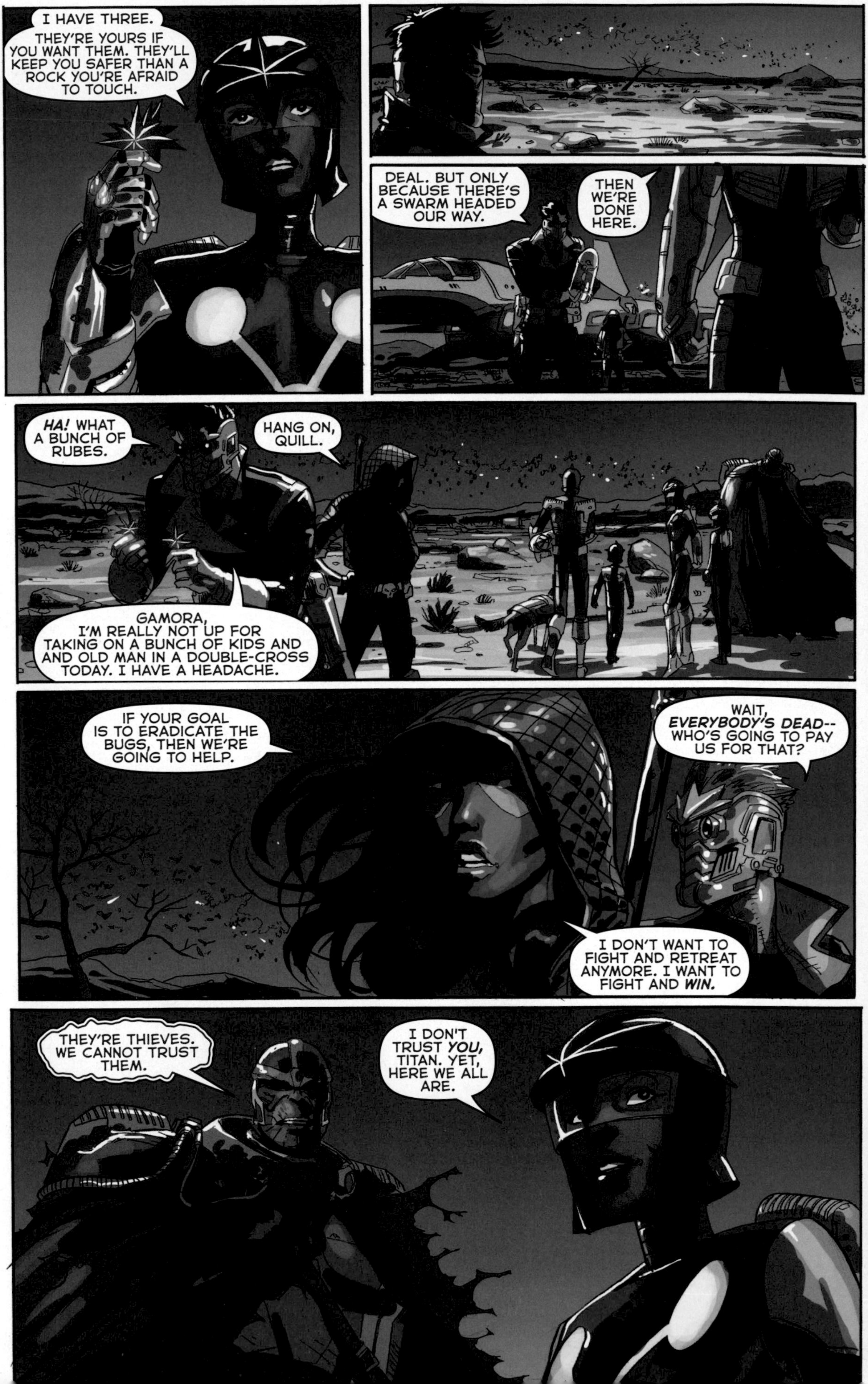
I HAVE THREE.
THEY'RE YOURS IF YOU WANT THEM. THEY'LL KEEP YOU SAFER THAN A ROCK YOU'RE AFRAID TO TOUCH.
DEAL. BUT ONLY BECAUSE THERE'S A SWARM HEADED OUR WAY.
THEN WE'RE DONE HERE.
HA! WHAT A BUNCH OF RUBES.
HANG ON, QUILL.
GAMORA, I'M REALLY NOT UP FOR TAKING ON A BUNCH OF KIDS AND AND OLD MAN IN A DOUBLE-CROSS TODAY. I HAVE A HEADACHE.
IF YOUR GOAL IS TO ERADICATE THE BUGS, THEN WE'RE GOING TO HELP.
WAIT, EVERYBODY'S DEAD-- WHO'S GOING TO PAY US FOR THAT?
I DON'T WANT TO FIGHT AND RETREAT ANYMORE. I WANT TO FIGHT AND WIN.
THEY'RE THIEVES. WE CANNOT TRUST THEM.
I DON'T TRUST YOU, TITAN. YET, HERE WE ALL ARE.

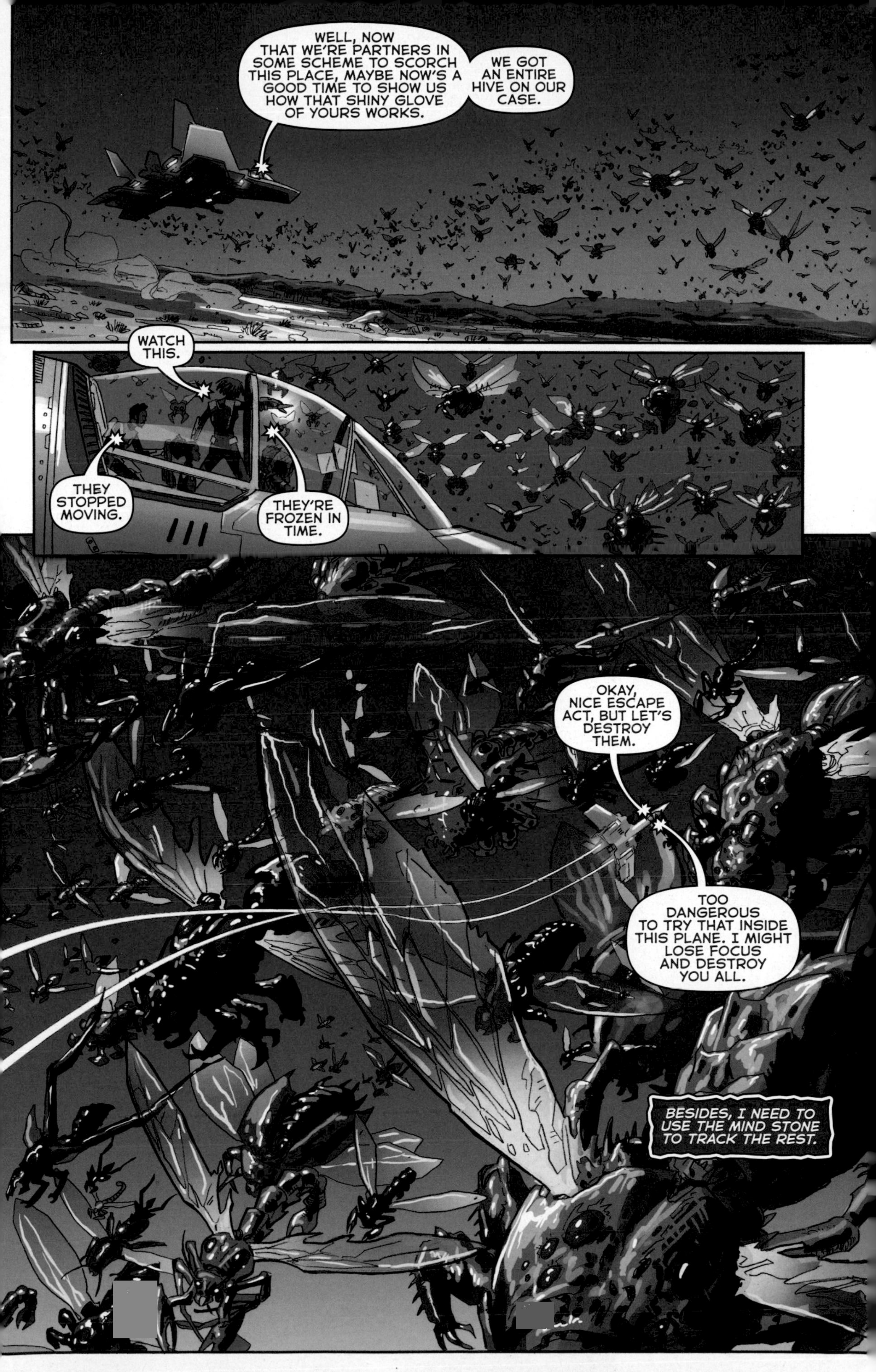
WELL, NOW THAT WE'RE PARTNERS IN SOME SCHEME TO SCORCH THIS PLACE, MAYBE NOW'S A GOOD TIME TO SHOW US HOW THAT SHINY GLOVE OF YOURS WORKS.
WE GOT AN ENTIRE HIVE ON OUR CASE.
WATCH THIS.
THEY STOPPED MOVING.
THEY'RE FROZEN IN TIME.
OKAY, NICE ESCAPE ACT, BUT LET'S DESTROY THEM.
TOO DANGEROUS TO TRY THAT INSIDE THIS PLANE. I MIGHT LOSE FOCUS AND DESTROY YOU ALL.
BESIDES, I NEED TO USE THE MIND STONE TO TRACK THE REST.

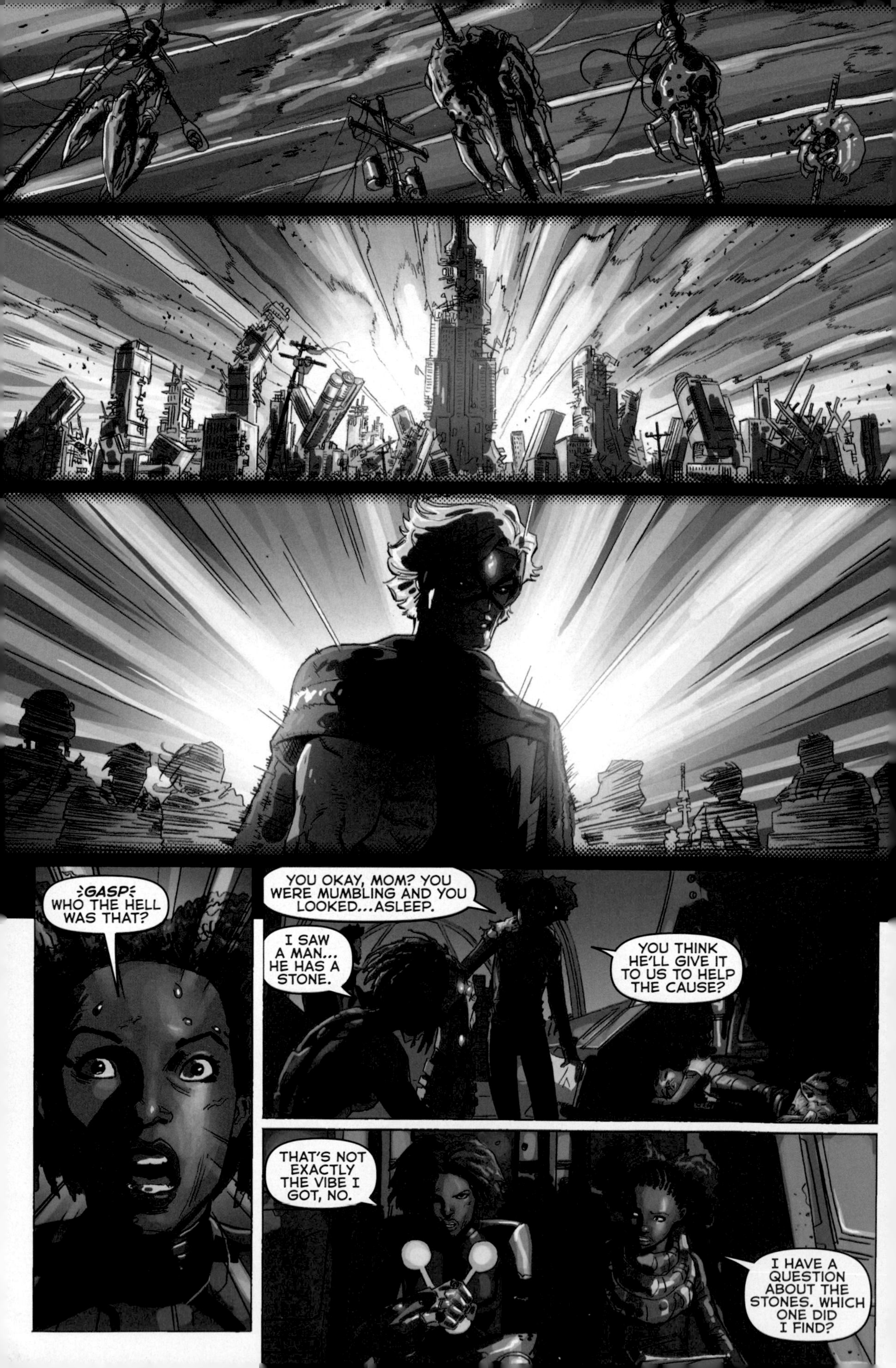
GASP
WHO THE HELL WAS THAT?
YOU OKAY, MOM? YOU WERE MUMBLING AND YOU LOOKED...ASLEEP.
I SAW A MAN... HE HAS A STONE.
YOU THINK HE'LL GIVE IT TO US TO HELP THE CAUSE?
THAT'S NOT EXACTLY THE VIBE I GOT, NO.
I HAVE A QUESTION ABOUT THE STONES. WHICH ONE DID I FIND?

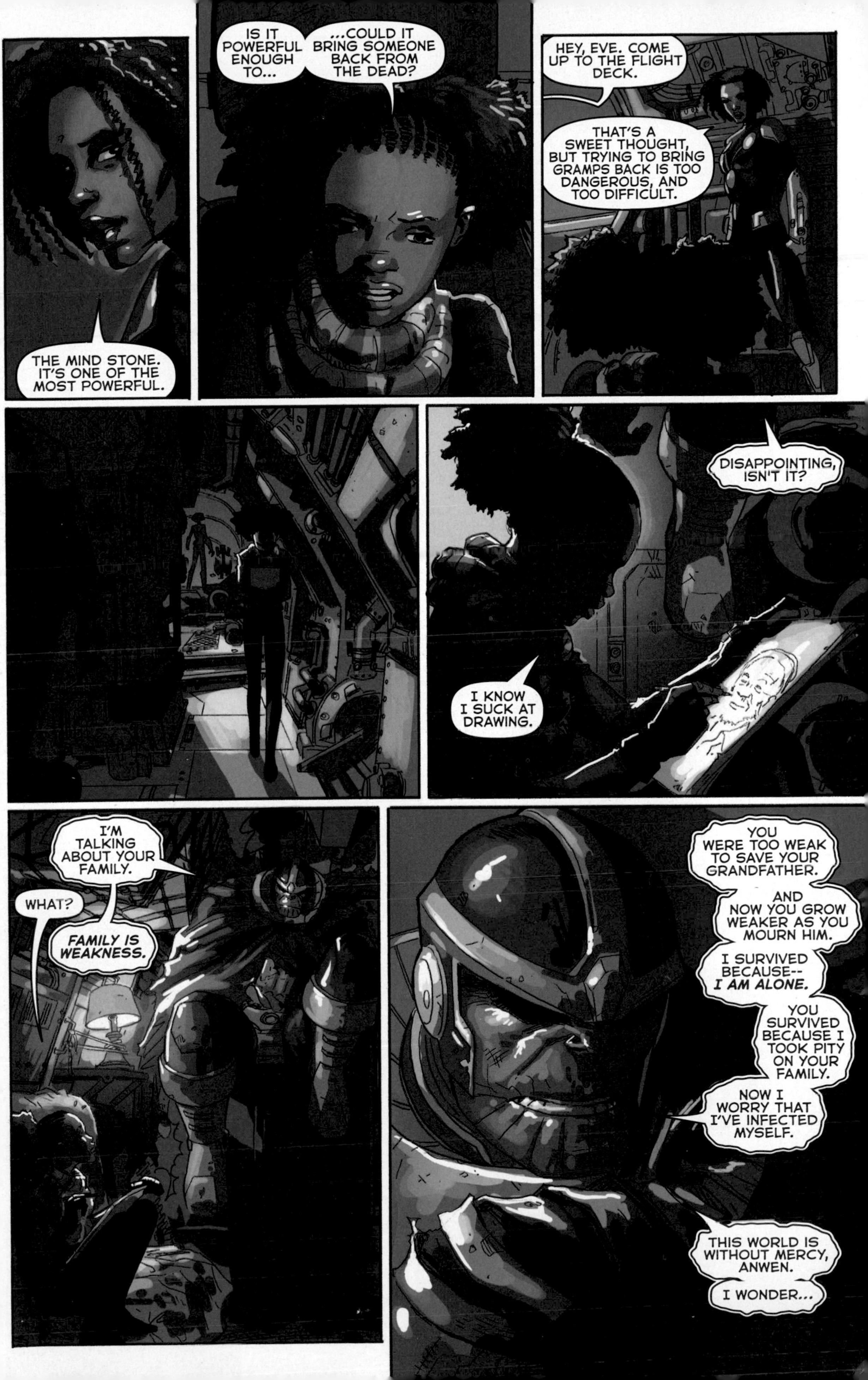
THE MIND STONE. IT'S ONE OF THE MOST POWERFUL.
IS IT POWERFUL ENOUGH TO...
...COULD IT BRING SOMEONE BACK FROM THE DEAD?
HEY, EVE. COME UP TO THE FLIGHT DECK.
THAT'S A SWEET THOUGHT, BUT TRYING TO BRING GRAMPS BACK IS TOO DANGEROUS, AND TOO DIFFICULT.
DISAPPOINTING, ISN'T IT?
I KNOW I SUCK AT DRAWING.
I'M TALKING ABOUT YOUR FAMILY.
WHAT?
FAMILY IS WEAKNESS.
YOU WERE TOO WEAK TO SAVE YOUR GRANDFATHER.
AND NOW YOU GROW WEAKER AS YOU MOURN HIM.
I SURVIVED BECAUSE-- I AM ALONE.
YOU SURVIVED BECAUSE I TOOK PITY ON YOUR FAMILY.
NOW I WORRY THAT I'VE INFECTED MYSELF.
THIS WORLD IS WITHOUT MERCY, ANWEN.
I WONDER...

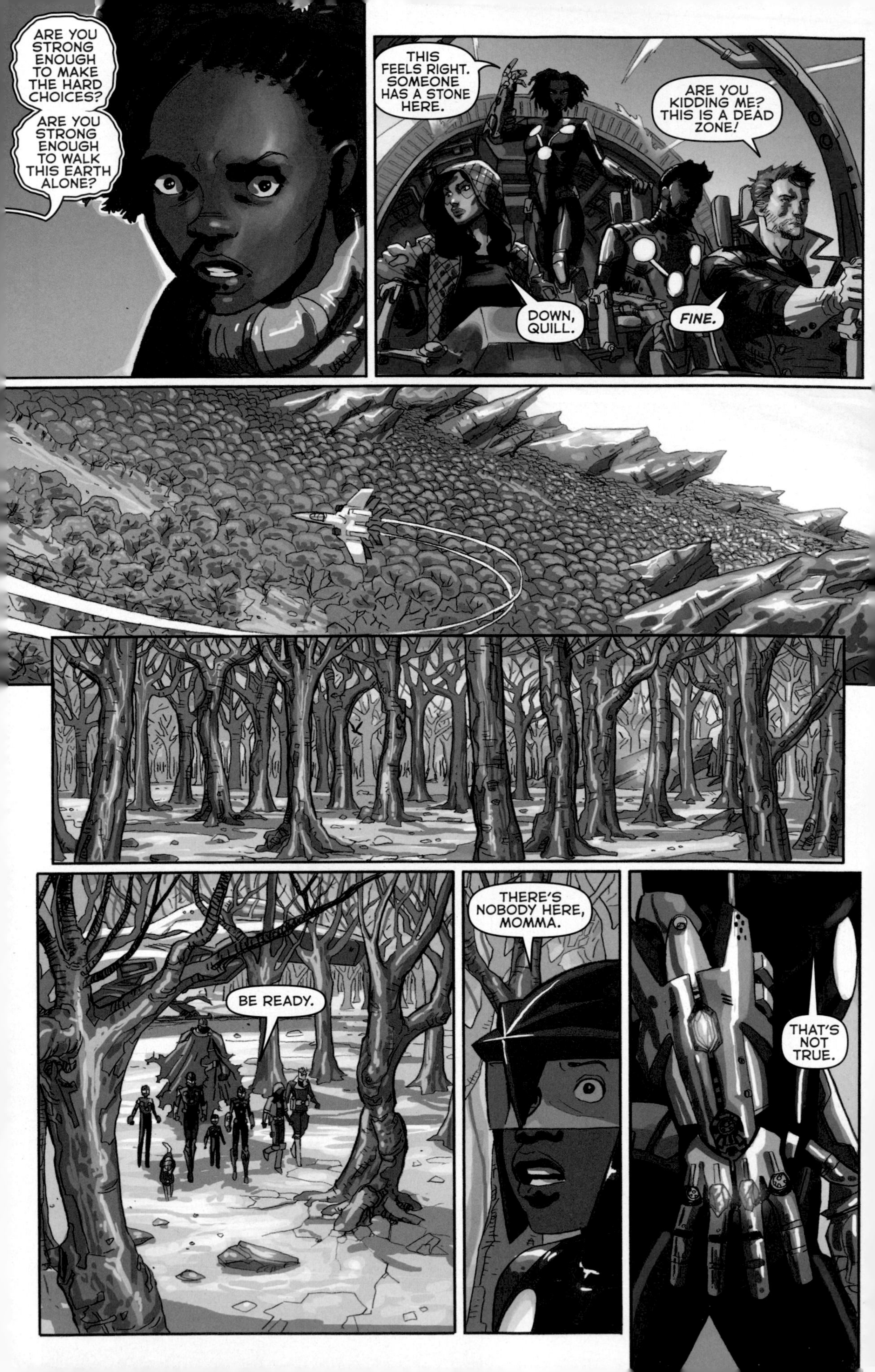
ARE YOU STRONG ENOUGH TO MAKE THE HARD CHOICES?
ARE YOU STRONG ENOUGH TO WALK THIS EARTH ALONE?
THIS FEELS RIGHT. SOMEONE HAS A STONE HERE.
ARE YOU KIDDING ME? THIS IS A DEAD ZONE!
DOWN, QUILL.
FINE.
BE READY.
THERE'S NOBODY HERE, MOMMA.
THAT'S NOT TRUE.

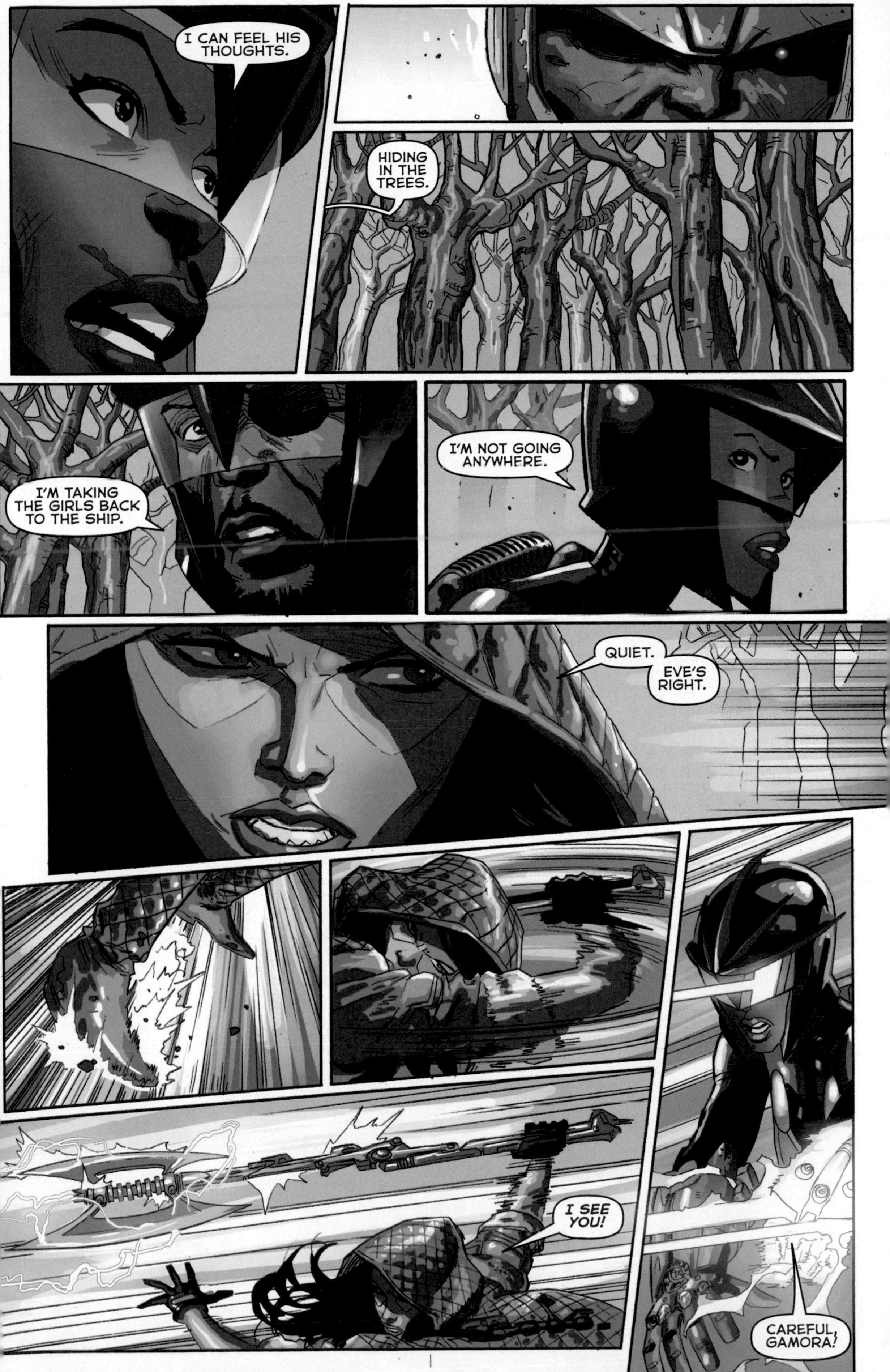
I CAN FEEL HIS THOUGHTS.
HIDING IN THE TREES.
I'M TAKING THE GIRLS BACK TO THE SHIP.
I'M NOT GOING ANYWHERE.
QUIET.
EVE'S RIGHT.
I SEE YOU!
CAREFUL, GAMORA!

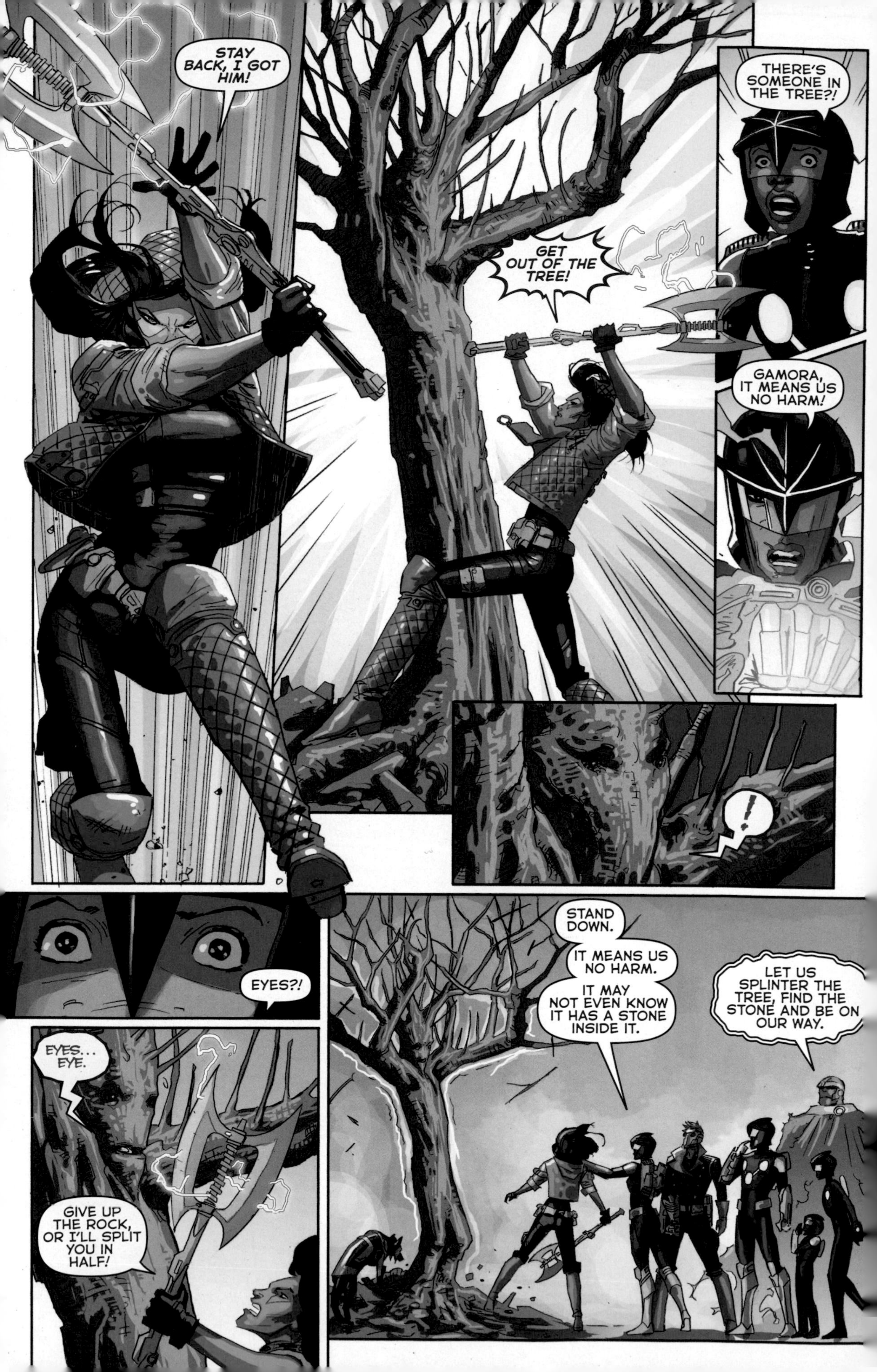
STAY BACK, I GOT HIM!
GET OUT OF THE TREE!
THERE'S SOMEONE IN THE TREE?!
GAMORA, IT MEANS US NO HARM!
!
EYES?!
EYES... EYE.
GIVE UP THE ROCK, OR I'LL SPLIT YOU IN HALF!
STAND DOWN.
IT MEANS US NO HARM.
IT MAY NOT EVEN KNOW IT HAS A STONE INSIDE IT.
LET US SPLINTER THE TREE, FIND THE STONE AND BE ON OUR WAY.

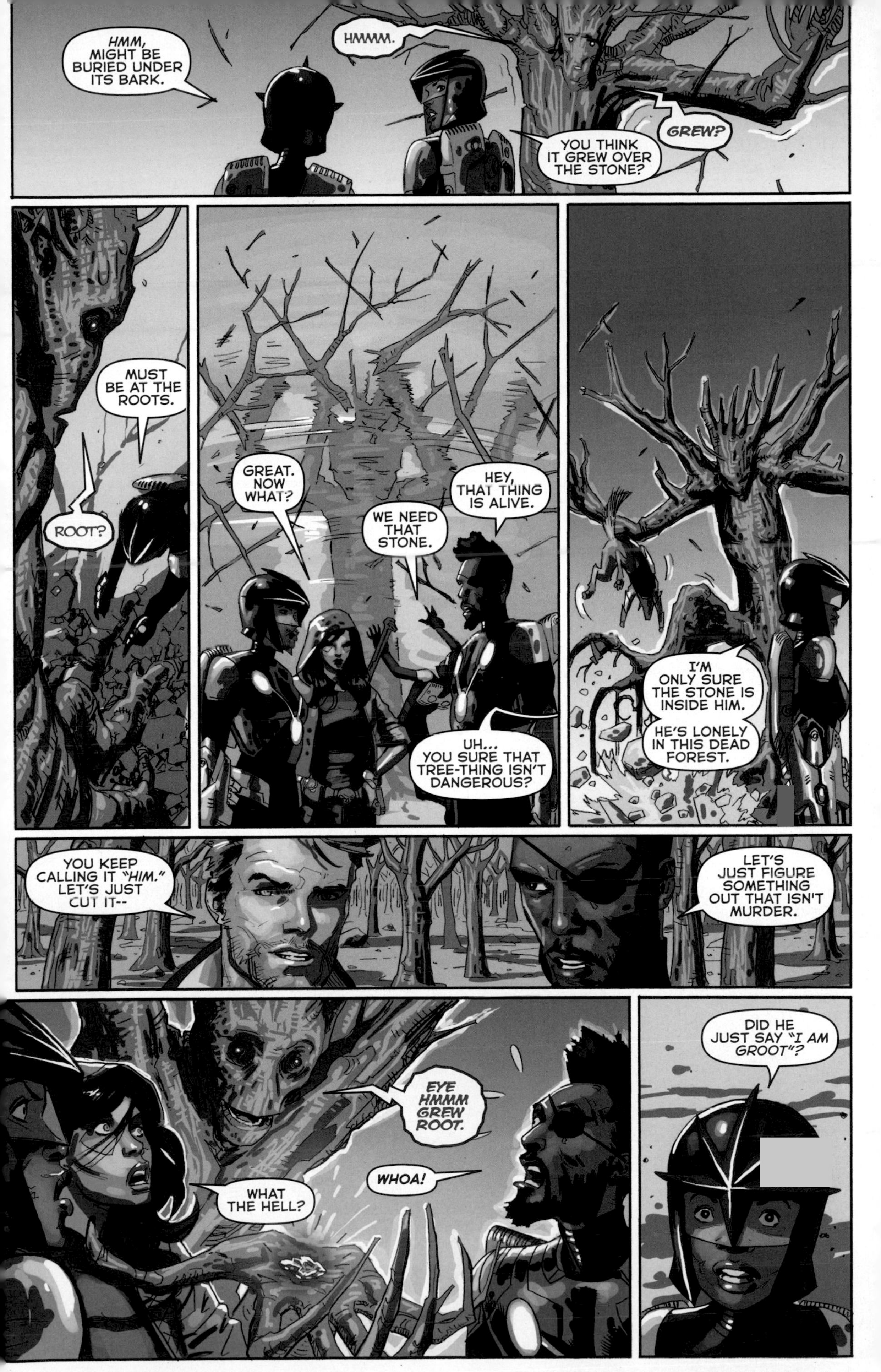
HMM, MIGHT BE BURIED UNDER ITS BARK.
HMMM.
YOU THINK IT GREW OVER THE STONE?
GREW?
MUST BE AT THE ROOTS.
ROOT?
GREAT. NOW WHAT?
HEY, THAT THING IS ALIVE.
WE NEED THAT STONE.
UH... YOU SURE THAT TREE-THING ISN'T DANGEROUS?
I'M ONLY SURE THE STONE IS INSIDE HIM.
HE'S LONELY IN THIS DEAD FOREST.
YOU KEEP CALLING IT "HIM." LET'S JUST CUT IT--
LET'S JUST FIGURE SOMETHING OUT THAT ISN'T MURDER.
EYE HMMM GREW ROOT.
WHOA!
WHAT THE HELL?
DID HE JUST SAY "I AM GROOT"?

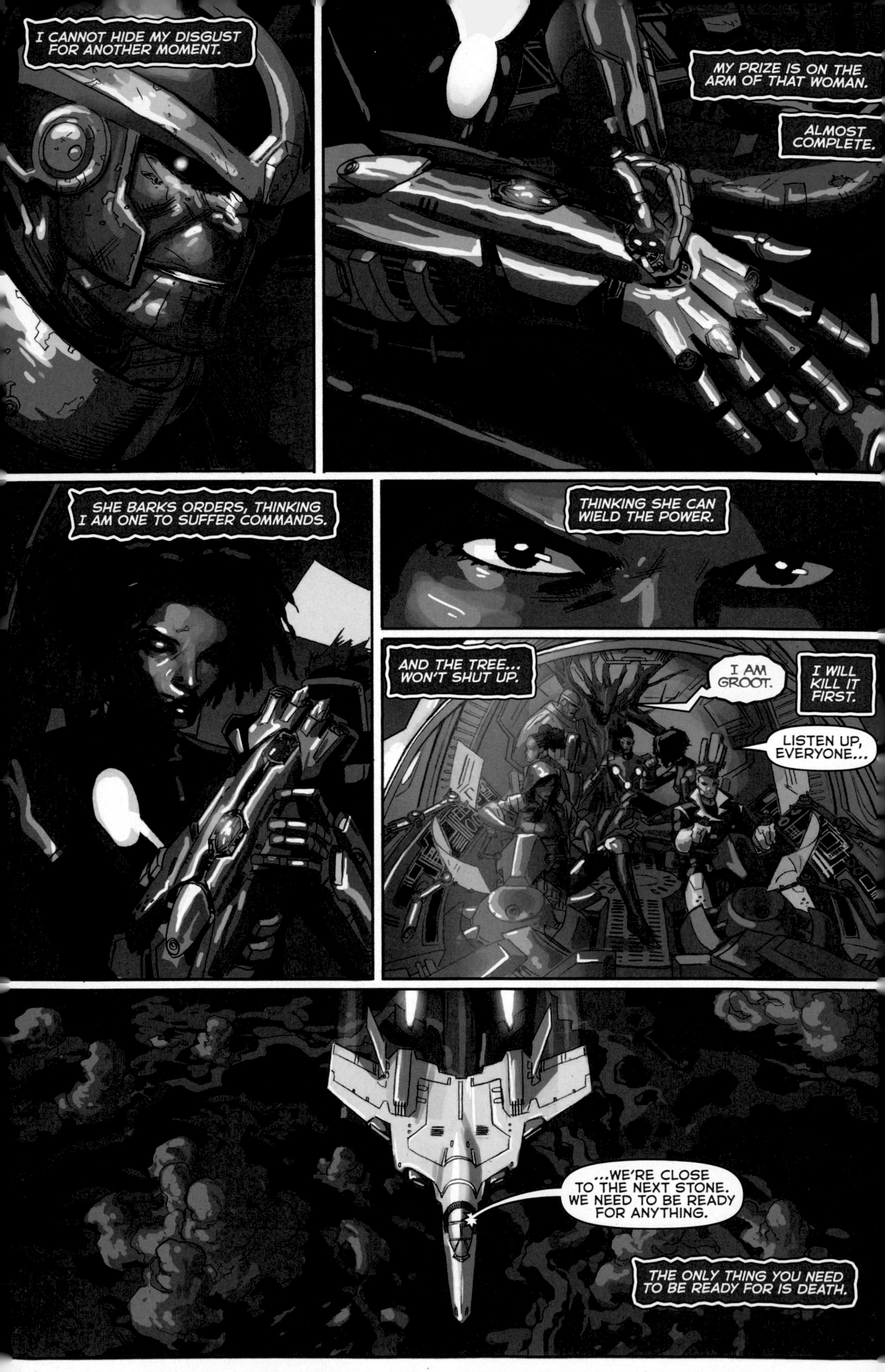

I CANNOT HIDE MY DISGUST FOR ANOTHER MOMENT.
MY PRIZE IS ON THE ARM OF THAT WOMAN.
ALMOST COMPLETE.
SHE BARKS ORDERS, THINKING I AM ONE TO SUFFER COMMANDS.
THINKING SHE CAN WIELD THE POWER.
AND THE TREE... WON'T SHUT UP.
I AM GROOT.
I WILL KILL IT FIRST.
LISTEN UP, EVERYONE...
...WE'RE CLOSE TO THE NEXT STONE. WE NEED TO BE READY FOR ANYTHING.
THE ONLY THING YOU NEED TO BE READY FOR IS DEATH.

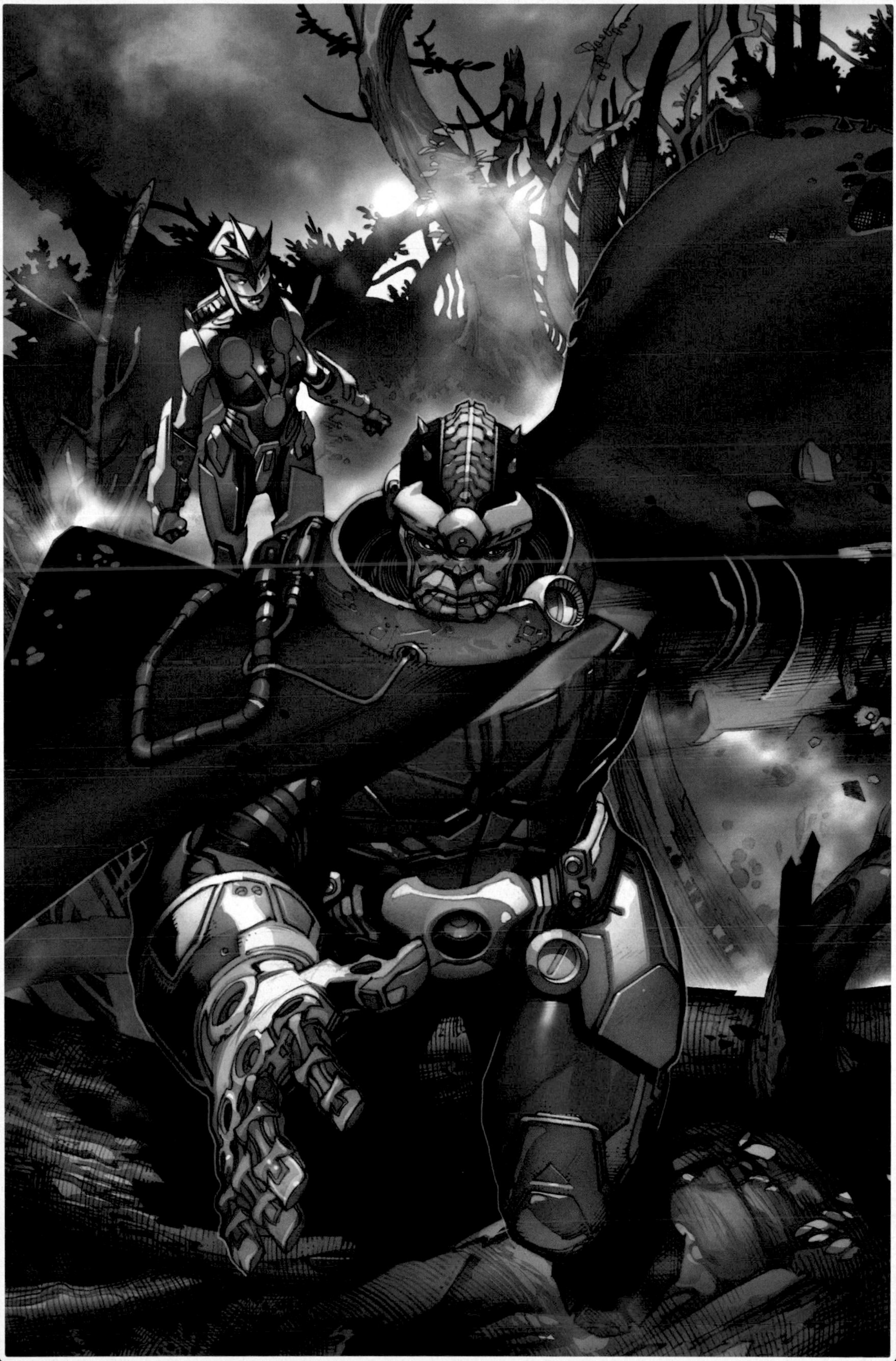

INFINITY GAUNTLET 3
VARIANT COVER BY SIMONE BIANCHI & DAVID CURIEL

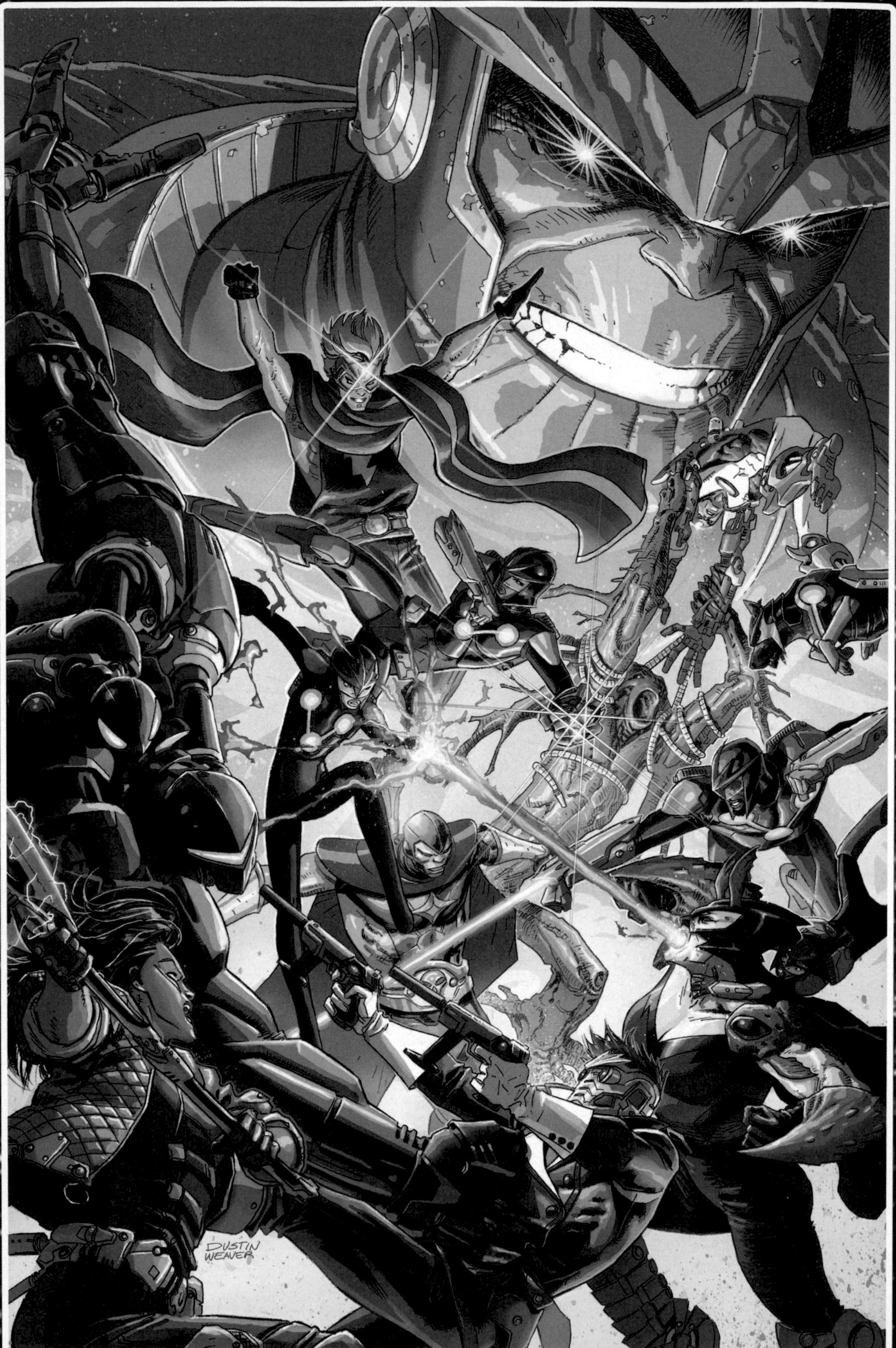
DUSTIN WEAVER

4

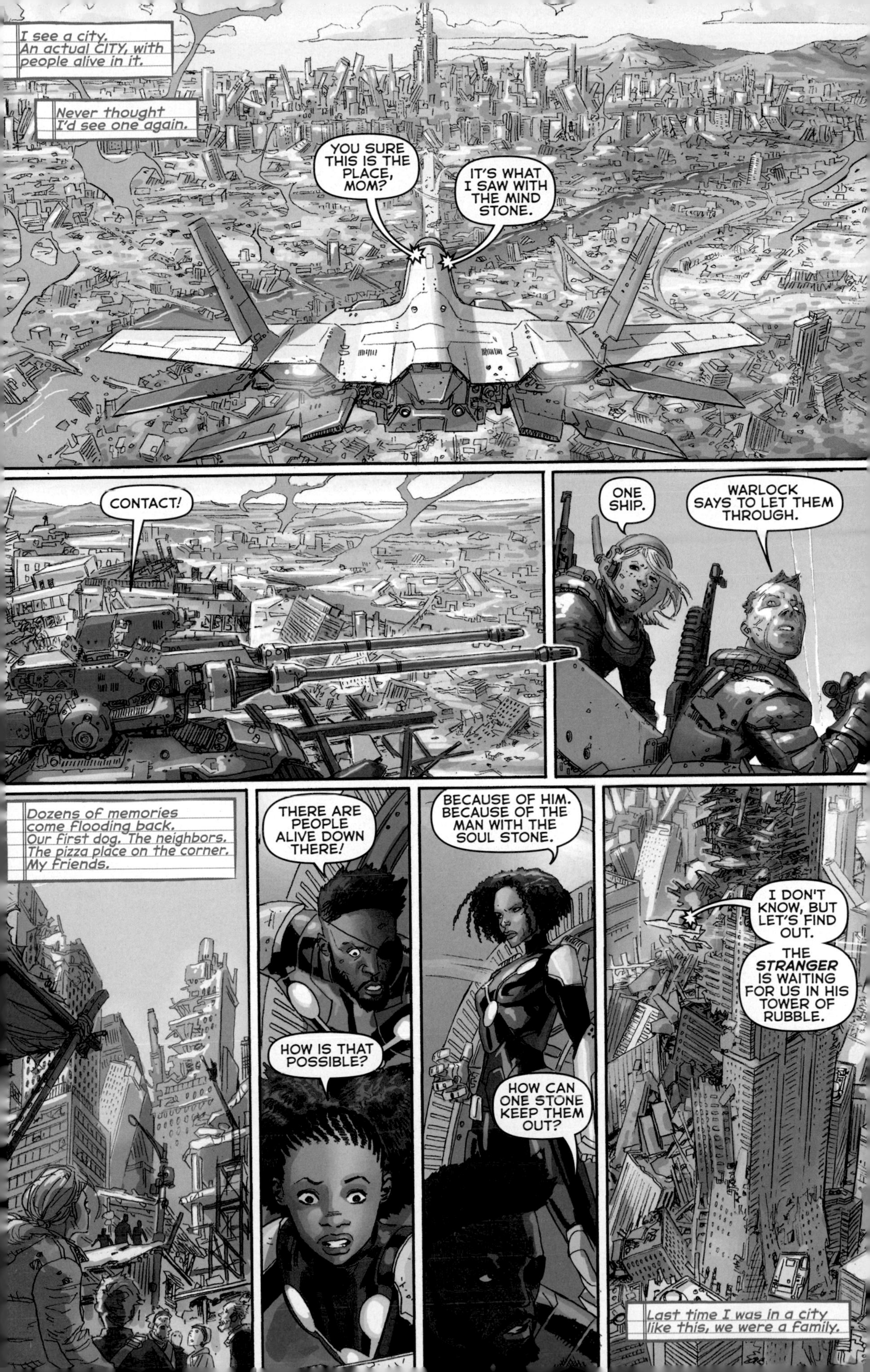
I see a city. An actual CITY, with people alive in it.
Never thought I'd see one again.
YOU SURE THIS IS THE PLACE, MOM?
IT'S WHAT I SAW WITH THE MIND STONE.
CONTACT!
ONE SHIP.
WARLOCK SAYS TO LET THEM THROUGH.
Dozens of memories come flooding back. Our first dog. The neighbors. The pizza place on the corner. My friends.
THERE ARE PEOPLE ALIVE DOWN THERE!
HOW IS THAT POSSIBLE?
BECAUSE OF HIM. BECAUSE OF THE MAN WITH THE SOUL STONE.
HOW CAN ONE STONE KEEP THEM OUT?
I DON'T KNOW, BUT LET'S FIND OUT.
THE STRANGER IS WAITING FOR US IN HIS TOWER OF RUBBLE.
Last time I was in a city like this, we were a family.

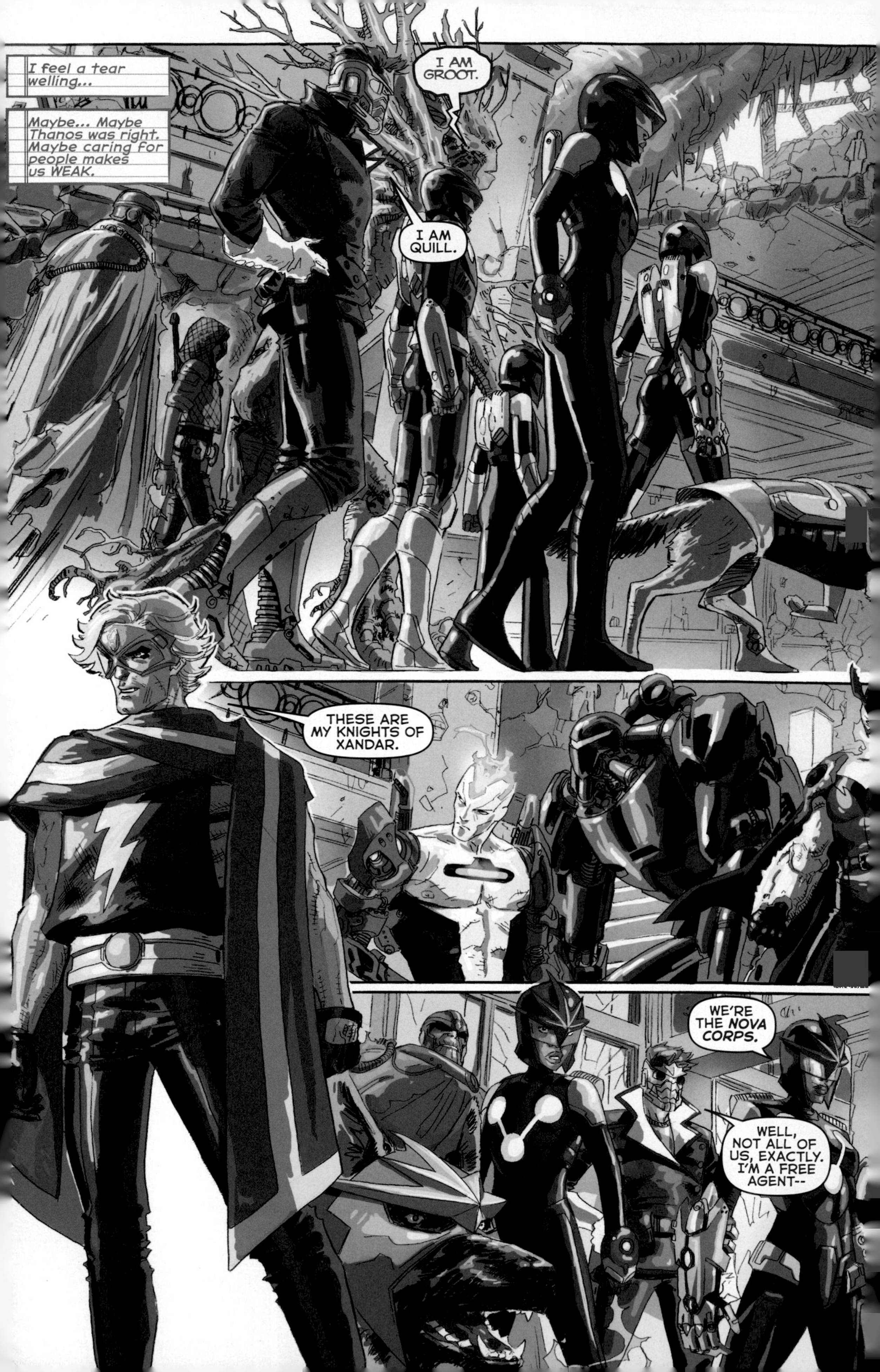
I feel a tear welling...
Maybe... Maybe Thanos was right. Maybe caring for people makes us WEAK.
I AM GROOT.
I AM QUILL.
THESE ARE MY KNIGHTS OF XANDAR.
WE'RE THE NOVA CORPS.
WELL, NOT ALL OF US, EXACTLY. I'M A FREE AGENT--

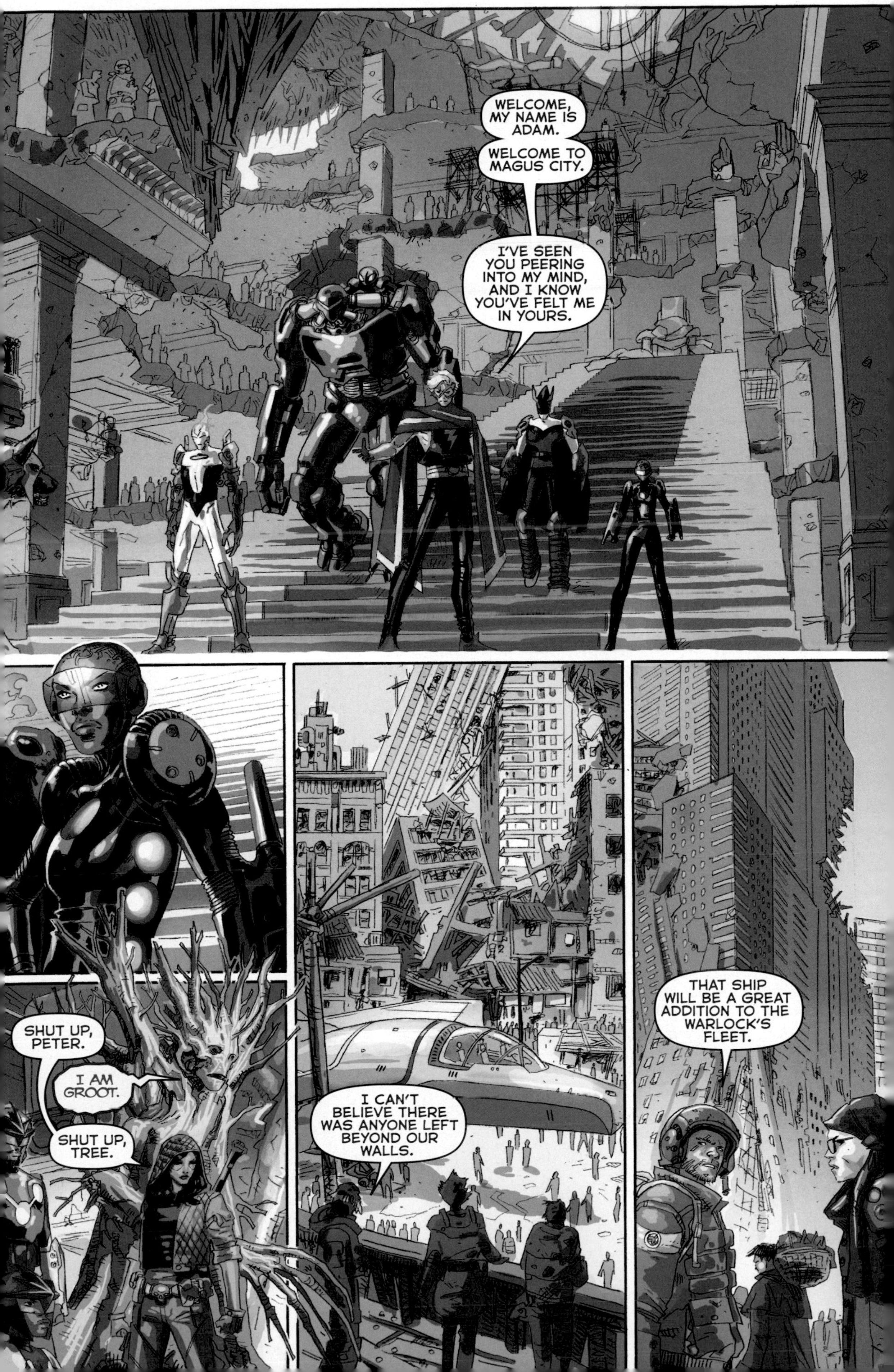
WELCOME, MY NAME IS ADAM.
WELCOME TO MAGUS CITY.
I'VE SEEN YOU PEERING INTO MY MIND, AND I KNOW YOU'VE FELT ME IN YOURS.
SHUT UP, PETER.
I AM GROOT.
SHUT UP, TREE.
I CAN'T BELIEVE THERE WAS ANYONE LEFT BEYOND OUR WALLS.
THAT SHIP WILL BE A GREAT ADDITION TO THE WARLOCK'S FLEET.

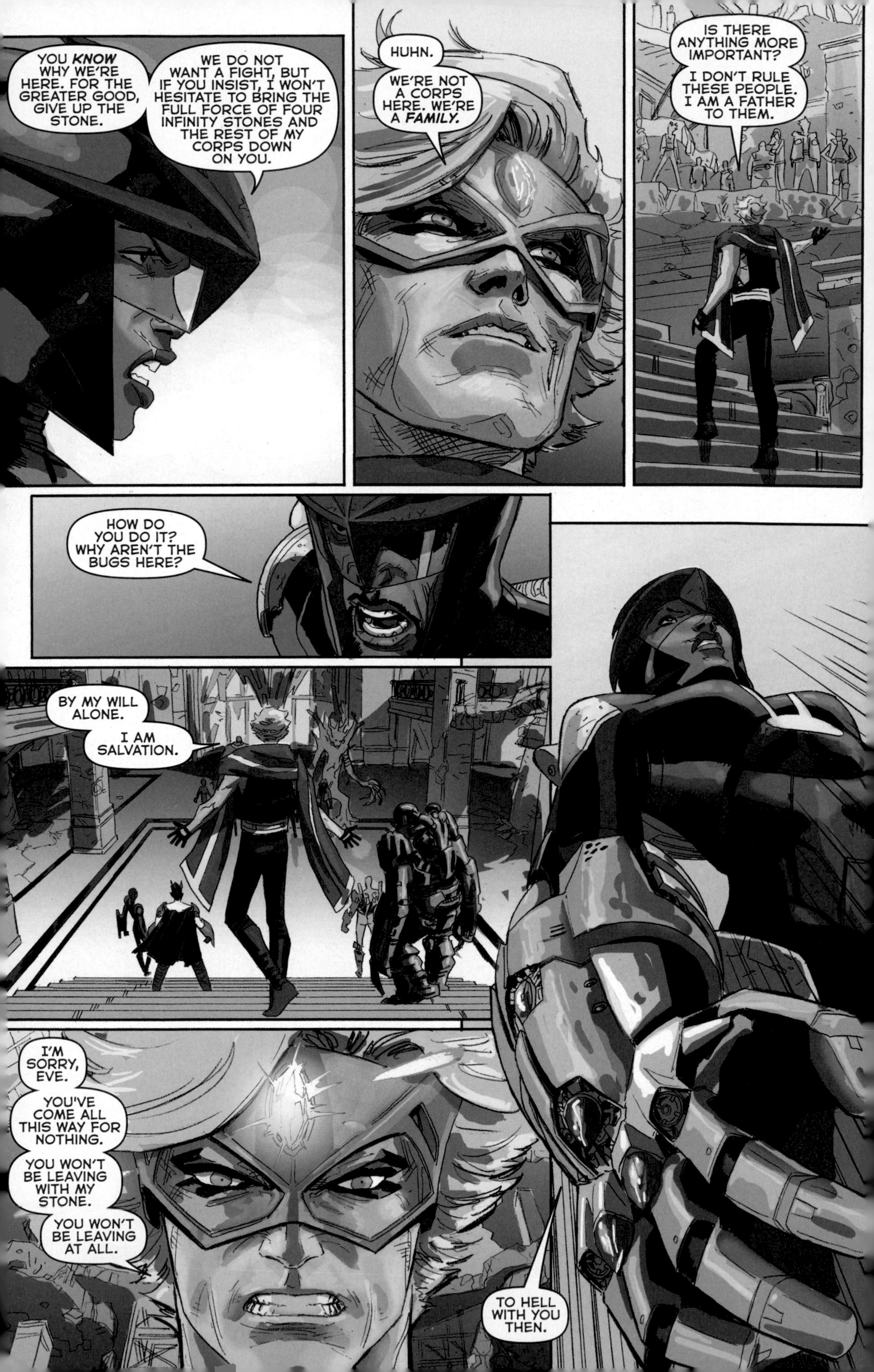
YOU *KNOW* WHY WE'RE HERE. FOR THE GREATER GOOD, GIVE UP THE STONE.
WE DO NOT WANT A FIGHT, BUT IF YOU INSIST, I WON'T HESITATE TO BRING THE FULL FORCE OF FOUR INFINITY STONES AND THE REST OF MY CORPS DOWN ON YOU.
HUHN.
WE'RE NOT A CORPS HERE. WE'RE A *FAMILY.*
IS THERE ANYTHING MORE IMPORTANT?
I DON'T RULE THESE PEOPLE. I AM A FATHER TO THEM.
HOW DO YOU DO IT? WHY AREN'T THE BUGS HERE?
BY MY WILL ALONE.
I AM SALVATION.
I'M SORRY, EVE.
YOU'VE COME ALL THIS WAY FOR NOTHING.
YOU WON'T BE LEAVING WITH MY STONE.
YOU WON'T BE LEAVING AT ALL.
TO HELL WITH YOU THEN.

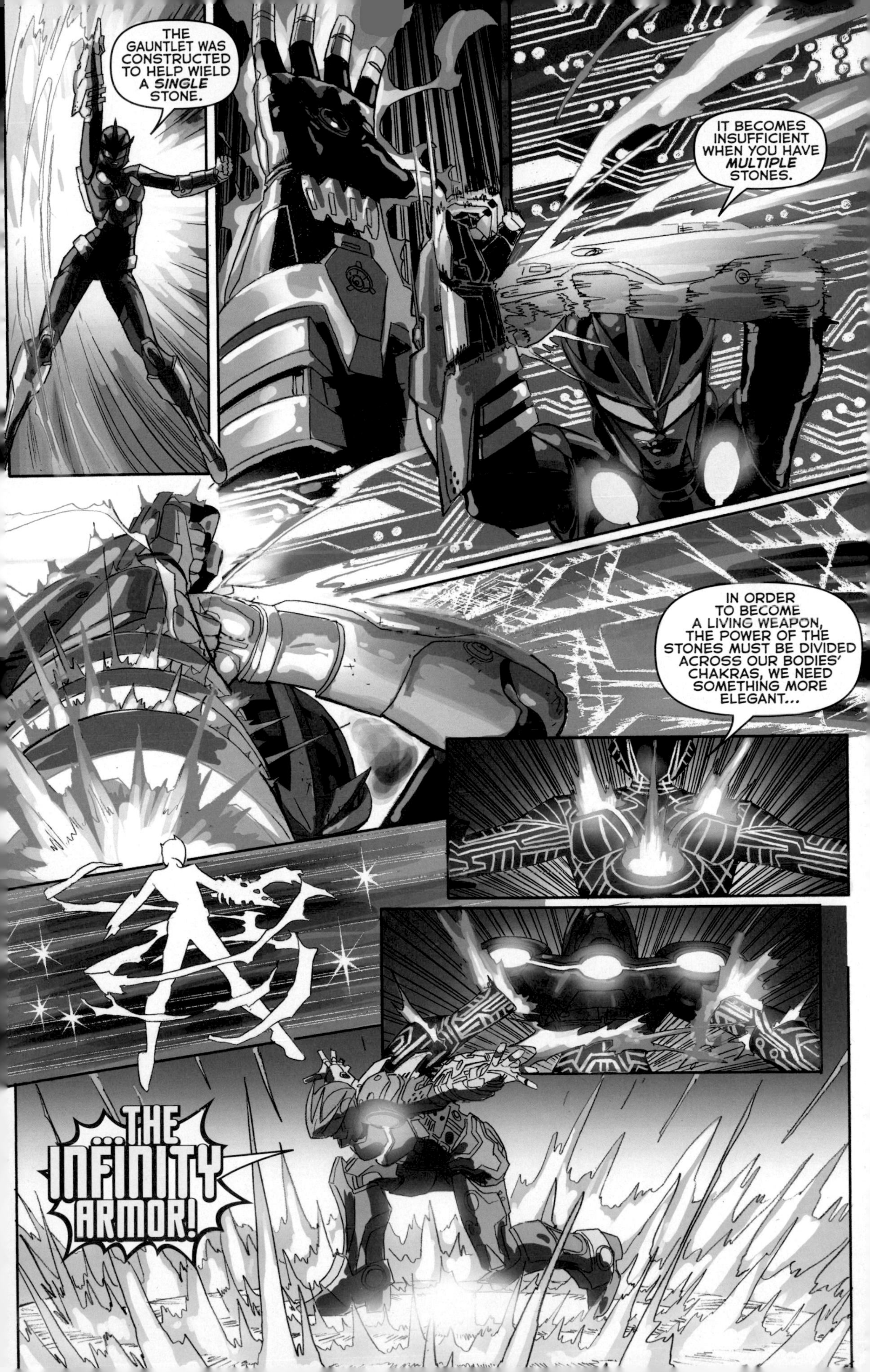
THE GAUNTLET WAS CONSTRUCTED TO HELP WIELD A *SINGLE* STONE.
IT BECOMES INSUFFICIENT WHEN YOU HAVE *MULTIPLE* STONES.
IN ORDER TO BECOME A LIVING WEAPON, THE POWER OF THE STONES MUST BE DIVIDED ACROSS OUR BODIES' CHAKRAS, WE NEED SOMETHING MORE ELEGANT...
...THE INFINITY ARMOR!

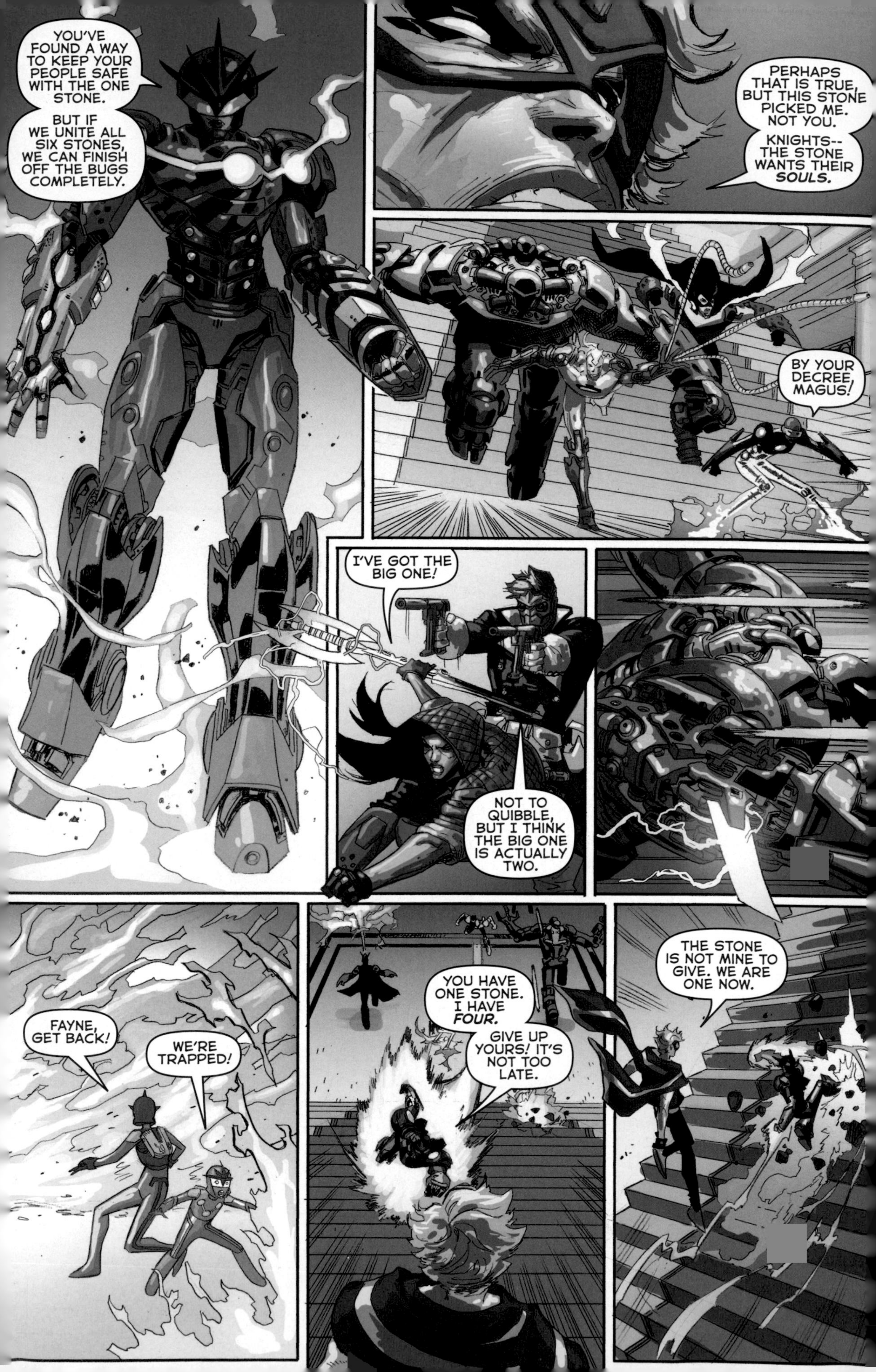
YOU'VE FOUND A WAY TO KEEP YOUR PEOPLE SAFE WITH THE ONE STONE.
BUT IF WE UNITE ALL SIX STONES, WE CAN FINISH OFF THE BUGS COMPLETELY.
PERHAPS THAT IS TRUE, BUT THIS STONE PICKED ME. NOT YOU.
KNIGHTS-- THE STONE WANTS THEIR *SOULS.*
BY YOUR DECREE, MAGUS!
I'VE GOT THE BIG ONE!
NOT TO QUIBBLE, BUT I THINK THE BIG ONE IS ACTUALLY TWO.
FAYNE, GET BACK!
WE'RE TRAPPED!
YOU HAVE ONE STONE. I HAVE *FOUR.*
GIVE UP YOURS! IT'S NOT TOO LATE.
THE STONE IS NOT MINE TO GIVE. WE ARE ONE NOW.

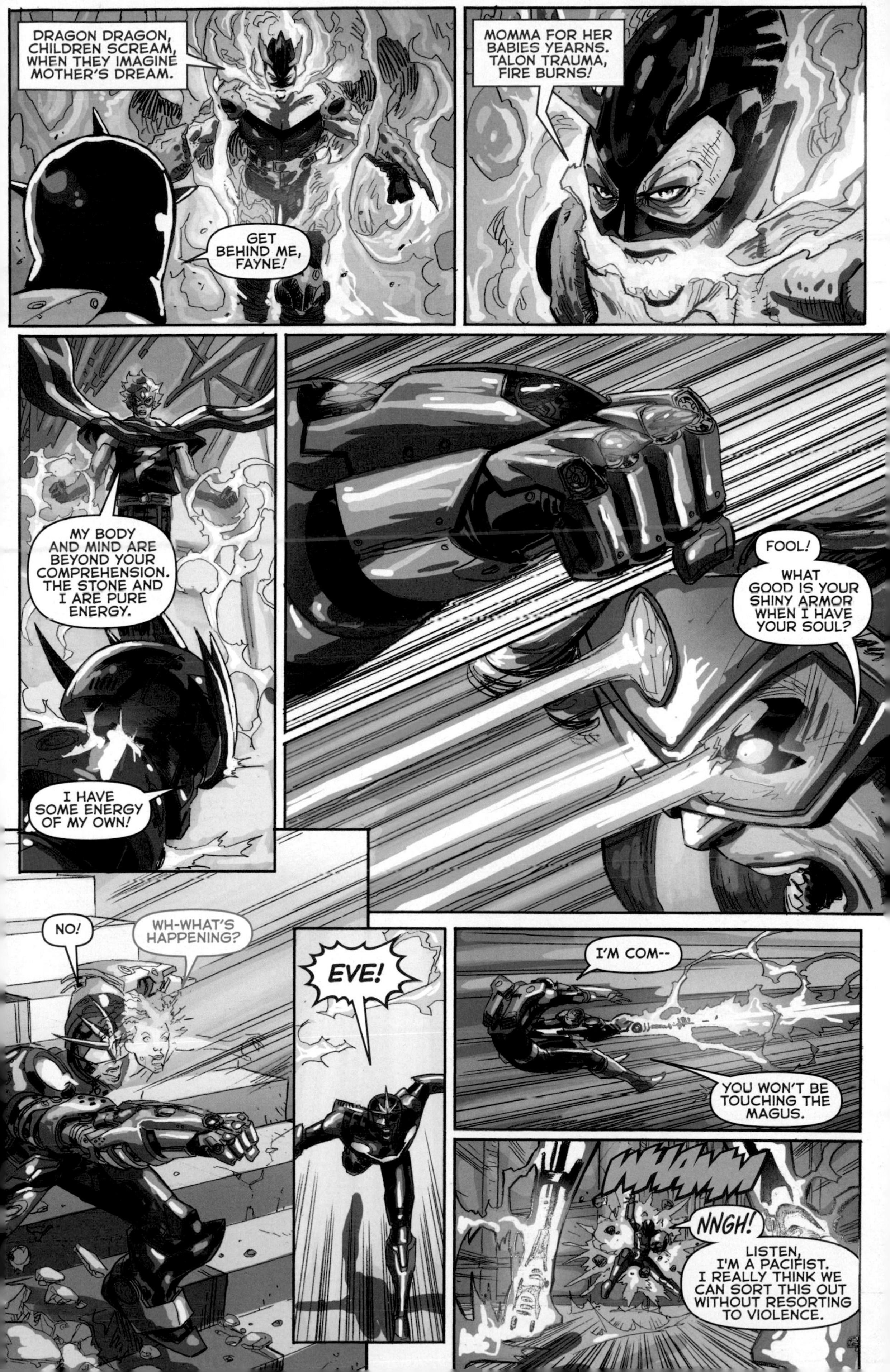
DRAGON DRAGON, CHILDREN SCREAM, WHEN THEY IMAGINE MOTHER'S DREAM.
GET BEHIND ME, FAYNE!
MOMMA FOR HER BABIES YEARNS. TALON TRAUMA, FIRE BURNS!
MY BODY AND MIND ARE BEYOND YOUR COMPREHENSION. THE STONE AND I ARE PURE ENERGY.
I HAVE SOME ENERGY OF MY OWN!
FOOL!
WHAT GOOD IS YOUR SHINY ARMOR WHEN I HAVE YOUR SOUL?
NO!
WH-WHAT'S HAPPENING?
EVE!
I'M COM--
YOU WON'T BE TOUCHING THE MAGUS.
NNGH!
LISTEN, I'M A PACIFIST. I REALLY THINK WE CAN SORT THIS OUT WITHOUT RESORTING TO VIOLENCE.

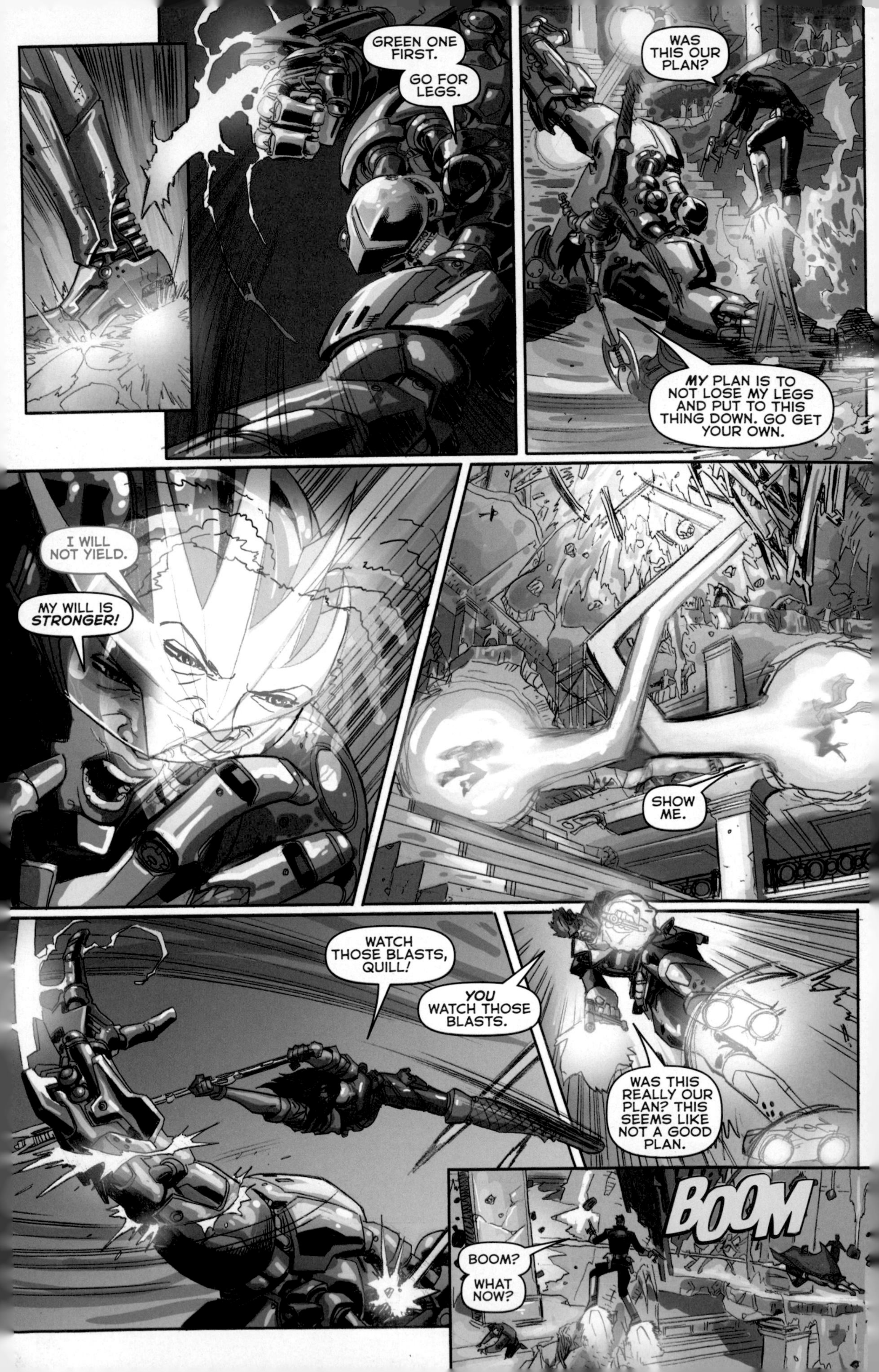
GREEN ONE FIRST.
GO FOR LEGS.
WAS THIS OUR PLAN?
MY PLAN IS TO NOT LOSE MY LEGS AND PUT TO THIS THING DOWN. GO GET YOUR OWN.
I WILL NOT YIELD.
MY WILL IS STRONGER!
SHOW ME.
WATCH THOSE BLASTS, QUILL!
YOU WATCH THOSE BLASTS.
WAS THIS REALLY OUR PLAN? THIS SEEMS LIKE NOT A GOOD PLAN.
BOOM
BOOM?
WHAT NOW?

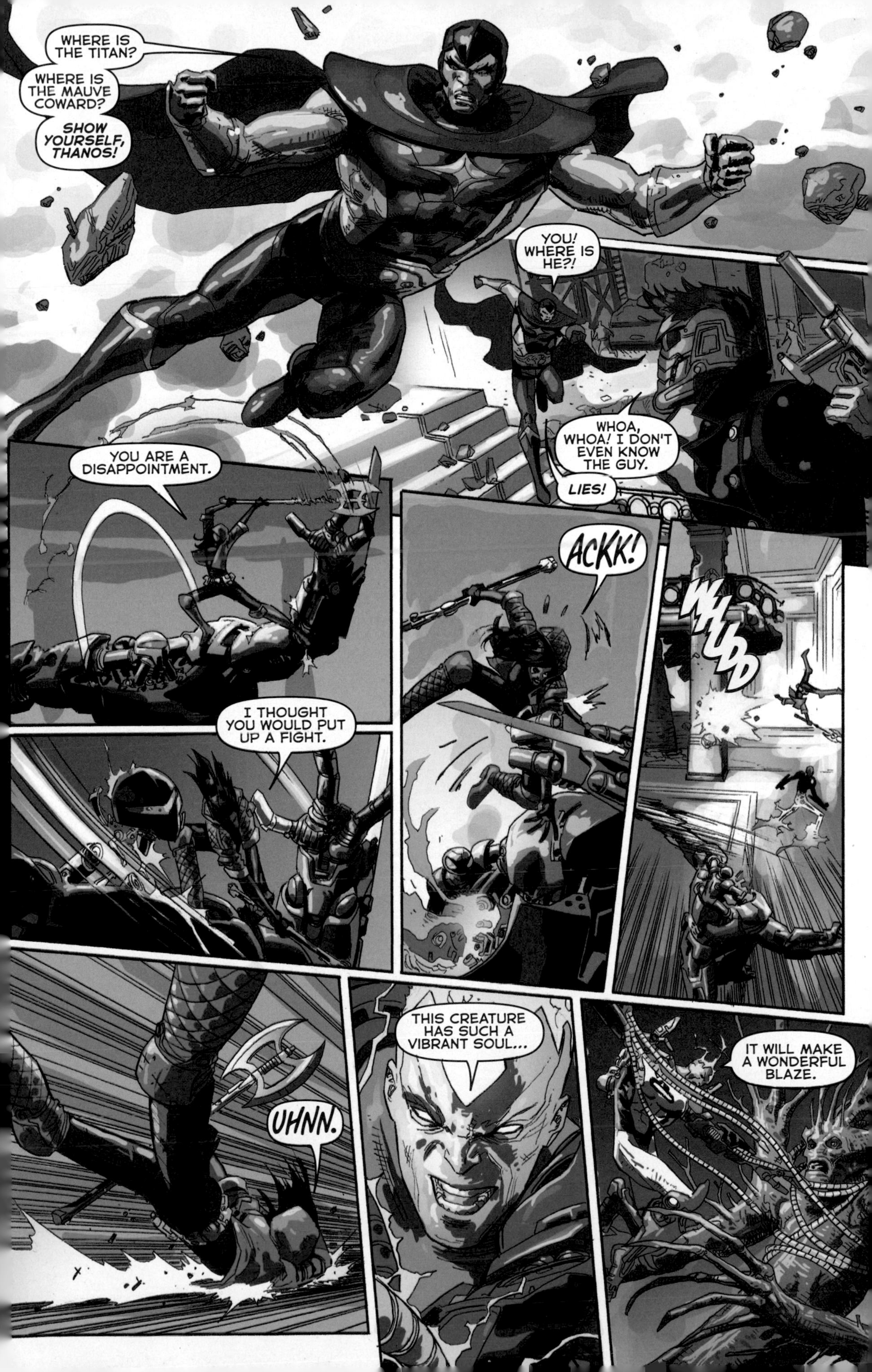
WHERE IS THE TITAN?
WHERE IS THE MAUVE COWARD?
SHOW YOURSELF, THANOS!
YOU! WHERE IS HE?!
WHOA, WHOA! I DON'T EVEN KNOW THE GUY.
LIES!
YOU ARE A DISAPPOINTMENT.
ACKK!
WHUDD
I THOUGHT YOU WOULD PUT UP A FIGHT.
UHNN.
THIS CREATURE HAS SUCH A VIBRANT SOUL...
IT WILL MAKE A WONDERFUL BLAZE.

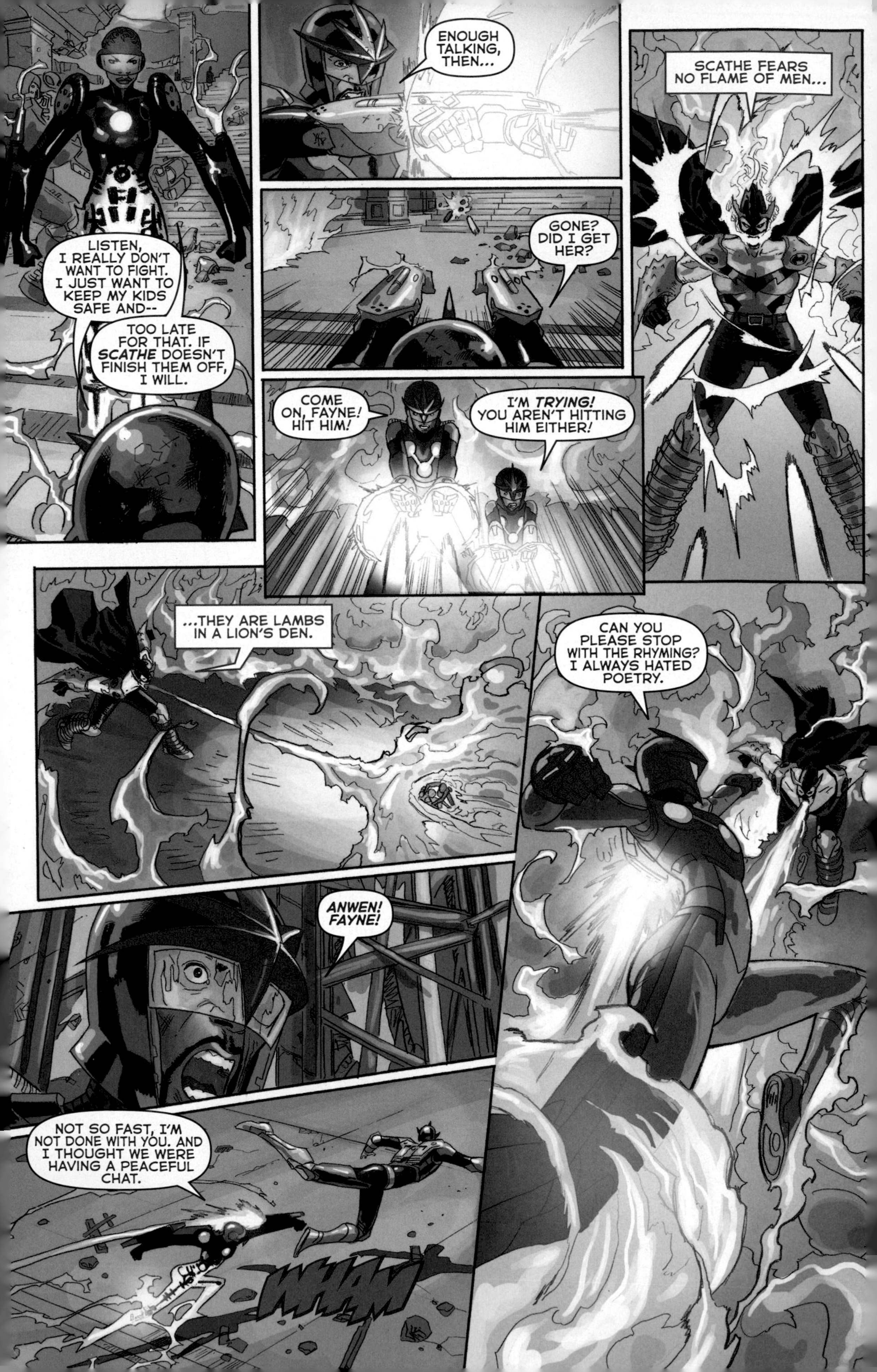
LISTEN, I REALLY DON'T WANT TO FIGHT. I JUST WANT TO KEEP MY KIDS SAFE AND--
TOO LATE FOR THAT. IF *SCATHE* DOESN'T FINISH THEM OFF, I WILL.
ENOUGH TALKING, THEN...
GONE? DID I GET HER?
COME ON, FAYNE! HIT HIM!
I'M *TRYING!* YOU AREN'T HITTING HIM EITHER!
SCATHE FEARS NO FLAME OF MEN...
...THEY ARE LAMBS IN A LION'S DEN.
CAN YOU PLEASE STOP WITH THE RHYMING? I ALWAYS HATED POETRY.
ANWEN! FAYNE!
NOT SO FAST, I'M NOT DONE WITH YOU. AND I THOUGHT WE WERE HAVING A PEACEFUL CHAT.
WHAM

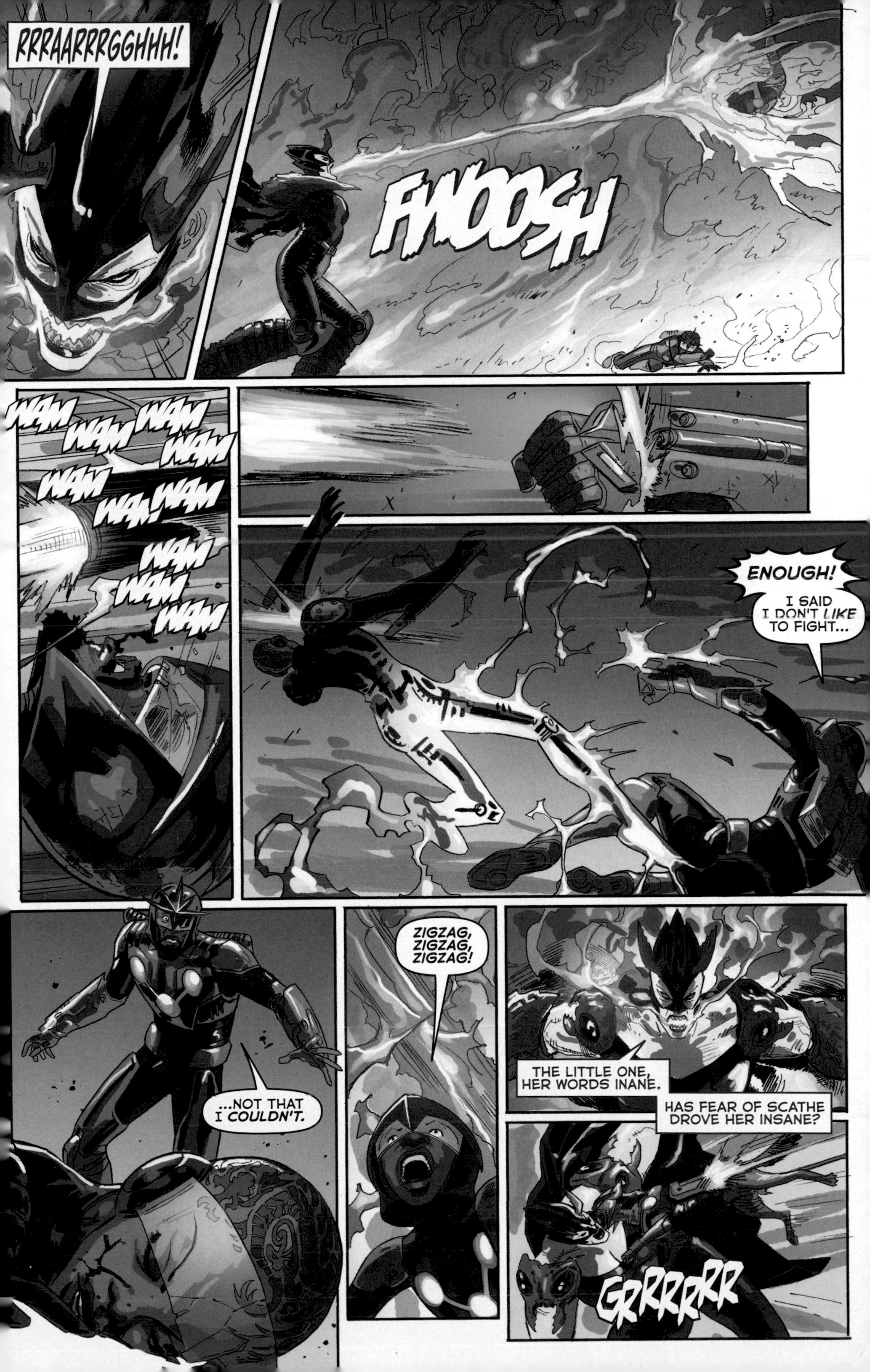
RRRAARRRGGHHH!
FWOOSH
WAM WAM WAM WAM WAM WAM WAM WAM WAM WAM WAM
ENOUGH!
I SAID I DON'T *LIKE* TO FIGHT...
...NOT THAT I *COULDN'T.*
ZIGZAG, ZIGZAG, ZIGZAG!
THE LITTLE ONE, HER WORDS INANE.
HAS FEAR OF SCATHE DROVE HER INSANE?
GRRRRRR

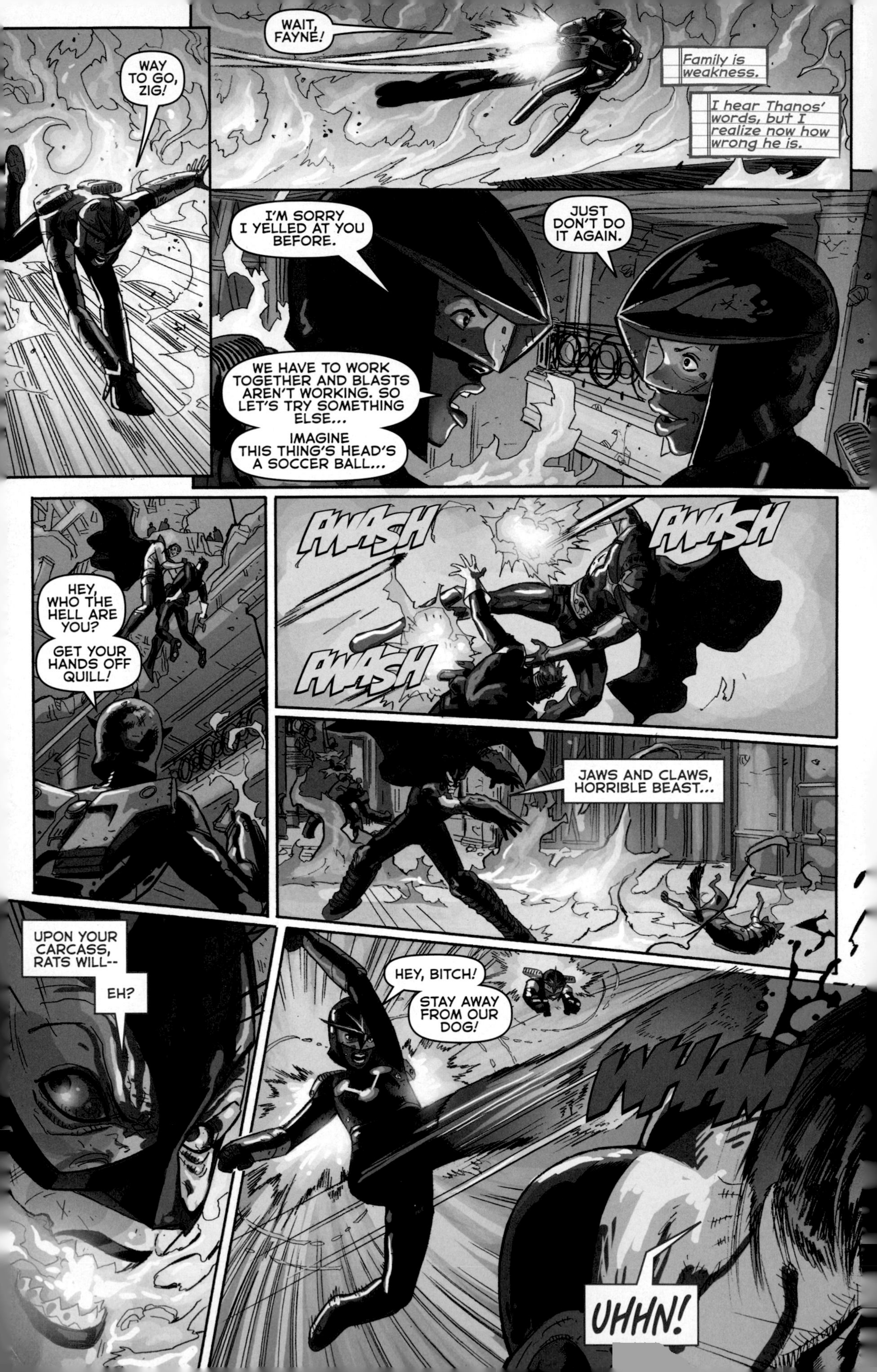
WAY TO GO, ZIG!
WAIT, FAYNE!
Family is weakness.
I hear Thanos' words, but I realize now how wrong he is.
I'M SORRY I YELLED AT YOU BEFORE.
JUST DON'T DO IT AGAIN.
WE HAVE TO WORK TOGETHER AND BLASTS AREN'T WORKING. SO LET'S TRY SOMETHING ELSE...
IMAGINE THIS THING'S HEAD'S A SOCCER BALL...
HEY, WHO THE HELL ARE YOU?
GET YOUR HANDS OFF QUILL!
AWASH
AWASH
AWASH
JAWS AND CLAWS, HORRIBLE BEAST...
UPON YOUR CARCASS, RATS WILL--
EH?
HEY, BITCH!
STAY AWAY FROM OUR DOG!
WHAM
UHHN!

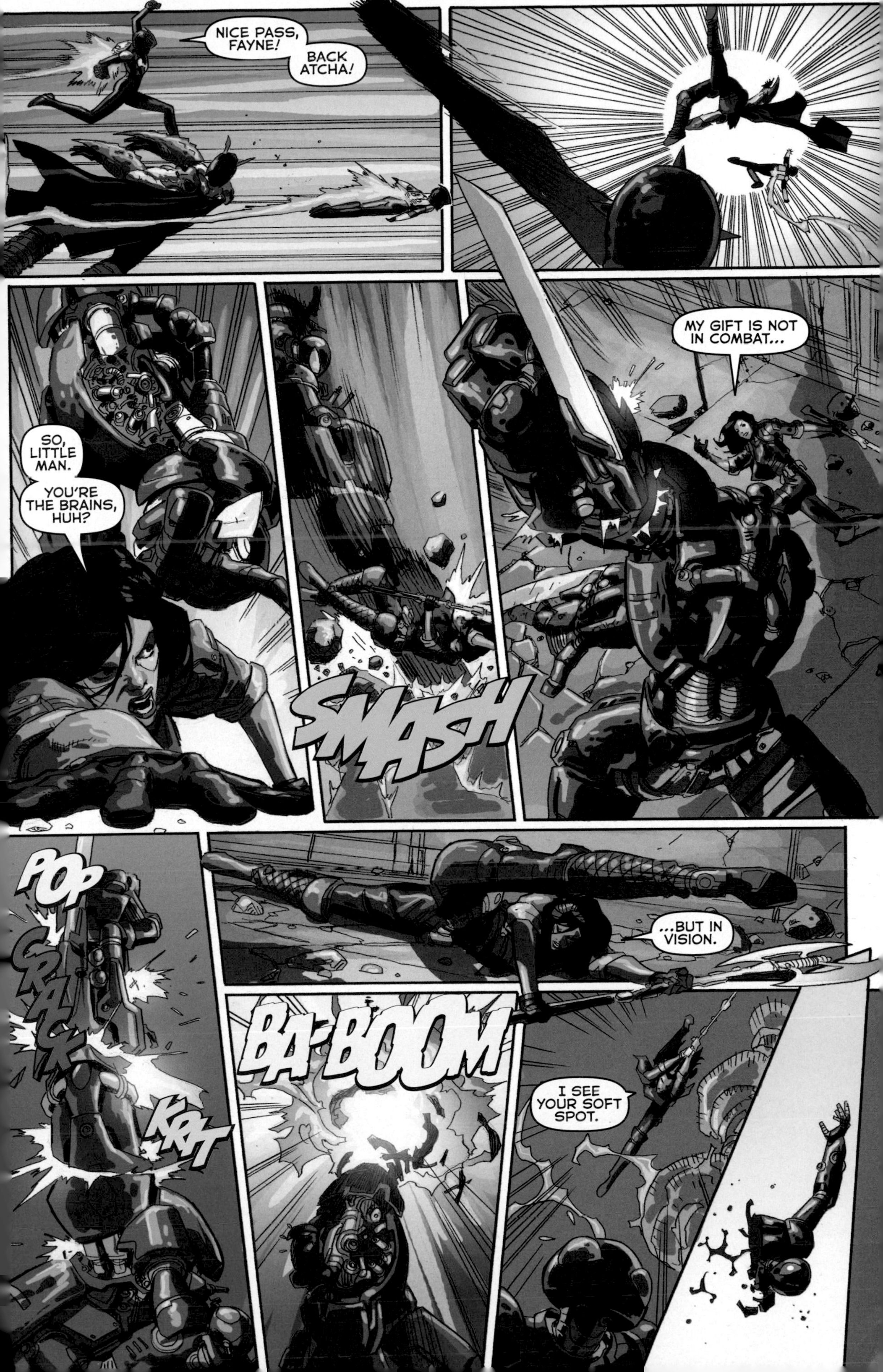
NICE PASS, FAYNE!
BACK ATCHA!
MY GIFT IS NOT IN COMBAT...
SO, LITTLE MAN.
YOU'RE THE BRAINS, HUH?
SMASH
POP
CRACK
KRKT
...BUT IN VISION.
BA-BOOM
I SEE YOUR SOFT SPOT.

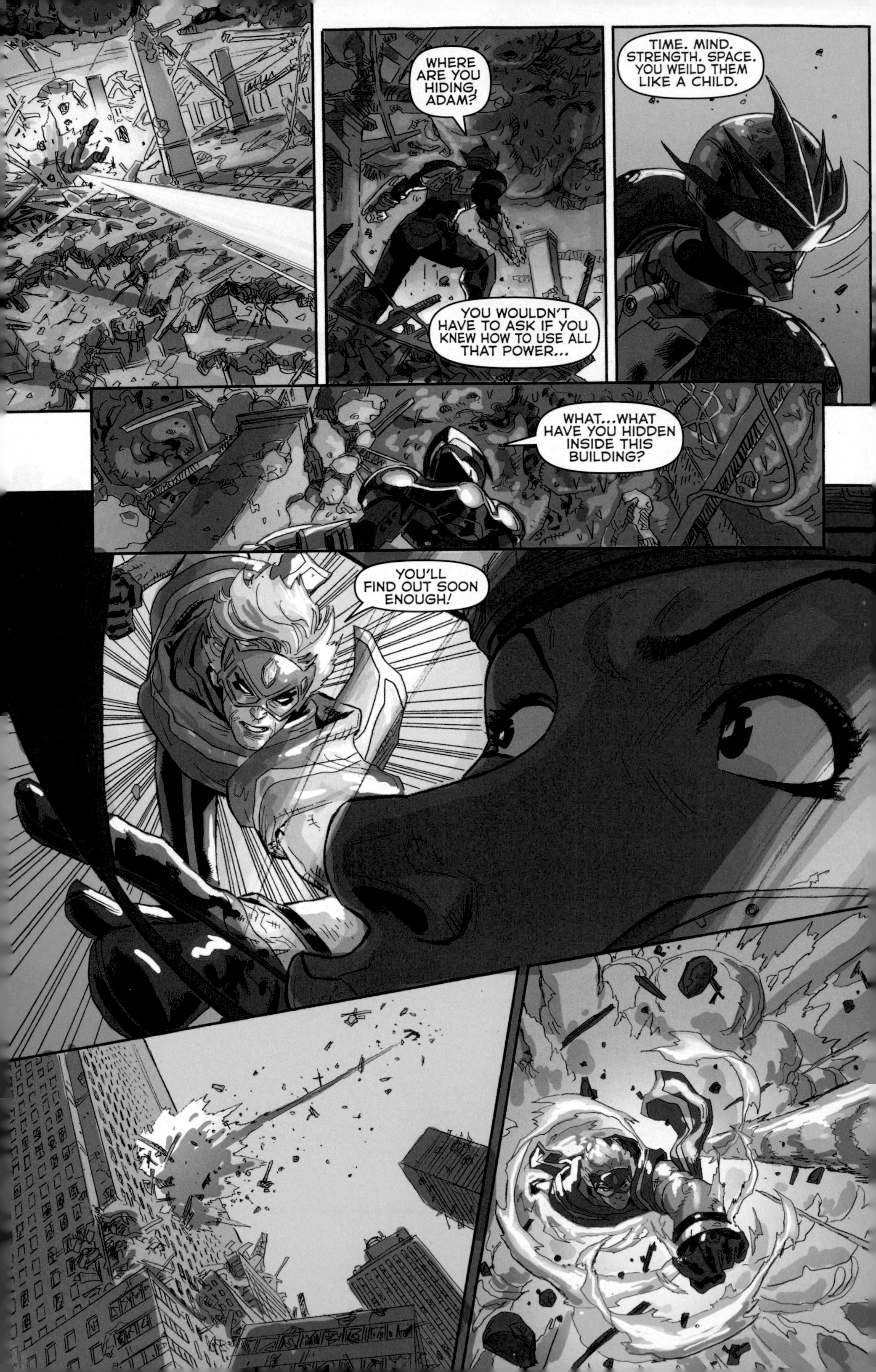
WHERE ARE YOU HIDING, ADAM?
YOU WOULDN'T HAVE TO ASK IF YOU KNEW HOW TO USE ALL THAT POWER...
TIME. MIND. STRENGTH. SPACE. YOU WEILD THEM LIKE A CHILD.
WHAT...WHAT HAVE YOU HIDDEN INSIDE THIS BUILDING?
YOU'LL FIND OUT SOON ENOUGH!

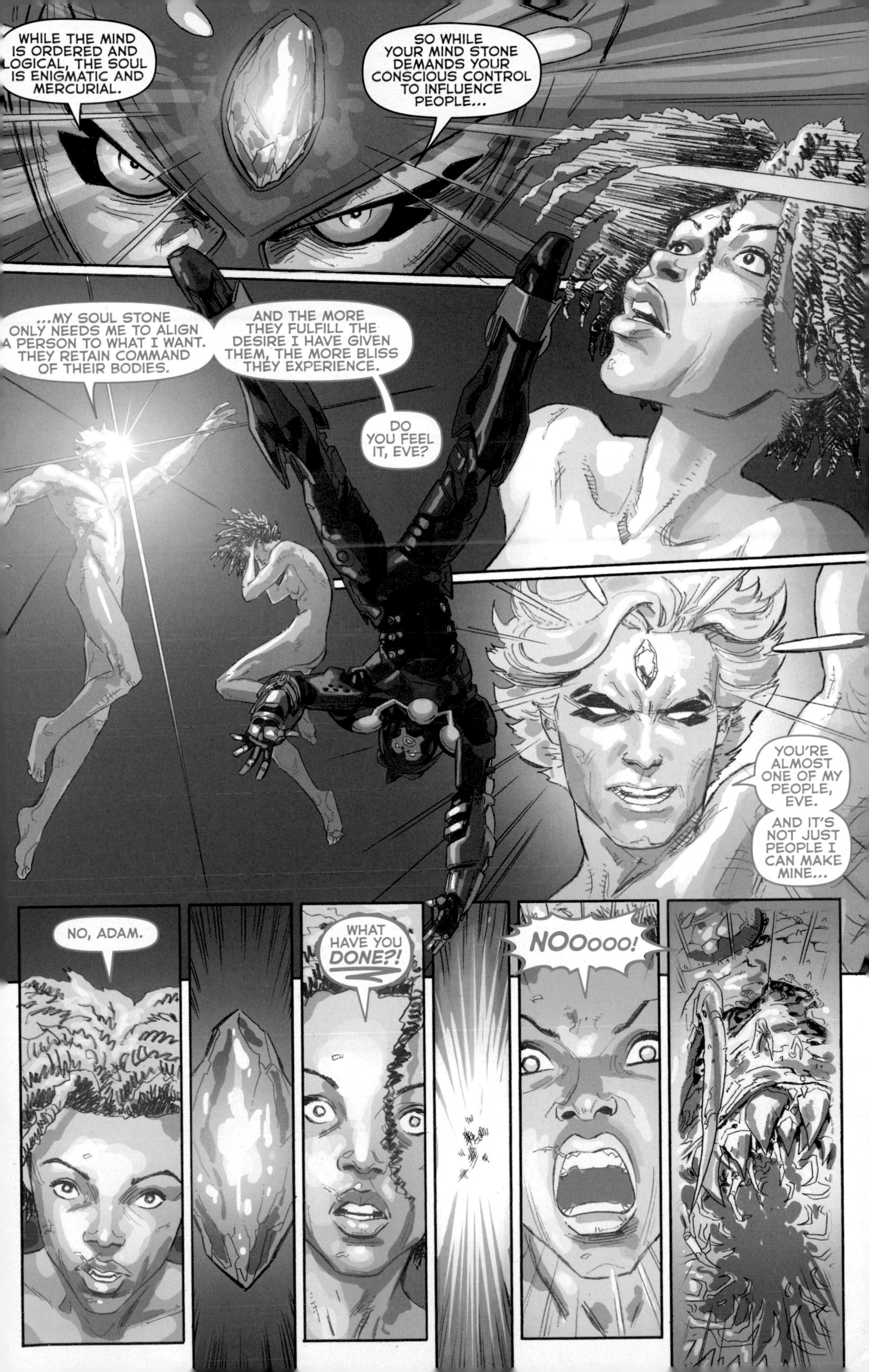
WHILE THE MIND IS ORDERED AND LOGICAL, THE SOUL IS ENIGMATIC AND MERCURIAL.
SO WHILE YOUR MIND STONE DEMANDS YOUR CONSCIOUS CONTROL TO INFLUENCE PEOPLE...
...MY SOUL STONE ONLY NEEDS ME TO ALIGN A PERSON TO WHAT I WANT. THEY RETAIN COMMAND OF THEIR BODIES.
AND THE MORE THEY FULFILL THE DESIRE I HAVE GIVEN THEM, THE MORE BLISS THEY EXPERIENCE.
DO YOU FEEL IT, EVE?
YOU'RE ALMOST ONE OF MY PEOPLE, EVE.
AND IT'S NOT JUST PEOPLE I CAN MAKE MINE...
NO, ADAM.
WHAT HAVE YOU DONE?!
NOOooo!

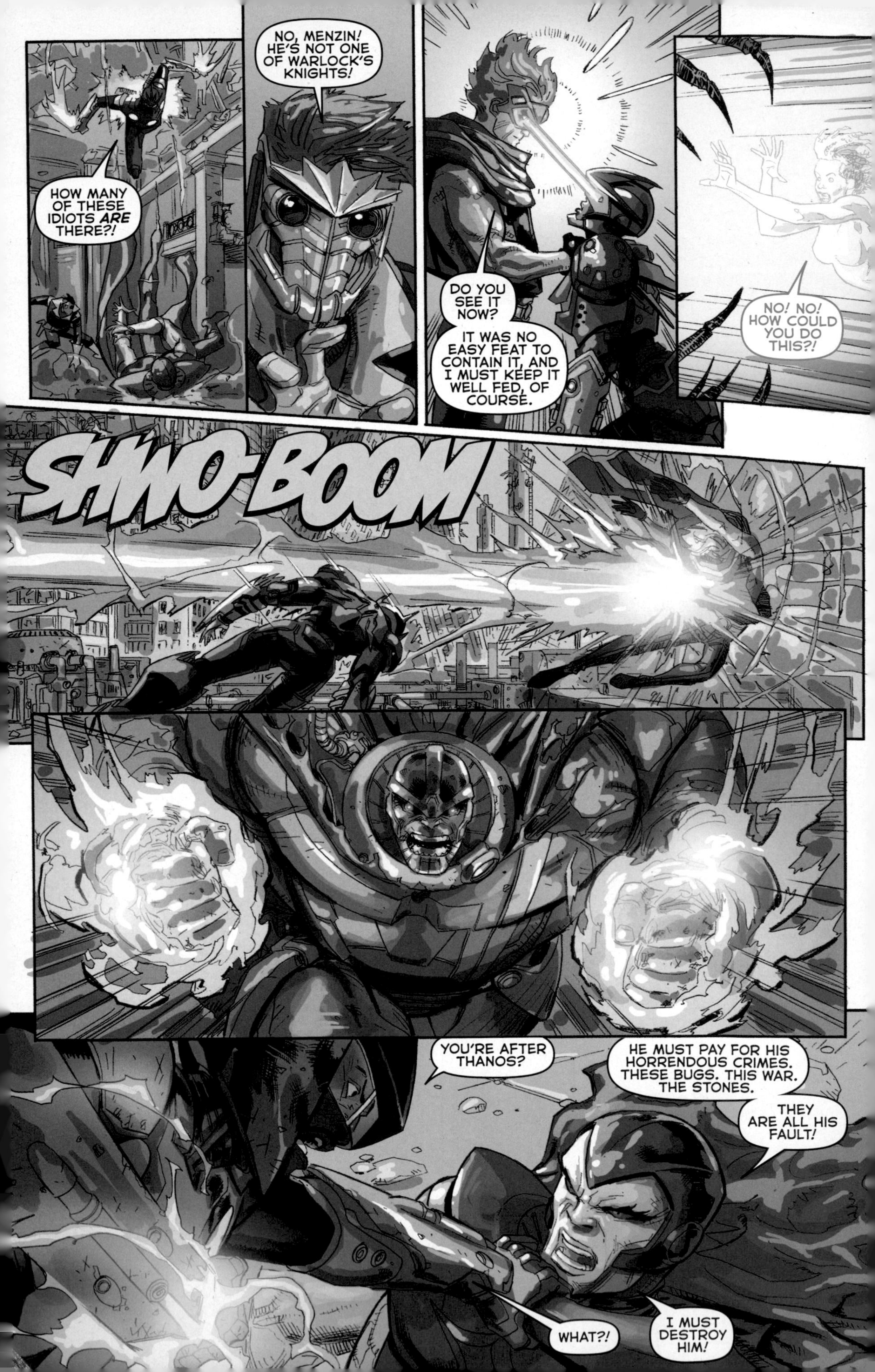
HOW MANY OF THESE IDIOTS *ARE* THERE?!
NO, MENZIN! HE'S NOT ONE OF WARLOCK'S KNIGHTS!
DO YOU SEE IT NOW?
IT WAS NO EASY FEAT TO CONTAIN IT, AND I MUST KEEP IT WELL FED, OF COURSE.
NO! NO! HOW COULD YOU DO THIS?!
SHWO-BOOM
YOU'RE AFTER THANOS?
HE MUST PAY FOR HIS HORRENDOUS CRIMES. THESE BUGS. THIS WAR. THE STONES.
THEY ARE ALL HIS FAULT!
WHAT?!
I MUST DESTROY HIM!

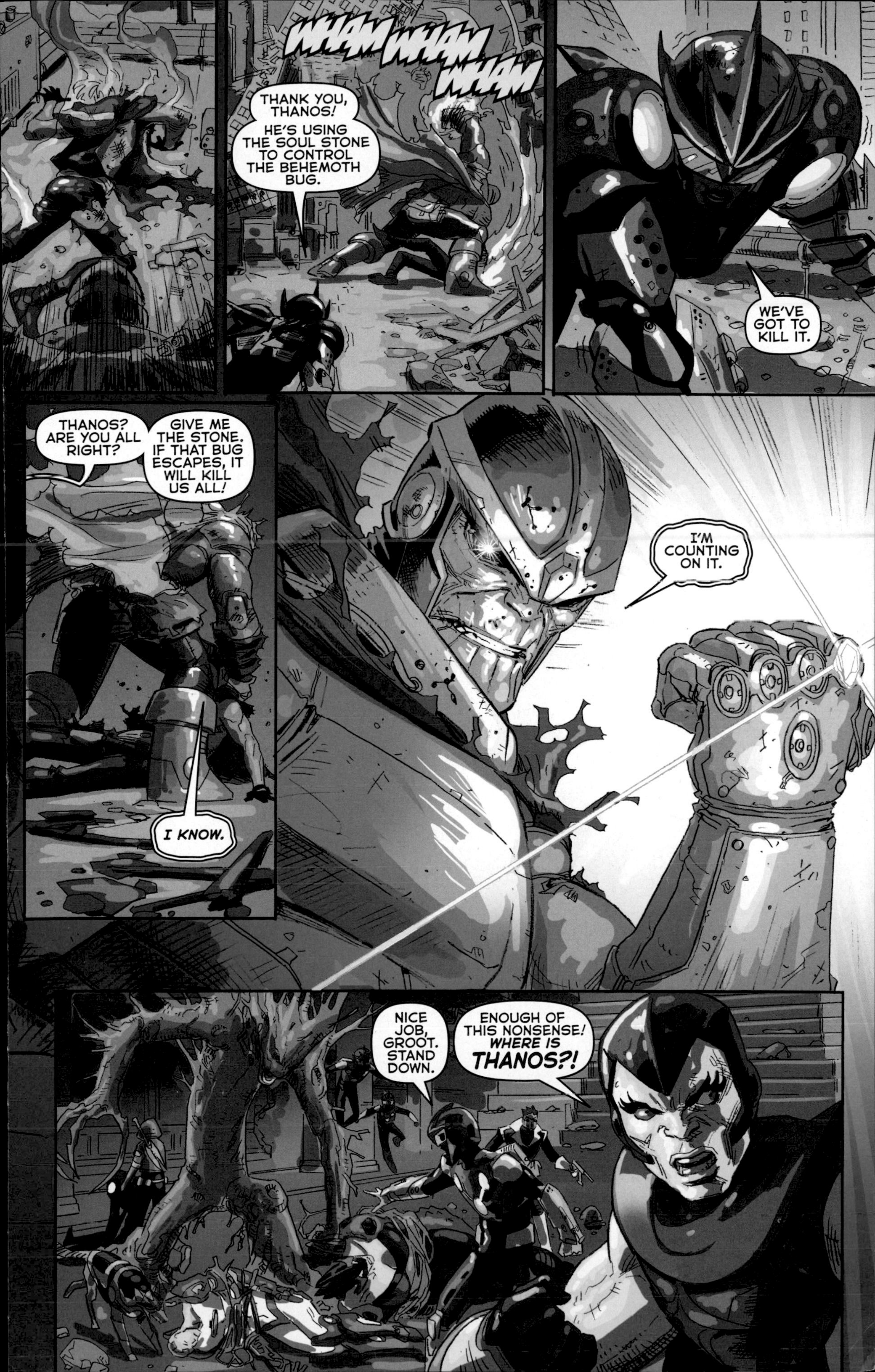
WHAM WHAM WHAM
THANK YOU, THANOS! HE'S USING THE SOUL STONE TO CONTROL THE BEHEMOTH BUG.
WE'VE GOT TO KILL IT.
THANOS? ARE YOU ALL RIGHT?
GIVE ME THE STONE. IF THAT BUG ESCAPES, IT WILL KILL US ALL!
I KNOW.
I'M COUNTING ON IT.
NICE JOB, GROOT. STAND DOWN.
ENOUGH OF THIS NONSENSE! WHERE IS THANOS?!

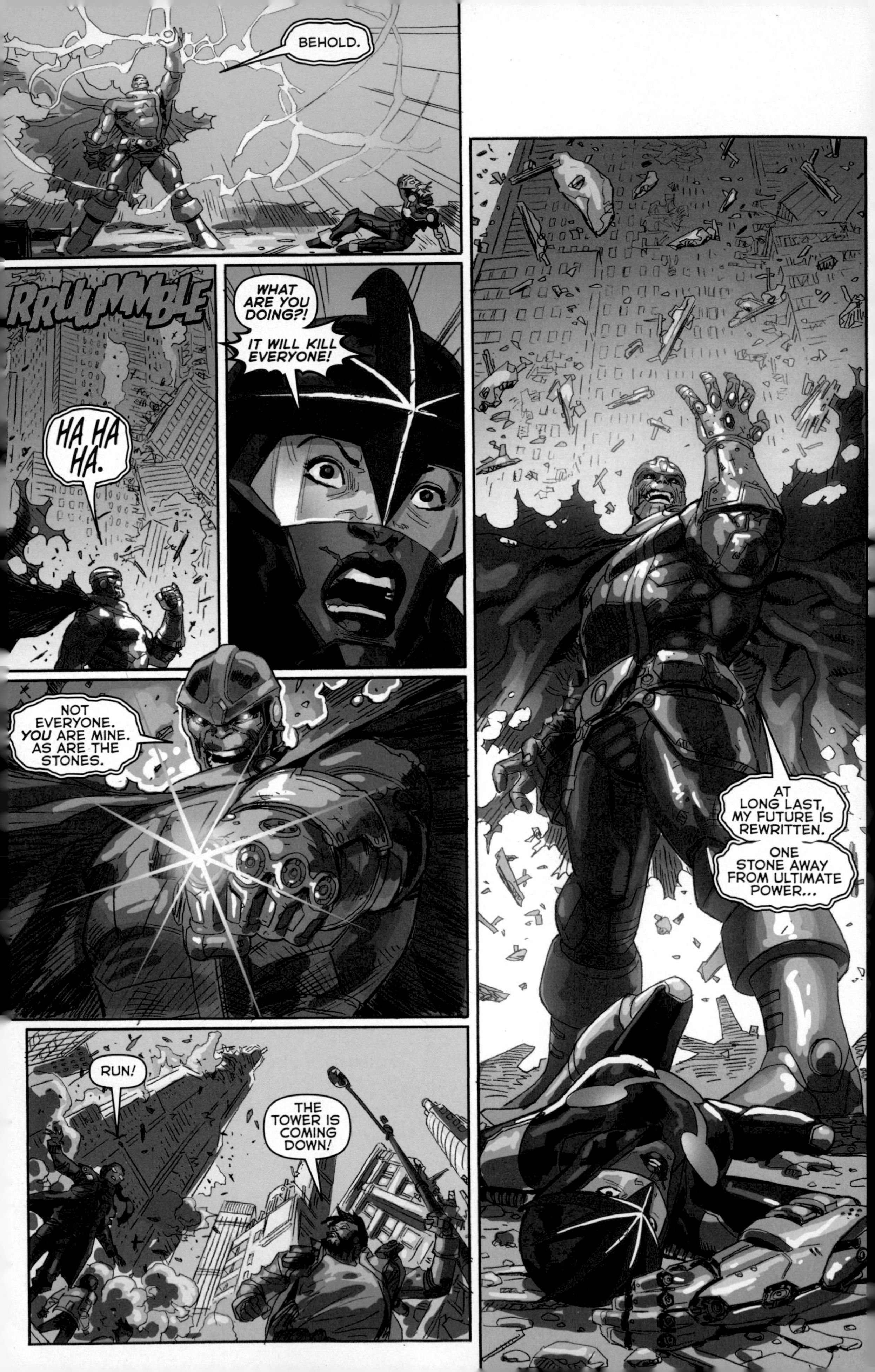
BEHOLD.
RRUUMMBLE
HA HA HA.
WHAT ARE YOU DOING?!
IT WILL KILL EVERYONE!
NOT EVERYONE. YOU ARE MINE. AS ARE THE STONES.
RUN!
THE TOWER IS COMING DOWN!
AT LONG LAST, MY FUTURE IS REWRITTEN.
ONE STONE AWAY FROM ULTIMATE POWER...

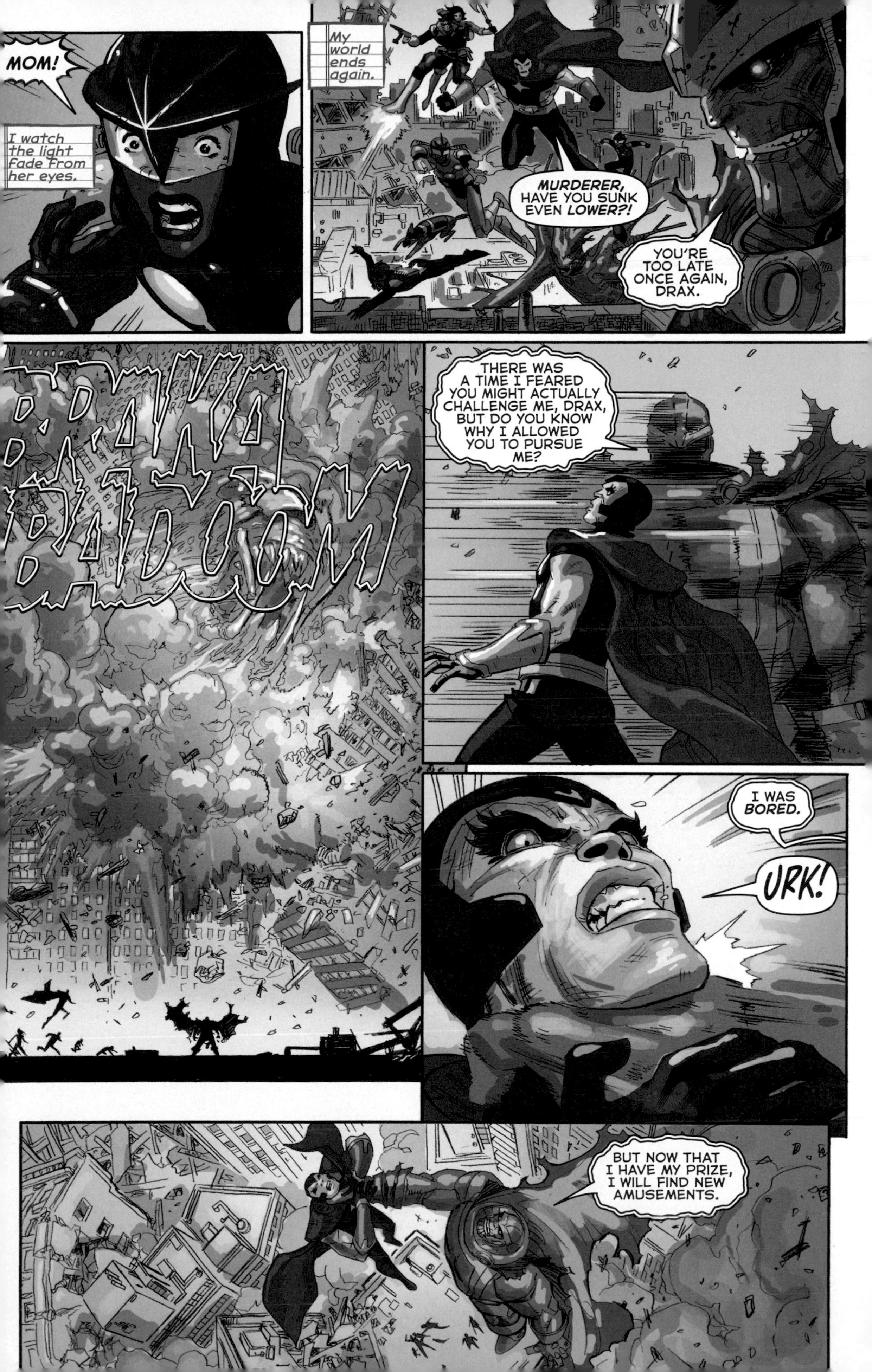
MOM!
I watch the light fade from her eyes.
My world ends again.
MURDERER, HAVE YOU SUNK EVEN LOWER?!
YOU'RE TOO LATE ONCE AGAIN, DRAX.
THERE WAS A TIME I FEARED YOU MIGHT ACTUALLY CHALLENGE ME, DRAX, BUT DO YOU KNOW WHY I ALLOWED YOU TO PURSUE ME?
I WAS BORED.
URK!
BUT NOW THAT I HAVE MY PRIZE, I WILL FIND NEW AMUSEMENTS.

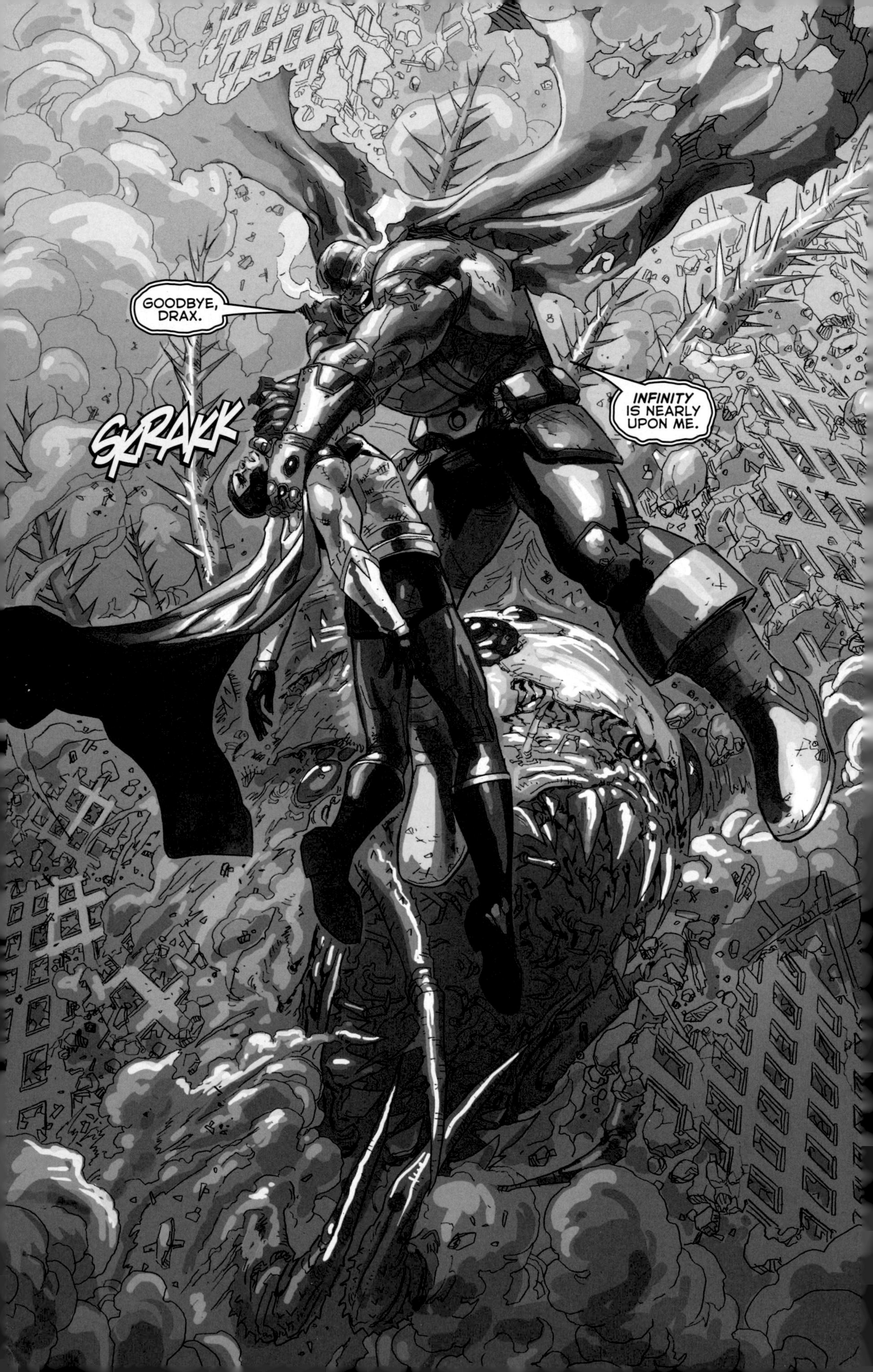
GOODBYE, DRAX.
SKRAKK
INFINITY IS NEARLY UPON ME.

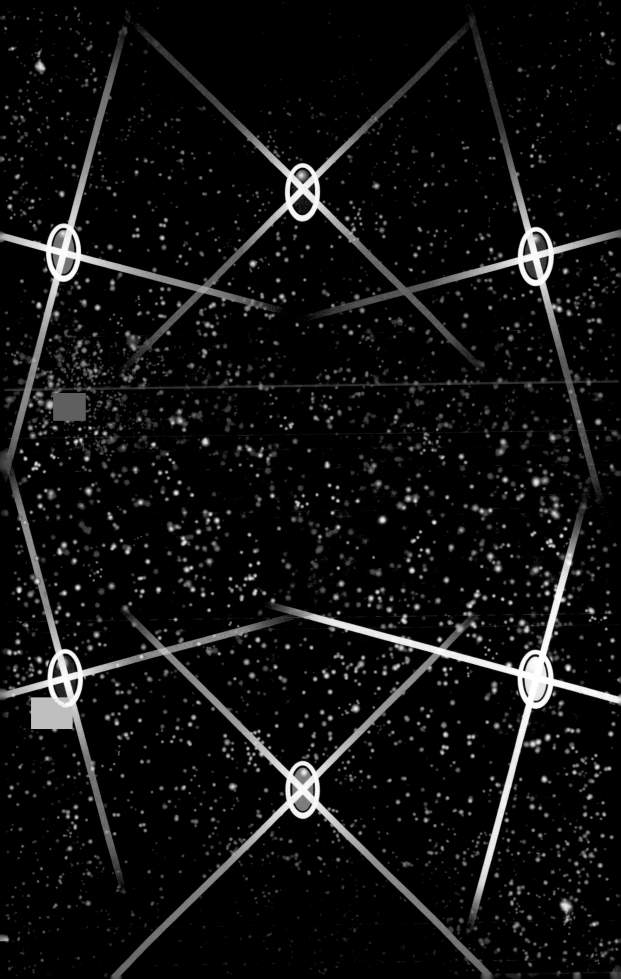

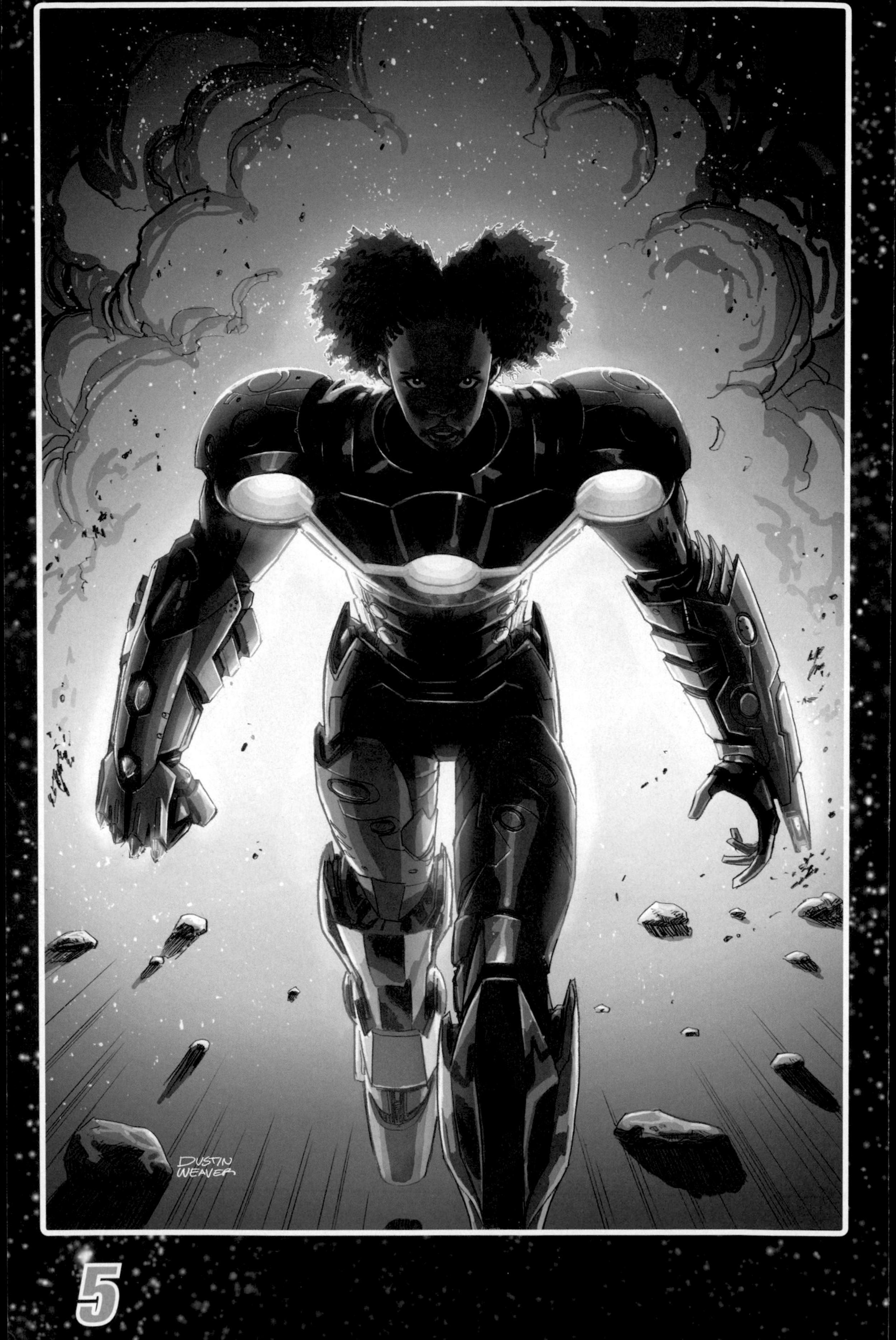
DUSTIN
WEAVER

5

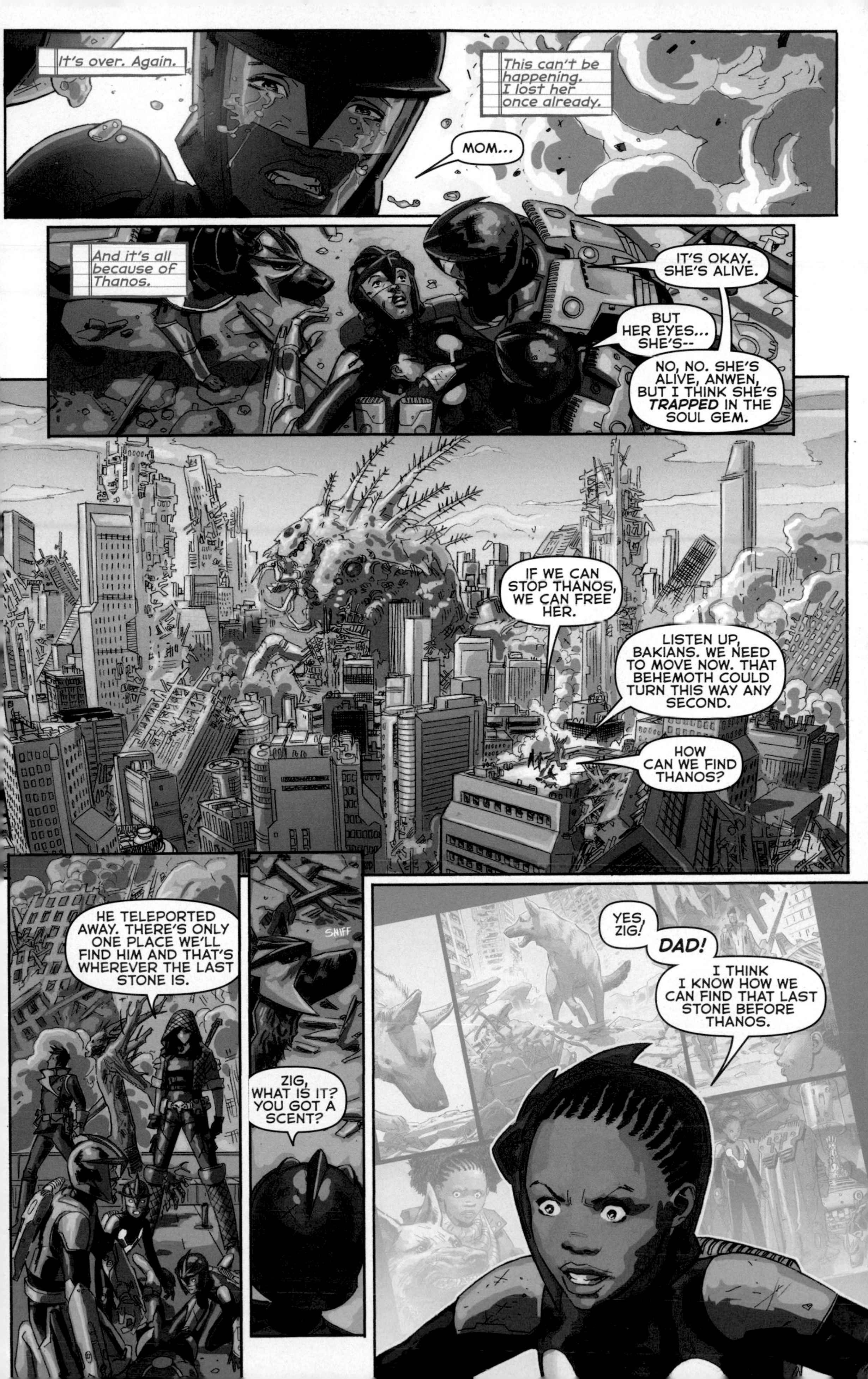
It's over. Again.
This can't be happening. I lost her once already.
MOM...
And it's all because of Thanos.
IT'S OKAY. SHE'S ALIVE.
BUT HER EYES... SHE'S--
NO, NO. SHE'S ALIVE, ANWEN, BUT I THINK SHE'S TRAPPED IN THE SOUL GEM.
IF WE CAN STOP THANOS, WE CAN FREE HER.
LISTEN UP, BAKIANS. WE NEED TO MOVE NOW. THAT BEHEMOTH COULD TURN THIS WAY ANY SECOND.
HOW CAN WE FIND THANOS?
HE TELEPORTED AWAY. THERE'S ONLY ONE PLACE WE'LL FIND HIM AND THAT'S WHEREVER THE LAST STONE IS.
SNIFF
ZIG, WHAT IS IT? YOU GOT A SCENT?
YES, ZIG!
DAD!
I THINK I KNOW HOW WE CAN FIND THAT LAST STONE BEFORE THANOS.

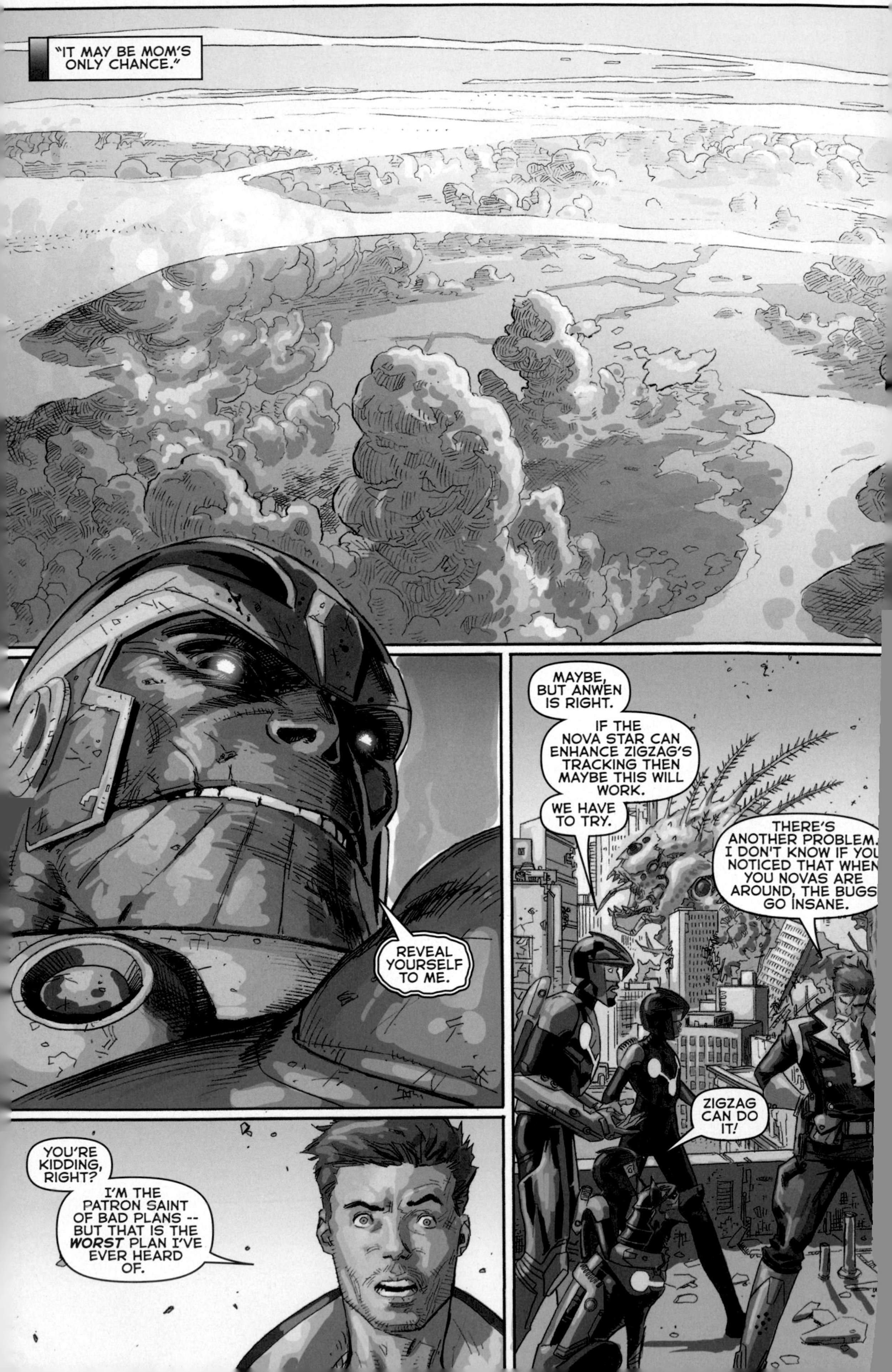
"IT MAY BE MOM'S ONLY CHANCE."
REVEAL YOURSELF TO ME.
MAYBE, BUT ANWEN IS RIGHT.
IF THE NOVA STAR CAN ENHANCE ZIGZAG'S TRACKING THEN MAYBE THIS WILL WORK.
WE HAVE TO TRY.
THERE'S ANOTHER PROBLEM. I DON'T KNOW IF YOU NOTICED THAT WHEN YOU NOVAS ARE AROUND, THE BUGS GO INSANE.
ZIGZAG CAN DO IT!
YOU'RE KIDDING, RIGHT?
I'M THE PATRON SAINT OF BAD PLANS -- BUT THAT IS THE WORST PLAN I'VE EVER HEARD OF.

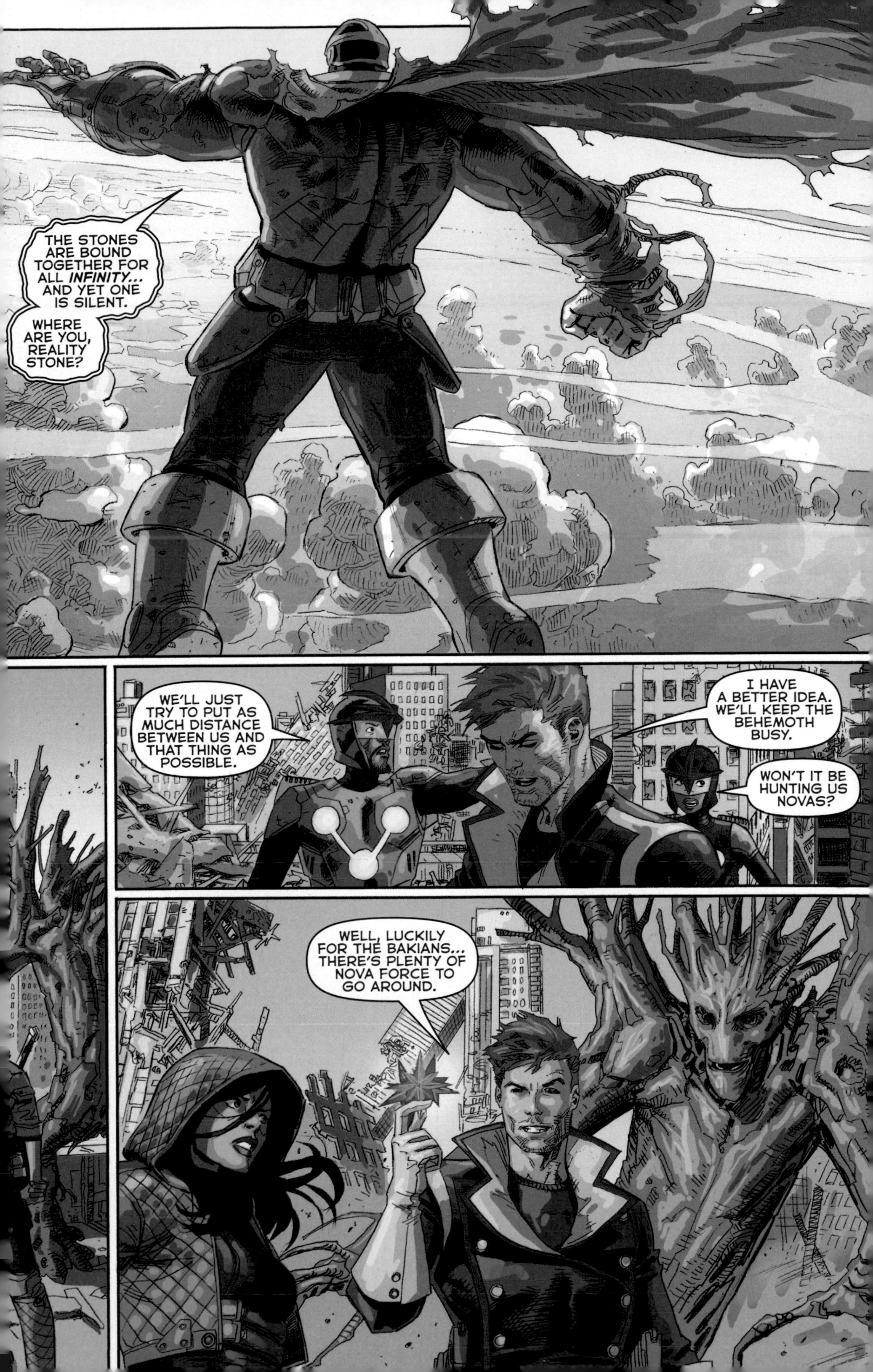
THE STONES ARE BOUND TOGETHER FOR ALL *INFINITY*... AND YET ONE IS SILENT.
WHERE ARE YOU, REALITY STONE?
WE'LL JUST TRY TO PUT AS MUCH DISTANCE BETWEEN US AND THAT THING AS POSSIBLE.
I HAVE A BETTER IDEA. WE'LL KEEP THE BEHEMOTH BUSY.
WON'T IT BE HUNTING US NOVAS?
WELL, LUCKILY FOR THE BAKIANS... THERE'S PLENTY OF NOVA FORCE TO GO AROUND.

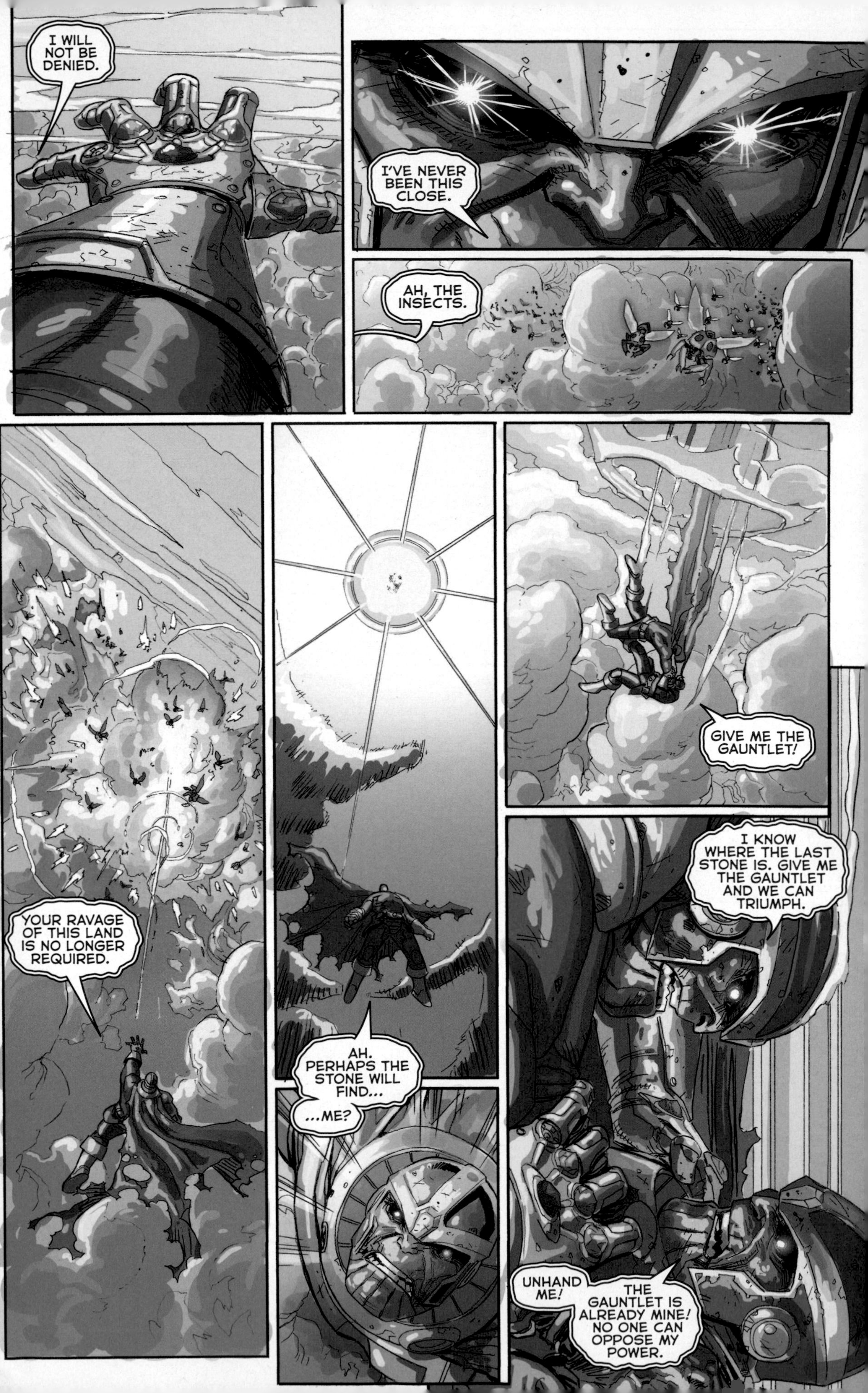
I WILL NOT BE DENIED.
I'VE NEVER BEEN THIS CLOSE.
AH, THE INSECTS.
YOUR RAVAGE OF THIS LAND IS NO LONGER REQUIRED.
AH. PERHAPS THE STONE WILL FIND...
...ME?
GIVE ME THE GAUNTLET!
I KNOW WHERE THE LAST STONE IS. GIVE ME THE GAUNTLET AND WE CAN TRIUMPH.
UNHAND ME!
THE GAUNTLET IS ALREADY MINE! NO ONE CAN OPPOSE MY POWER.

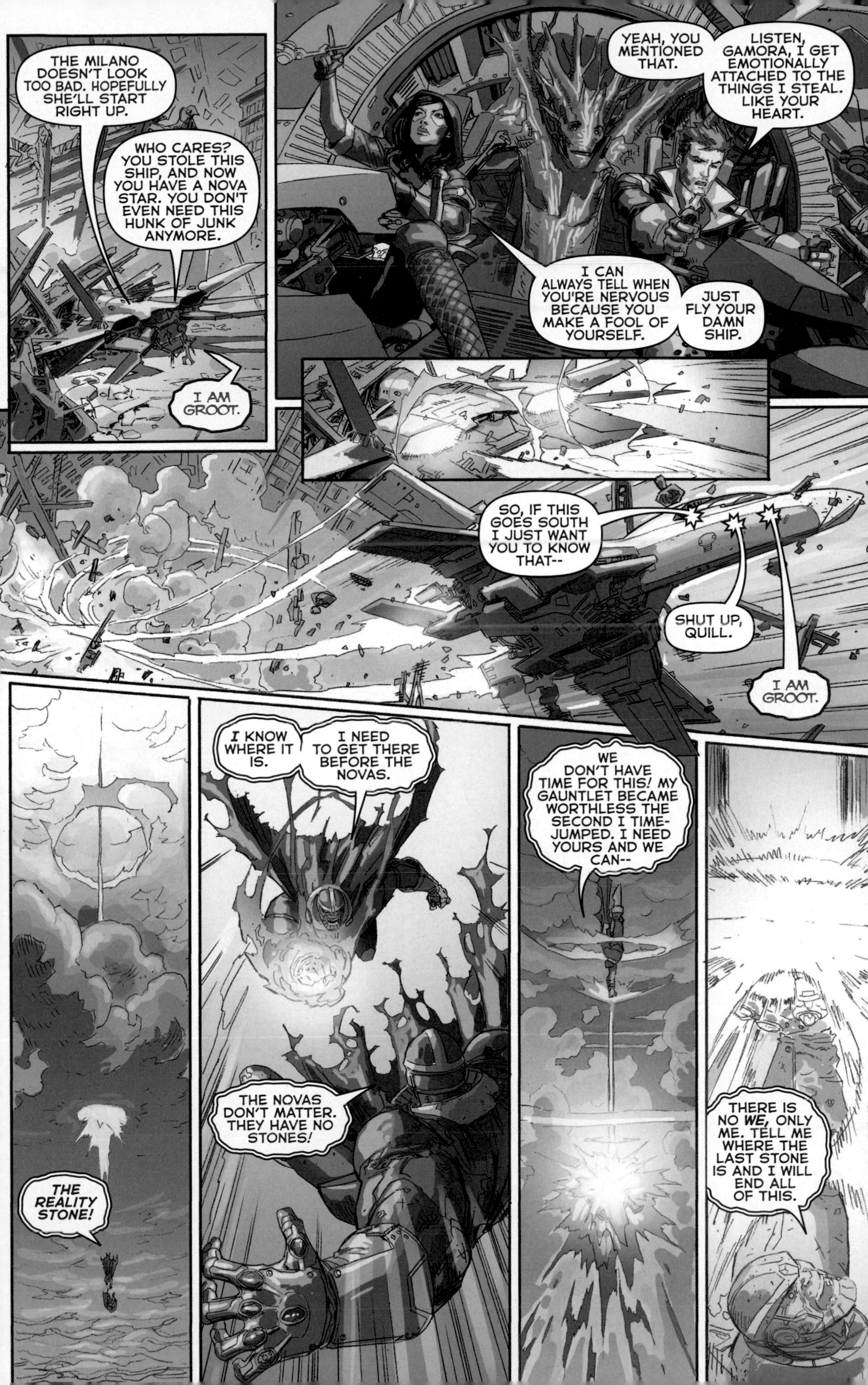

THE MILANO DOESN'T LOOK TOO BAD. HOPEFULLY SHE'LL START RIGHT UP.
WHO CARES? YOU STOLE THIS SHIP, AND NOW YOU HAVE A NOVA STAR. YOU DON'T EVEN NEED THIS HUNK OF JUNK ANYMORE.
I AM GROOT.
YEAH, YOU MENTIONED THAT.
LISTEN, GAMORA, I GET EMOTIONALLY ATTACHED TO THE THINGS I STEAL. LIKE YOUR HEART.
I CAN ALWAYS TELL WHEN YOU'RE NERVOUS BECAUSE YOU MAKE A FOOL OF YOURSELF.
JUST FLY YOUR DAMN SHIP.
SO, IF THIS GOES SOUTH I JUST WANT YOU TO KNOW THAT--
SHUT UP, QUILL.
I AM GROOT.
THE REALITY STONE!
I KNOW WHERE IT IS.
I NEED TO GET THERE BEFORE THE NOVAS.
THE NOVAS DON'T MATTER. THEY HAVE NO STONES!
WE DON'T HAVE TIME FOR THIS! MY GAUNTLET BECAME WORTHLESS THE SECOND I TIME-JUMPED. I NEED YOURS AND WE CAN--
THERE IS NO WE, ONLY ME. TELL ME WHERE THE LAST STONE IS AND I WILL END ALL OF THIS.

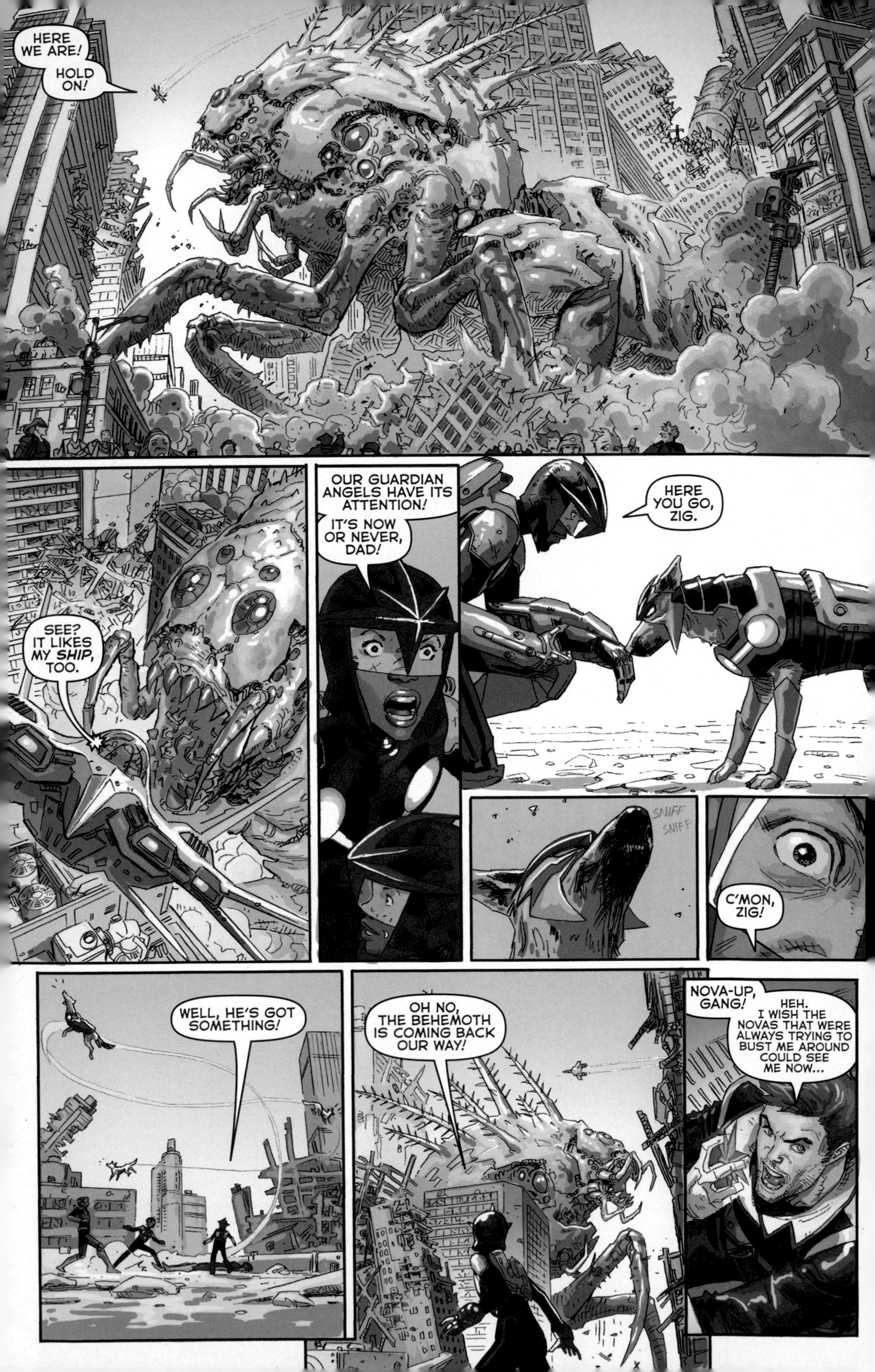
HERE WE ARE!
HOLD ON!
SEE? IT LIKES MY SHIP, TOO.
OUR GUARDIAN ANGELS HAVE ITS ATTENTION!
IT'S NOW OR NEVER, DAD!
HERE YOU GO, ZIG.
SNIFF SNIFF
C'MON, ZIG!
WELL, HE'S GOT SOMETHING!
OH NO, THE BEHEMOTH IS COMING BACK OUR WAY!
NOVA-UP, GANG!
HEH. I WISH THE NOVAS THAT WERE ALWAYS TRYING TO BUST ME AROUND COULD SEE ME NOW...

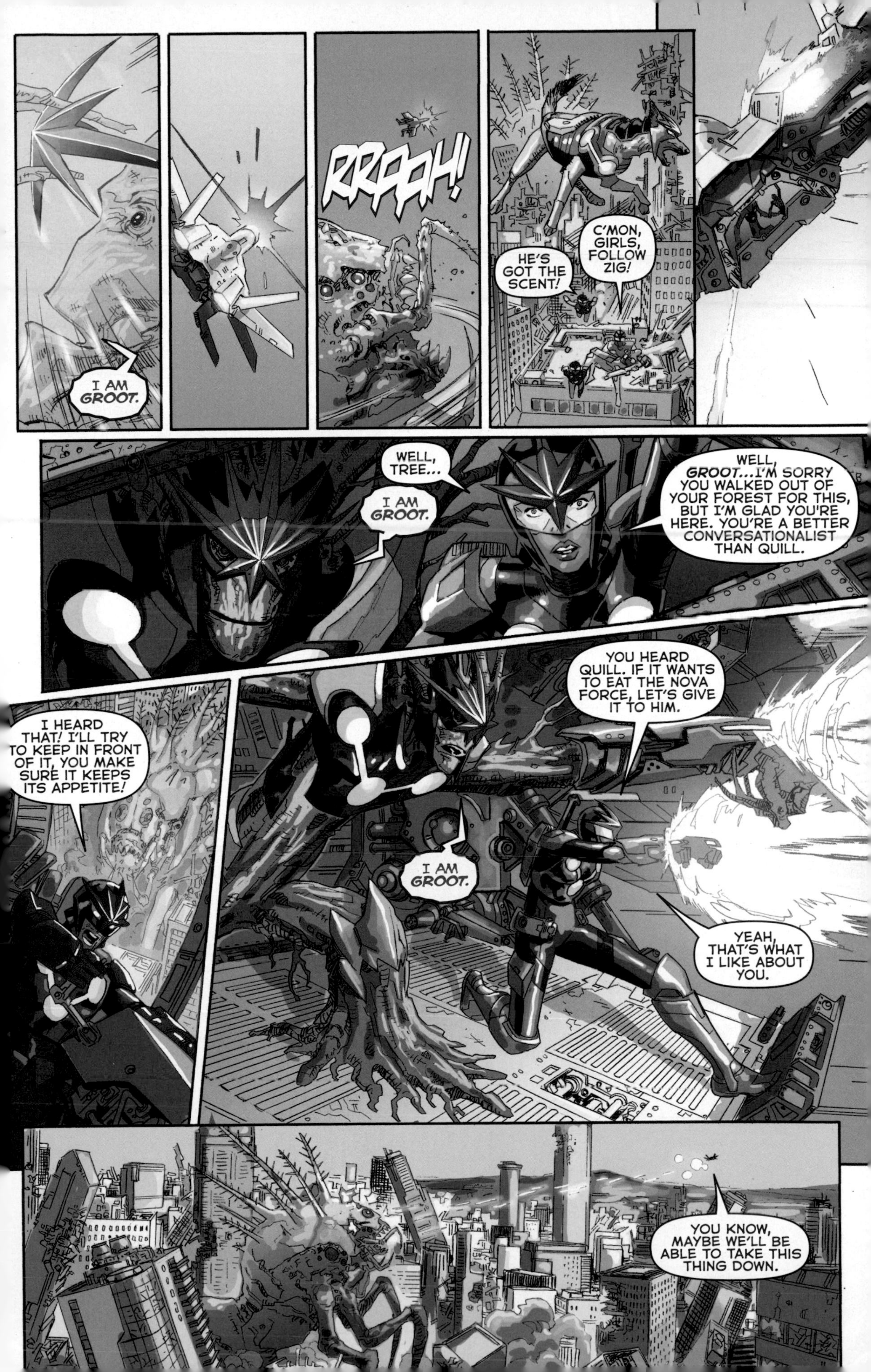
I AM GROOT.
RRRAAH!
C'MON, GIRLS, FOLLOW ZIG!
HE'S GOT THE SCENT!
WELL, TREE...
I AM GROOT.
WELL, GROOT...I'M SORRY YOU WALKED OUT OF YOUR FOREST FOR THIS, BUT I'M GLAD YOU'RE HERE. YOU'RE A BETTER CONVERSATIONALIST THAN QUILL.
I HEARD THAT! I'LL TRY TO KEEP IN FRONT OF IT, YOU MAKE SURE IT KEEPS ITS APPETITE!
YOU HEARD QUILL. IF IT WANTS TO EAT THE NOVA FORCE, LET'S GIVE IT TO HIM.
I AM GROOT.
YEAH, THAT'S WHAT I LIKE ABOUT YOU.
YOU KNOW, MAYBE WE'LL BE ABLE TO TAKE THIS THING DOWN.

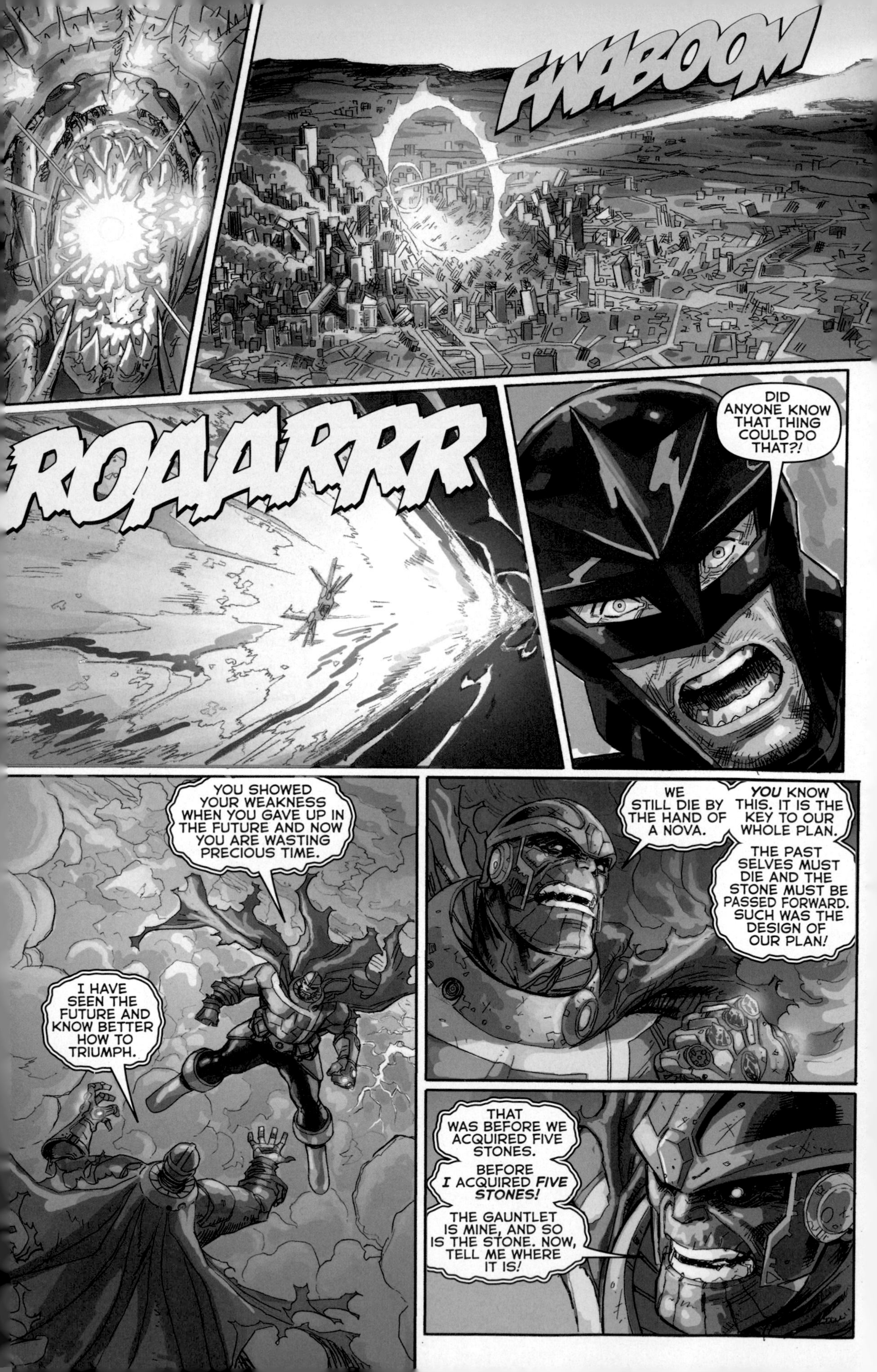
FWABOOM
ROAARRR
DID ANYONE KNOW THAT THING COULD DO THAT?!
YOU SHOWED YOUR WEAKNESS WHEN YOU GAVE UP IN THE FUTURE AND NOW YOU ARE WASTING PRECIOUS TIME.
I HAVE SEEN THE FUTURE AND KNOW BETTER HOW TO TRIUMPH.
WE STILL DIE BY THE HAND OF A NOVA.
YOU KNOW THIS. IT IS THE KEY TO OUR WHOLE PLAN.
THE PAST SELVES MUST DIE AND THE STONE MUST BE PASSED FORWARD. SUCH WAS THE DESIGN OF OUR PLAN!
THAT WAS BEFORE WE ACQUIRED FIVE STONES.
BEFORE I ACQUIRED FIVE STONES!
THE GAUNTLET IS MINE, AND SO IS THE STONE. NOW, TELL ME WHERE IT IS!

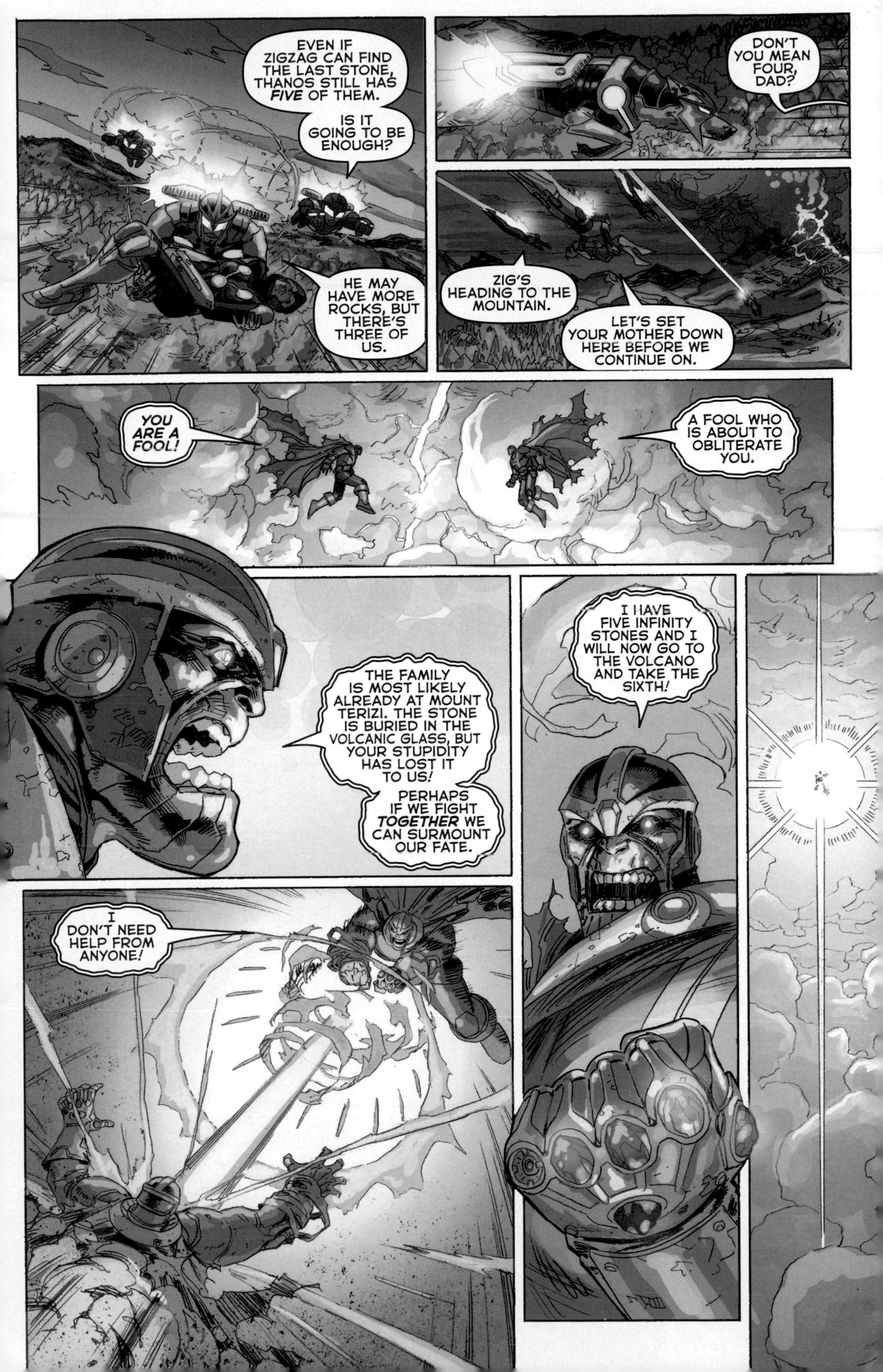
EVEN IF ZIGZAG CAN FIND THE LAST STONE, THANOS STILL HAS *FIVE* OF THEM.
IS IT GOING TO BE ENOUGH?
HE MAY HAVE MORE ROCKS, BUT THERE'S THREE OF US.
DON'T YOU MEAN FOUR, DAD?
ZIG'S HEADING TO THE MOUNTAIN.
LET'S SET YOUR MOTHER DOWN HERE BEFORE WE CONTINUE ON.
YOU ARE A FOOL!
A FOOL WHO IS ABOUT TO OBLITERATE YOU.
THE FAMILY IS MOST LIKELY ALREADY AT MOUNT TERIZI. THE STONE IS BURIED IN THE VOLCANIC GLASS, BUT YOUR STUPIDITY HAS LOST IT TO US!
PERHAPS IF WE FIGHT ***TOGETHER*** WE CAN SURMOUNT OUR FATE.
I HAVE FIVE INFINITY STONES AND I WILL NOW GO TO THE VOLCANO AND TAKE THE SIXTH!
I DON'T NEED HELP FROM ANYONE!

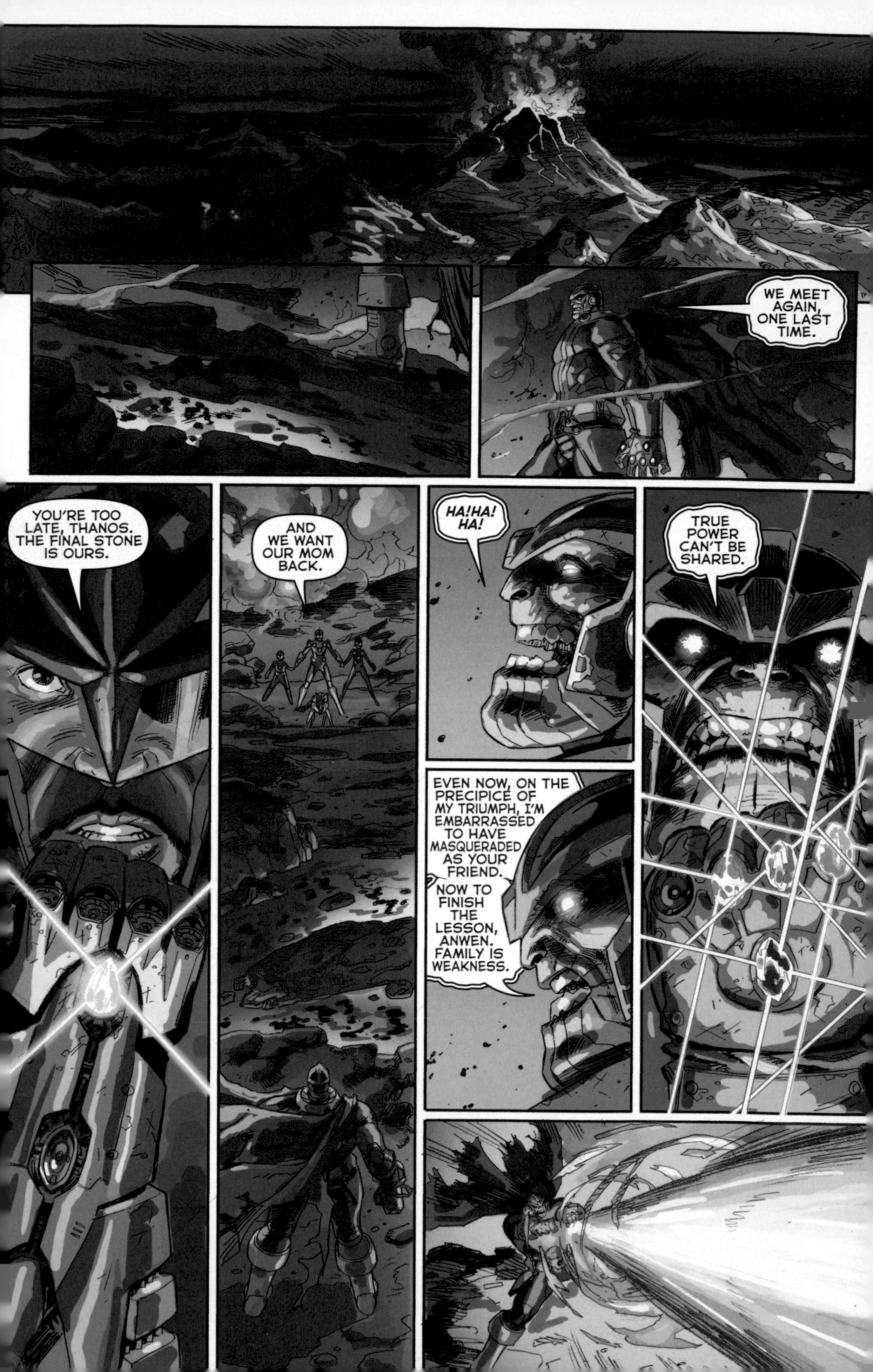
WE MEET AGAIN, ONE LAST TIME.
YOU'RE TOO LATE, THANOS. THE FINAL STONE IS OURS.
AND WE WANT OUR MOM BACK.
HA!HA! HA!
TRUE POWER CAN'T BE SHARED.
EVEN NOW, ON THE PRECIPICE OF MY TRIUMPH, I'M EMBARRASSED TO HAVE MASQUERADED AS YOUR FRIEND.
NOW TO FINISH THE LESSON, ANWEN. FAMILY IS WEAKNESS.

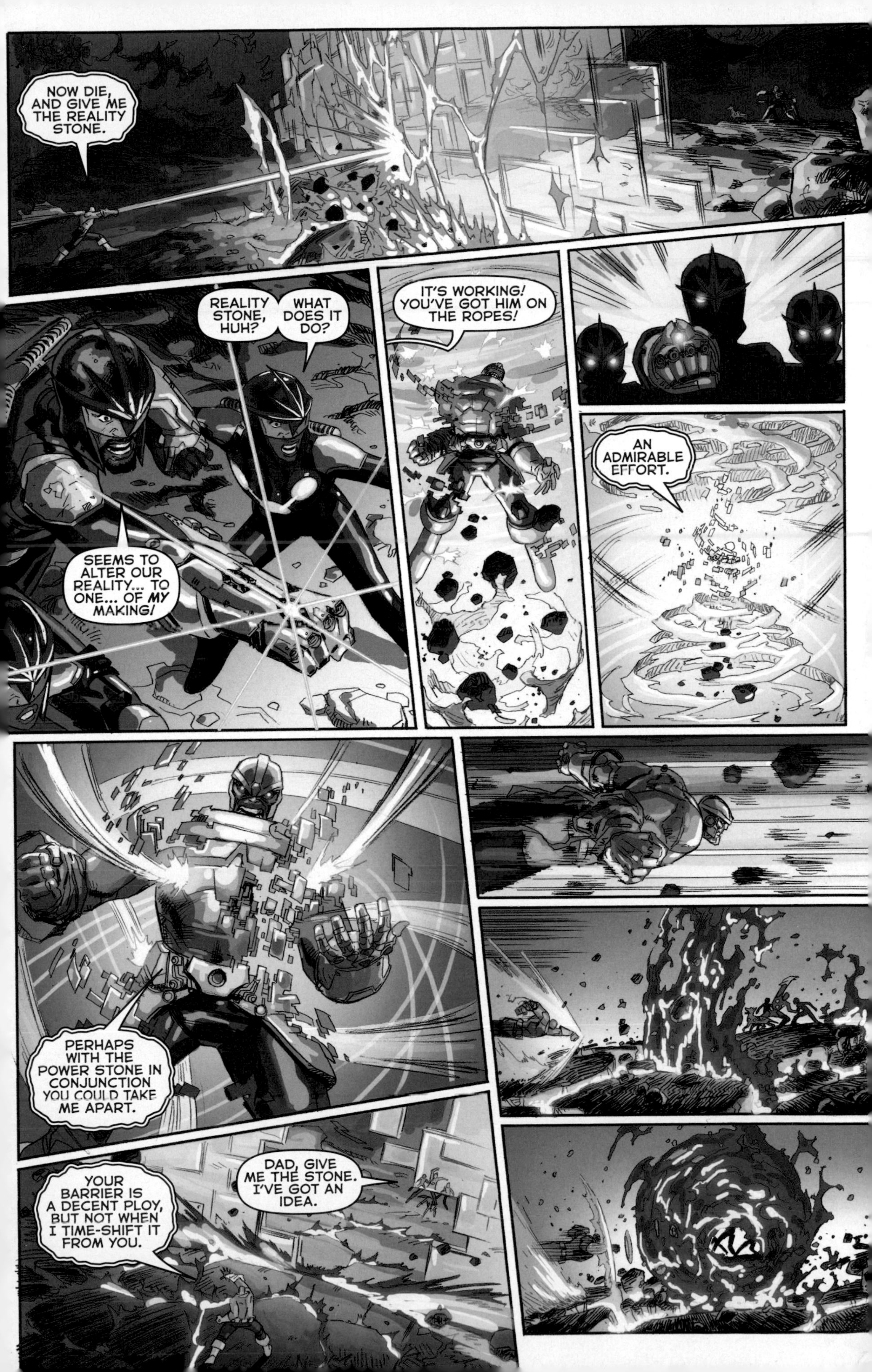
NOW DIE, AND GIVE ME THE REALITY STONE.
REALITY STONE, HUH?
WHAT DOES IT DO?
SEEMS TO ALTER OUR REALITY... TO ONE... OF MY MAKING!
IT'S WORKING! YOU'VE GOT HIM ON THE ROPES!
AN ADMIRABLE EFFORT.
PERHAPS WITH THE POWER STONE IN CONJUNCTION YOU COULD TAKE ME APART.
YOUR BARRIER IS A DECENT PLOY, BUT NOT WHEN I TIME-SHIFT IT FROM YOU.
DAD, GIVE ME THE STONE. I'VE GOT AN IDEA.

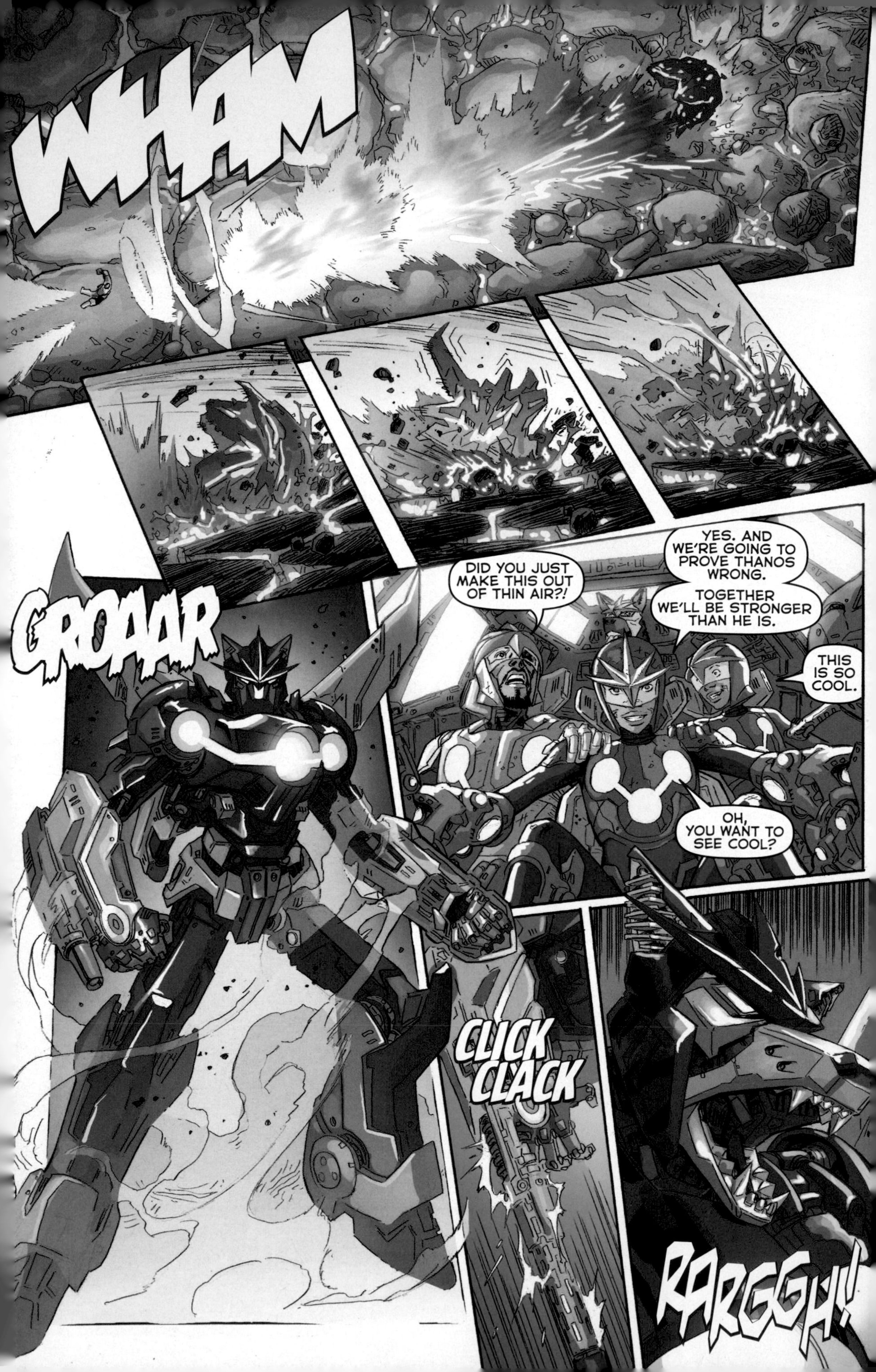
WHAM
GROAAR
DID YOU JUST MAKE THIS OUT OF THIN AIR?!
YES. AND WE'RE GOING TO PROVE THANOS WRONG.
TOGETHER WE'LL BE STRONGER THAN HE IS.
THIS IS SO COOL.
OH, YOU WANT TO SEE COOL?
CLICK CLACK
RARGGH!!

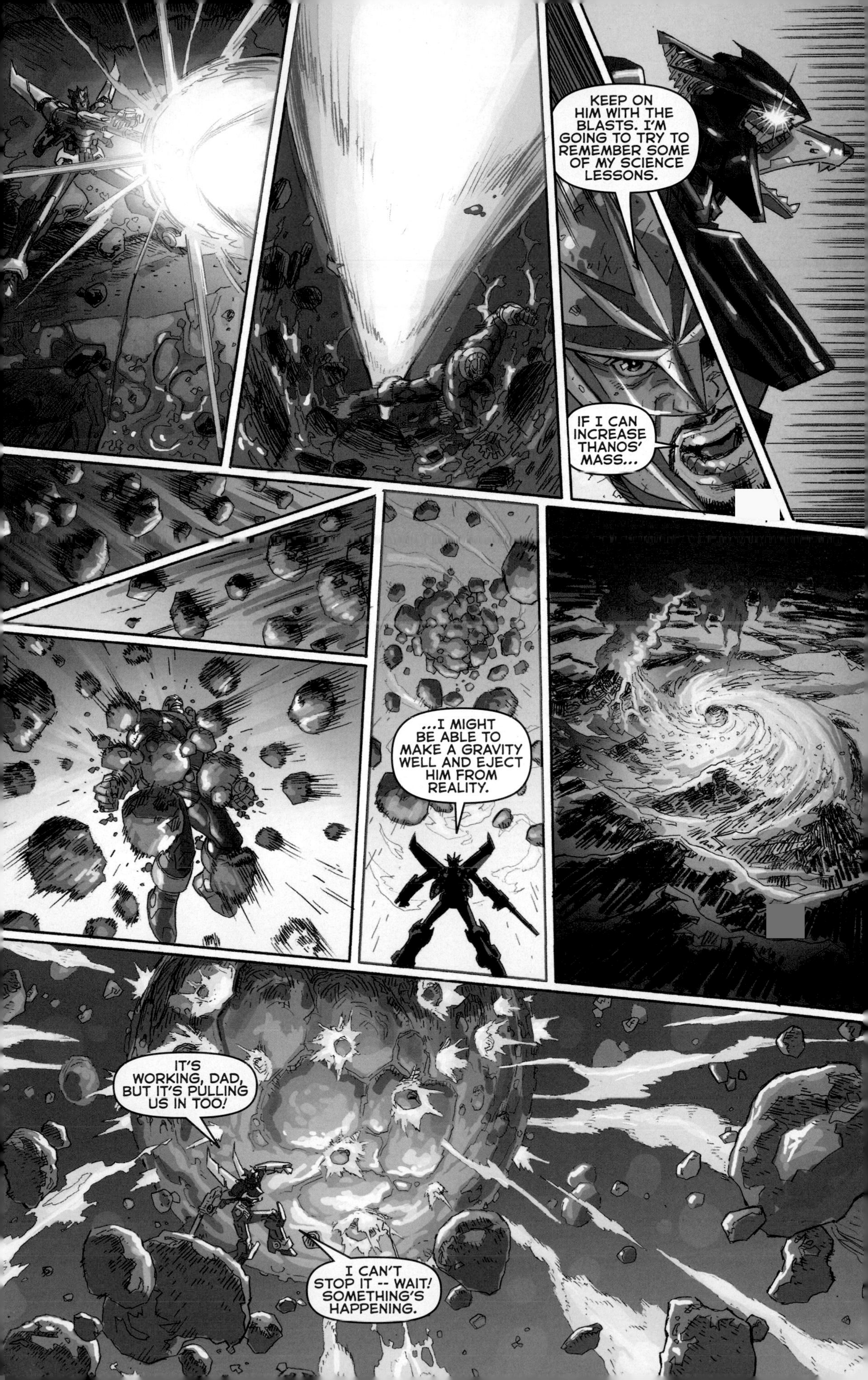
KEEP ON HIM WITH THE BLASTS. I'M GOING TO TRY TO REMEMBER SOME OF MY SCIENCE LESSONS.
IF I CAN INCREASE THANOS' MASS...
...I MIGHT BE ABLE TO MAKE A GRAVITY WELL AND EJECT HIM FROM REALITY.
IT'S WORKING, DAD, BUT IT'S PULLING US IN TOO!
I CAN'T STOP IT -- WAIT! SOMETHING'S HAPPENING.

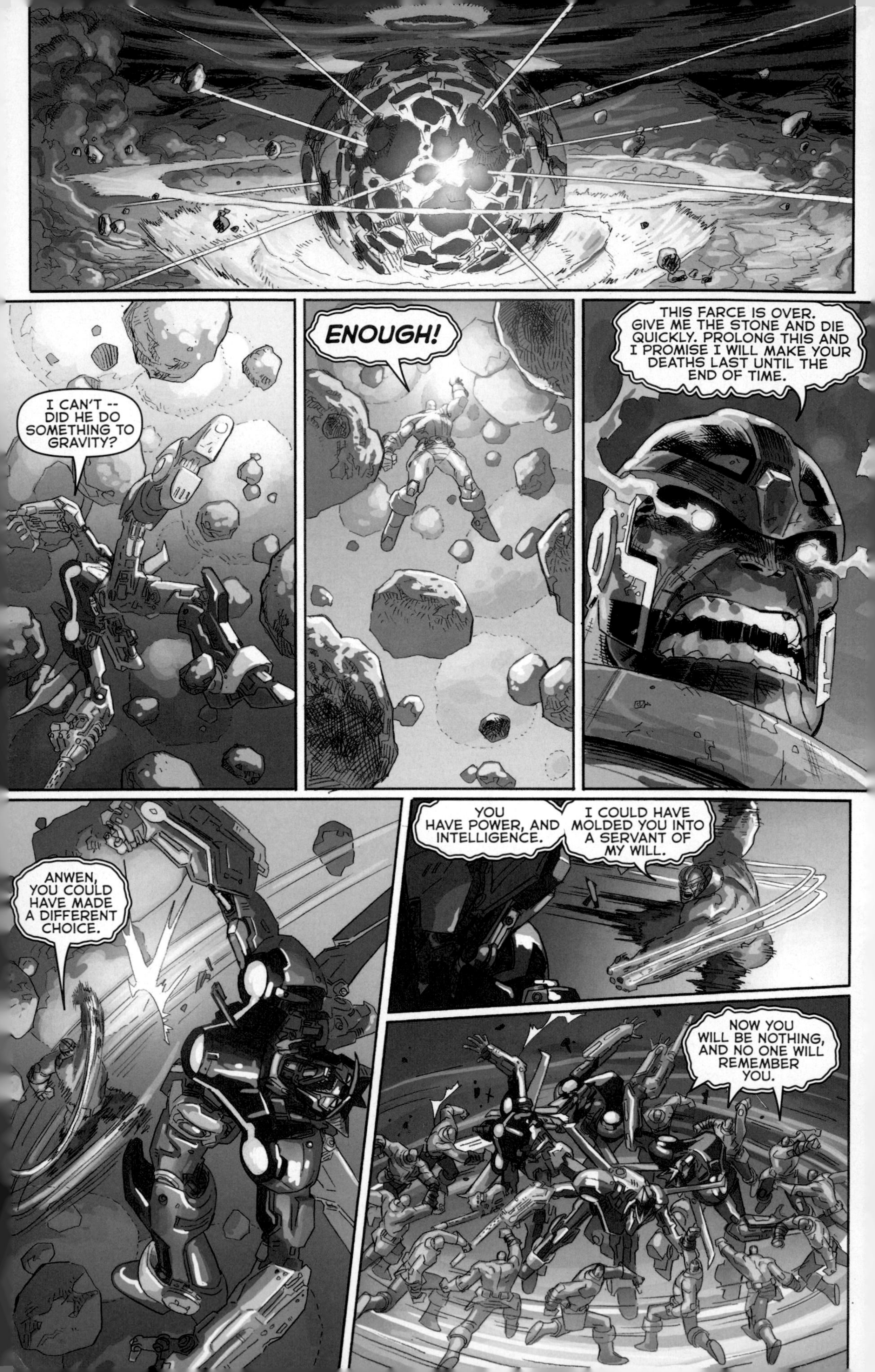
I CAN'T -- DID HE DO SOMETHING TO GRAVITY?
ENOUGH!
THIS FARCE IS OVER. GIVE ME THE STONE AND DIE QUICKLY. PROLONG THIS AND I PROMISE I WILL MAKE YOUR DEATHS LAST UNTIL THE END OF TIME.
ANWEN, YOU COULD HAVE MADE A DIFFERENT CHOICE.
YOU HAVE POWER, AND INTELLIGENCE.
I COULD HAVE MOLDED YOU INTO A SERVANT OF MY WILL.
NOW YOU WILL BE NOTHING, AND NO ONE WILL REMEMBER YOU.

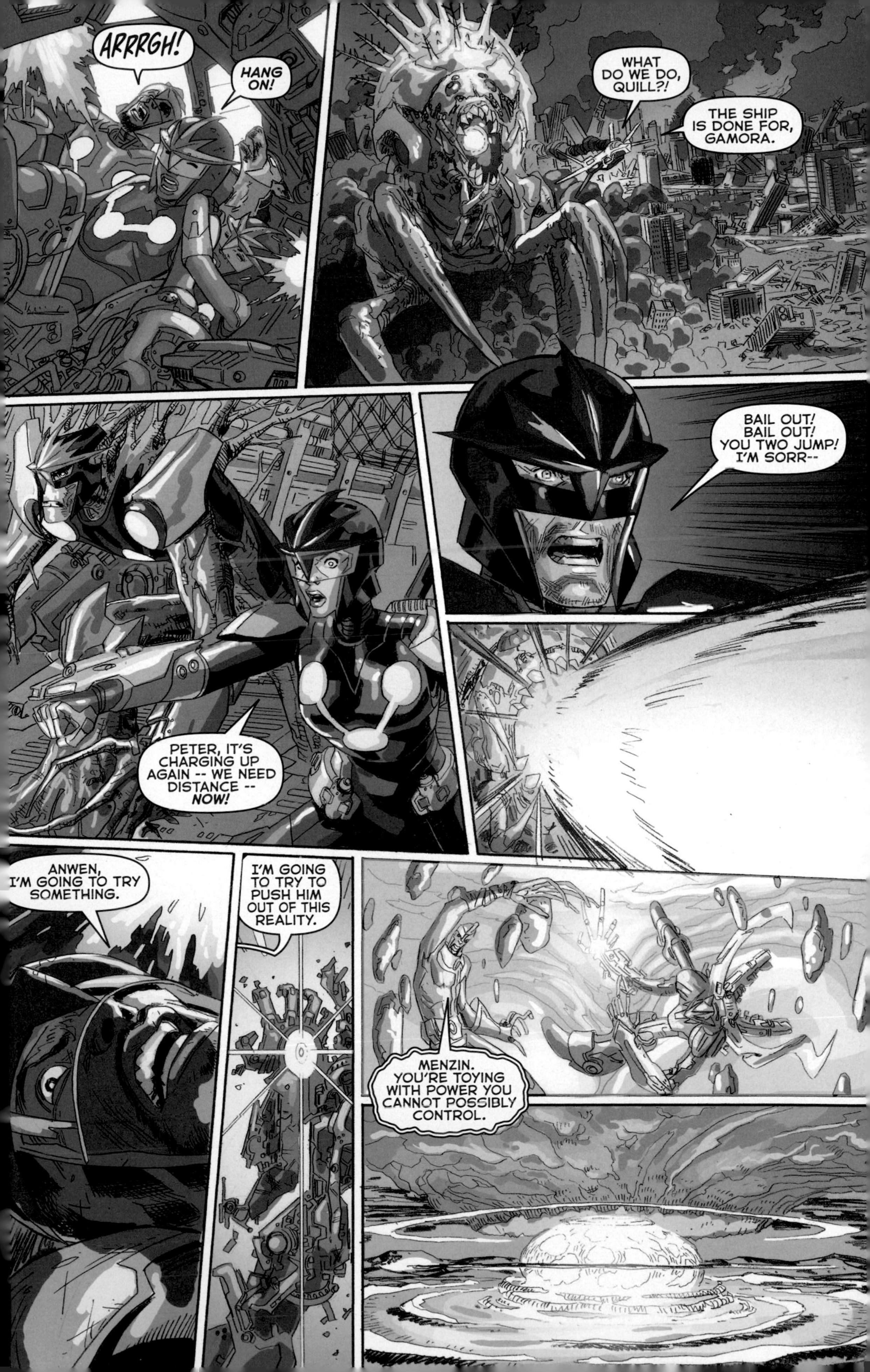
ARRRGH!
HANG ON!
WHAT DO WE DO, QUILL?!
THE SHIP IS DONE FOR, GAMORA.
BAIL OUT! BAIL OUT! YOU TWO JUMP! I'M SORR--
PETER, IT'S CHARGING UP AGAIN -- WE NEED DISTANCE -- *NOW!*
ANWEN, I'M GOING TO TRY SOMETHING.
I'M GOING TO TRY TO PUSH HIM OUT OF THIS REALITY.
MENZIN. YOU'RE TOYING WITH POWER YOU CANNOT POSSIBLY CONTROL.

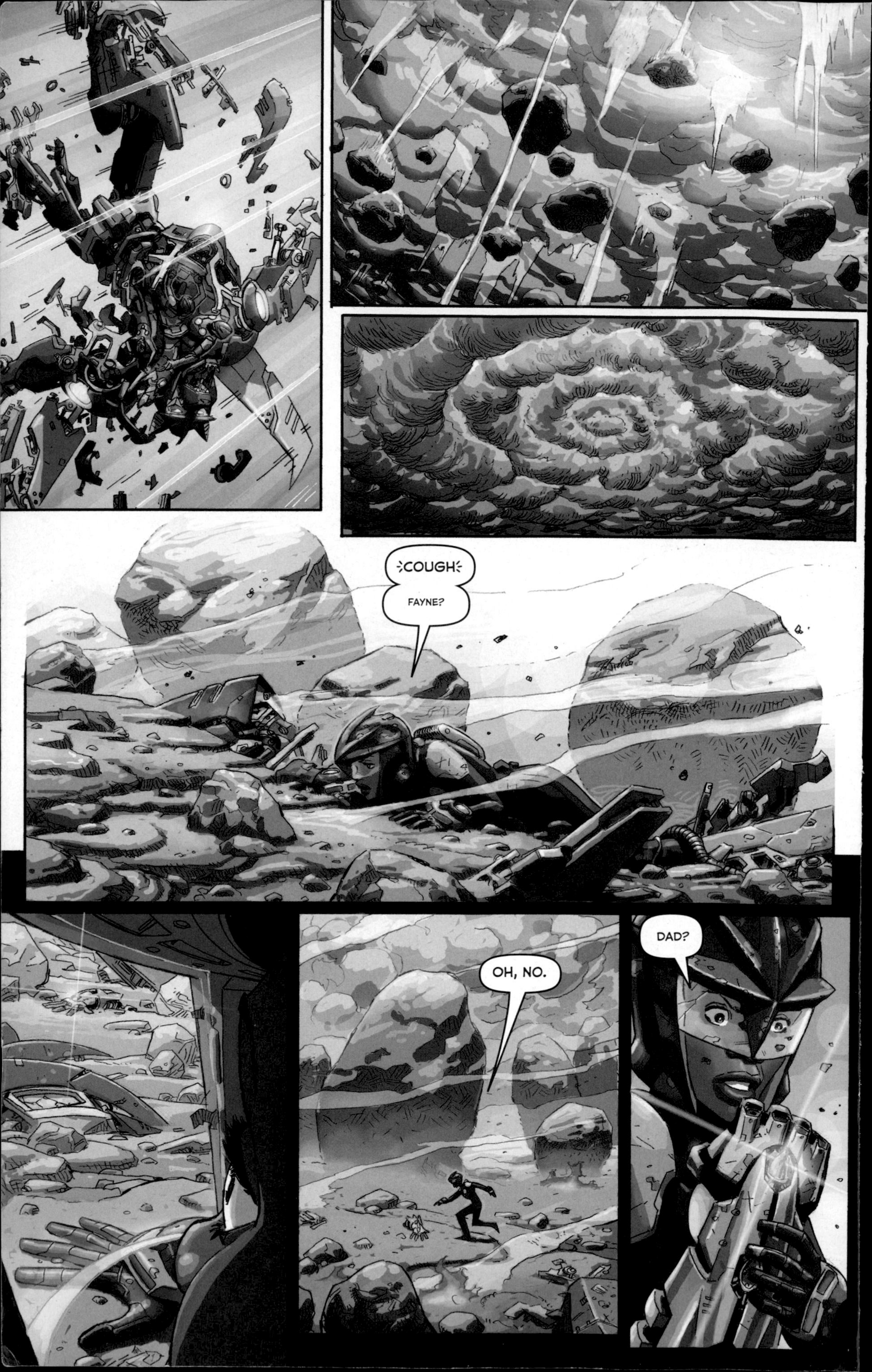
COUGH
FAYNE?
OH, NO.
DAD?

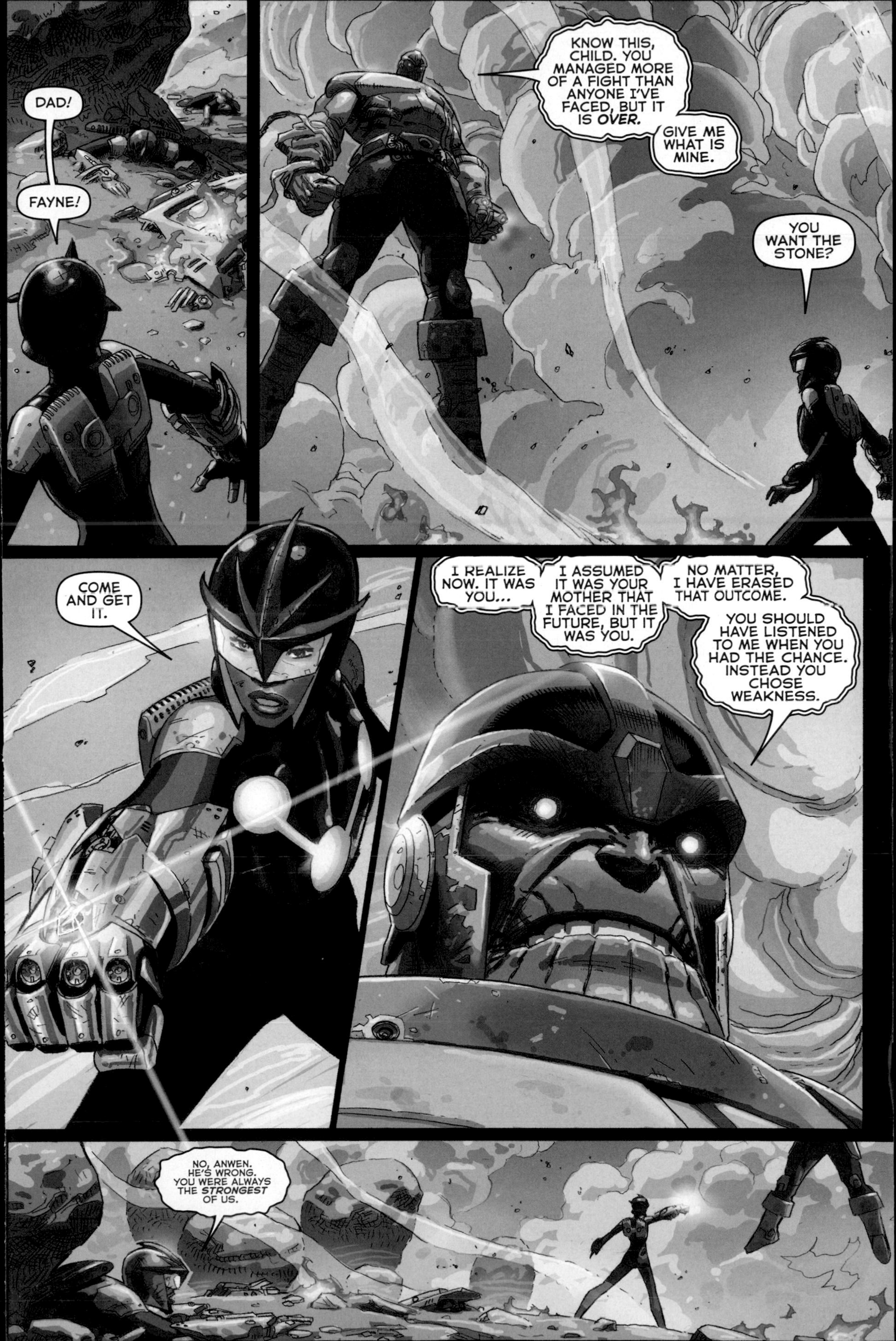
DAD!
FAYNE!
KNOW THIS, CHILD. YOU MANAGED MORE OF A FIGHT THAN ANYONE I'VE FACED, BUT IT IS *OVER.*
GIVE ME WHAT IS MINE.
YOU WANT THE STONE?
COME AND GET IT.
I REALIZE NOW. IT WAS YOU...
I ASSUMED IT WAS YOUR MOTHER THAT I FACED IN THE FUTURE, BUT IT WAS YOU.
NO MATTER, I HAVE ERASED THAT OUTCOME.
YOU SHOULD HAVE LISTENED TO ME WHEN YOU HAD THE CHANCE. INSTEAD YOU CHOSE WEAKNESS.
NO, ANWEN. HE'S WRONG. YOU WERE ALWAYS THE *STRONGEST* OF US.

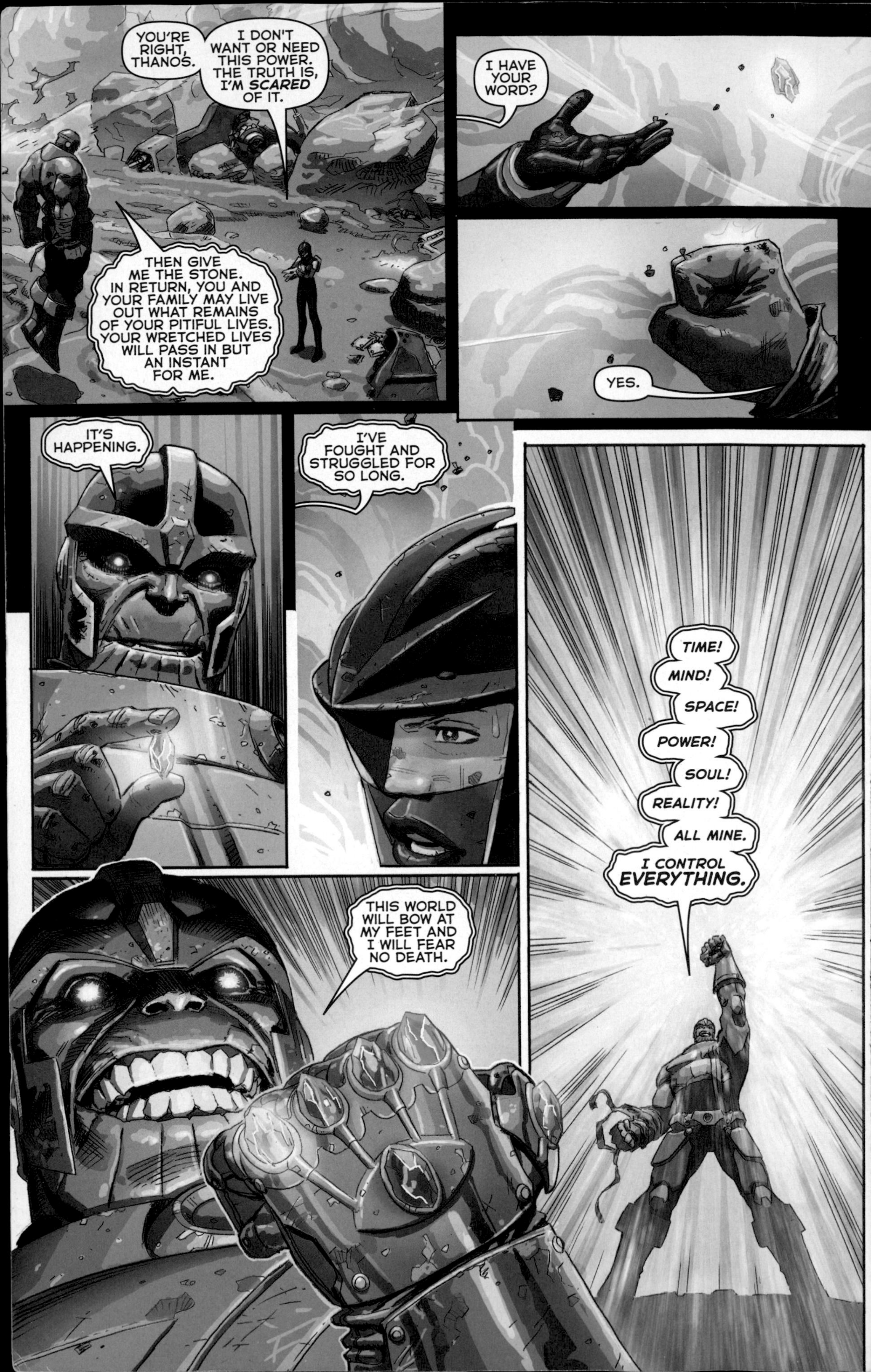

YOU'RE RIGHT, THANOS.
I DON'T WANT OR NEED THIS POWER. THE TRUTH IS, I'M *SCARED* OF IT.
THEN GIVE ME THE STONE. IN RETURN, YOU AND YOUR FAMILY MAY LIVE OUT WHAT REMAINS OF YOUR PITIFUL LIVES. YOUR WRETCHED LIVES WILL PASS IN BUT AN INSTANT FOR ME.
I HAVE YOUR WORD?
YES.
IT'S HAPPENING.
I'VE FOUGHT AND STRUGGLED FOR SO LONG.
THIS WORLD WILL BOW AT MY FEET AND I WILL FEAR NO DEATH.
TIME!
MIND!
SPACE!
POWER!
SOUL!
REALITY!
ALL MINE.
I CONTROL **EVERYTHING.**

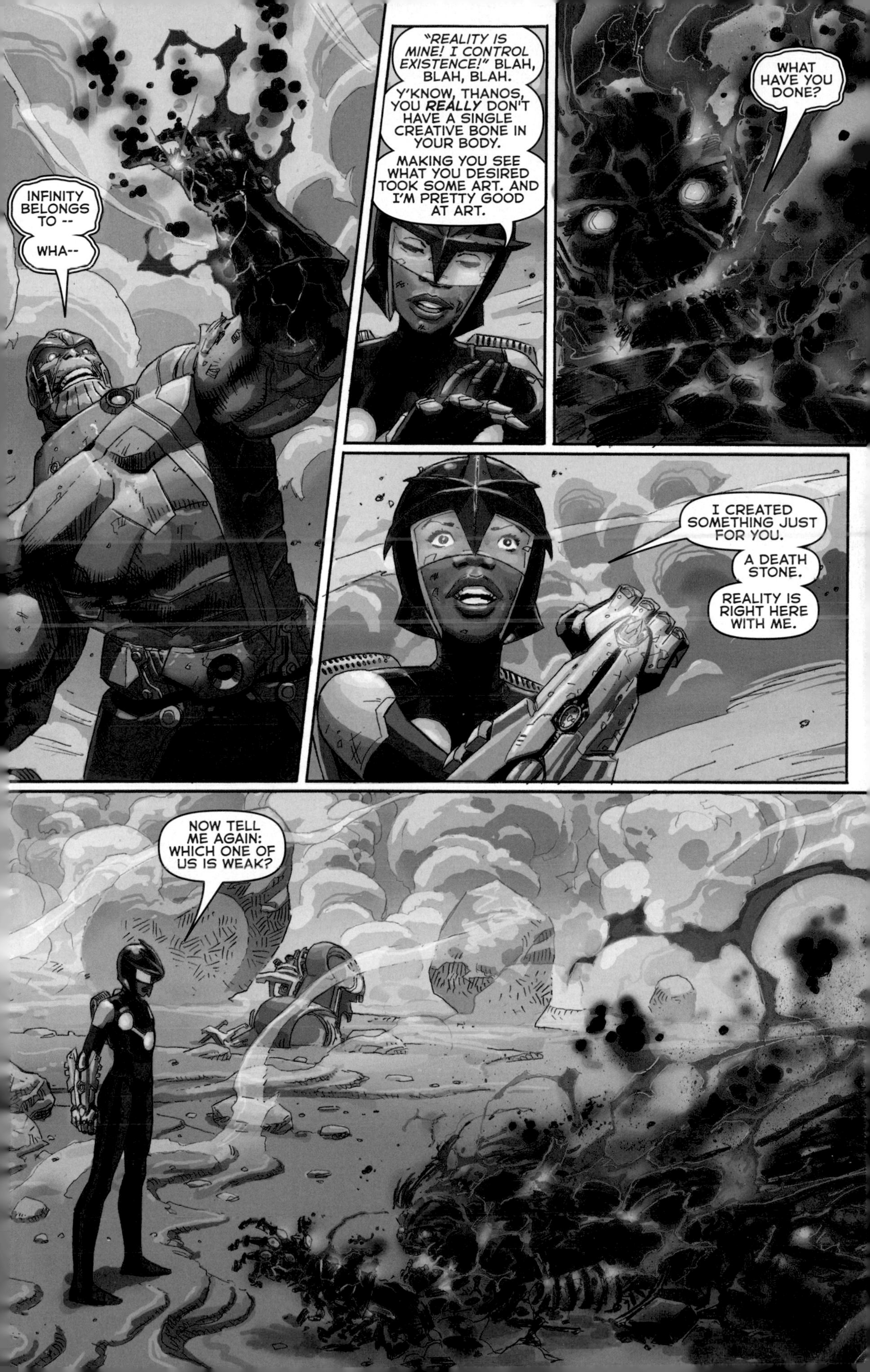
INFINITY BELONGS TO --
WHA--
"REALITY IS MINE! I CONTROL EXISTENCE!" BLAH, BLAH, BLAH.
Y'KNOW, THANOS, YOU REALLY DON'T HAVE A SINGLE CREATIVE BONE IN YOUR BODY.
MAKING YOU SEE WHAT YOU DESIRED TOOK SOME ART. AND I'M PRETTY GOOD AT ART.
WHAT HAVE YOU DONE?
I CREATED SOMETHING JUST FOR YOU.
A DEATH STONE.
REALITY IS RIGHT HERE WITH ME.
NOW TELL ME AGAIN: WHICH ONE OF US IS WEAK?

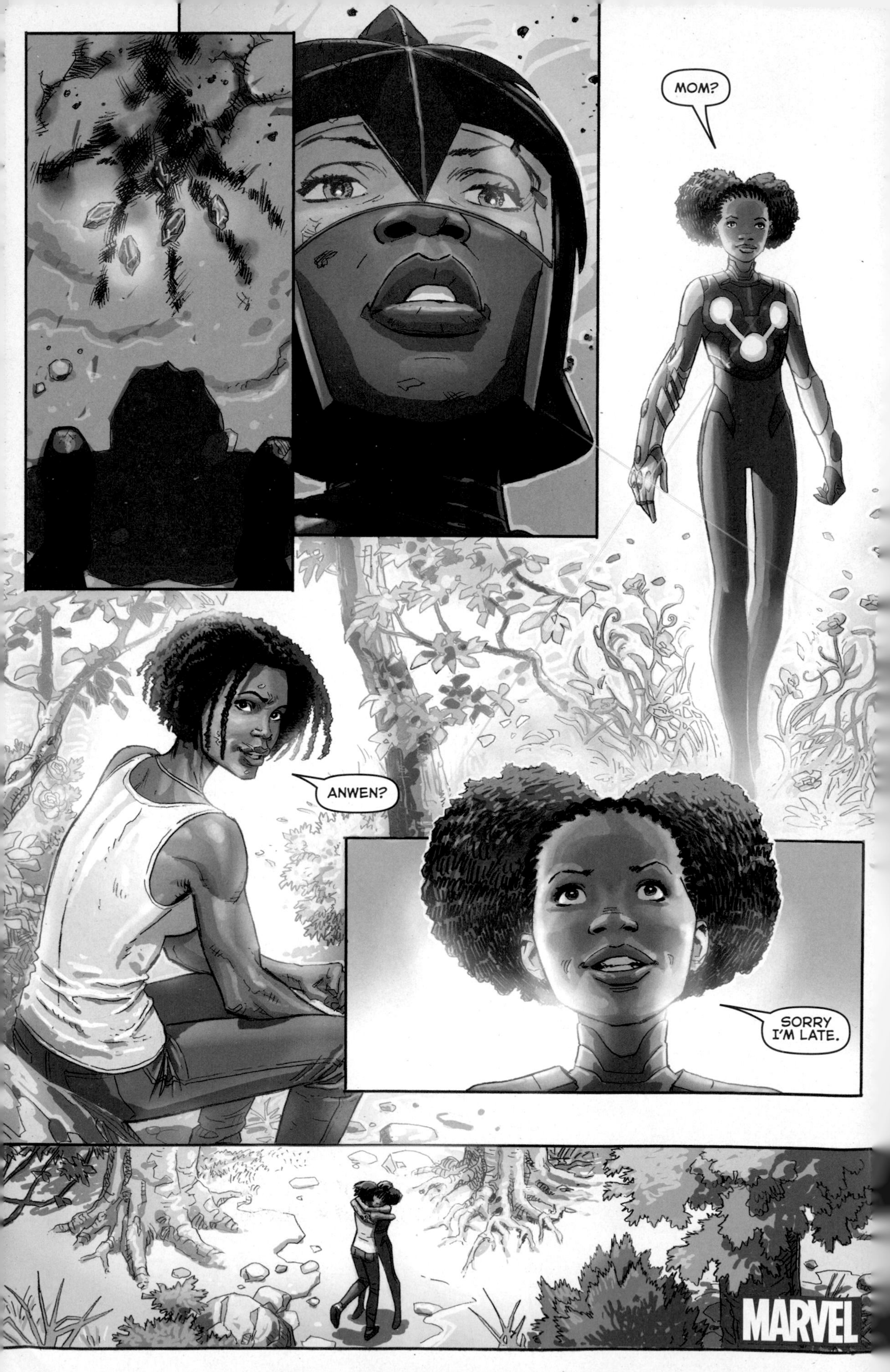
MOM?
ANWEN?
SORRY I'M LATE.
MARVEL